MICHIGAN
STATE PARKS

A Complete Recreation Guide

MICHIGAN STATE PARKS

A Complete Recreation Guide

SECOND EDITION

JIM DUFRESNE

THE
MOUNTAINEERS

Published by
The Mountaineers
1001 SW Klickitat Way, Suite 201
Seattle, WA 98134

First edition 1989
Second edition: first printing 1998, second printing 2000

Published simultaneously in Great Britain by Cordee, 3a DeMontfort Street, Leicester, England, LE1 7HD

Manufactured in Canada

Edited by Christine Clifton-Thornton
All photographs by the author unless otherwise noted.
Cover design by Watson Graphics
Book design by Gray Mouse Graphics
Typography by The Mountaineers Books

Cover photographs: (Clockwise from top left) *Mountain Bikers in Ionia Recreation Area; Upper Tahquamenon Falls; Backcountry skiers at the East Vista in the Porcupine Mountains Wilderness State Park; Lake of the Clouds at Porcupine Mountains Wilderness State Park* by Jim DuFresne
Frontispiece: *Whitetail deer* by David Kenyon (photo courtesy Michigan DNR)

Library of Congress Cataloging-in-Publication Data

DuFresne, Jim.
    Michigan state parks: a complete recreation guide / Jim DuFresne.
  —2nd ed.
      p.   cm.
    Includes index.
    ISBN   0-89886-544-1
    1. Outdoor recreation—Michigan—Guidebooks. 2. Parks—Michigan—Directories. I. Title.
GV191.42.M5D83 1998
333.78'3'025774—dc21
                                      97-43534
                                       CIP

Contents

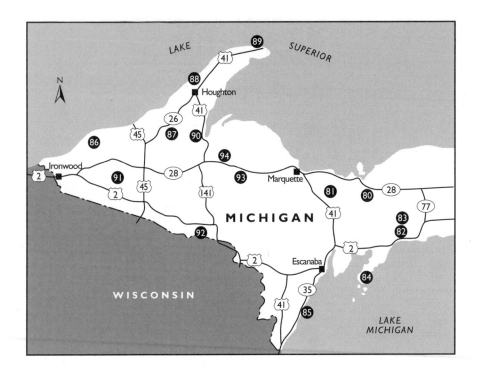

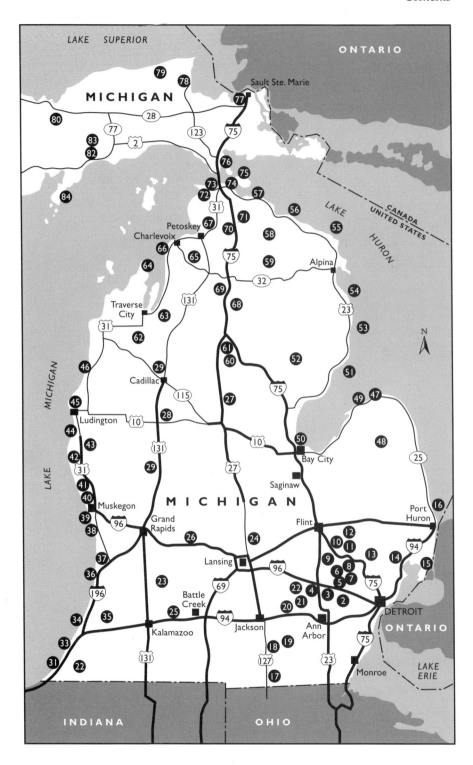

Map Key

1 Sterling State Park
2 Maybury State Park
3 Island Lake Recreation Area
4 Brighton Recreation Area
5 Proud Lake Recreation Area
6 Highland Recreation Area
7 Dodge No. 4 State Park
8 Pontiac Lake Recreation Area
9 Seven Lakes State Park
10 Holly Recreation Area
11 Ortonville Recreation Area
12 Metamora–Hadley Recreation Area
13 Bald Mountain Recreation Area
14 Wetzel State Park
15 Algonac State Park
16 Lakeport State Park
17 Lake Hudson Recreation Area
18 Cambridge State Historic Park
19 W. J. Hayes State Park
20 Waterloo Recreation Area
21 Pinckney Recreation Area
22 Lakelands Trail State Park
23 Yankee Springs Recreation Area
24 Sleepy Hollow State Park
25 Fort Custer Recreation Area
26 Ionia Recreation Area
27 Wilson State Park
28 White Pine Trail State Park
29 Mitchell State Park
30 Newaygo State Park
31 Warren Dunes State Park
32 Warren Woods Natural Area
33 Grand Mere State Park
34 Van Buren State Park
35 Kal–Haven Trail State Park
36 Saugatuck Dunes State Park
37 Holland State Park
38 Grand Haven State Park
39 P. J. Hoffmaster State Park
40 Muskegon State Park
41 Duck Lake State Park
42 Silver Lake State Park
43 Hart–Montague Trail State Park
44 Charles Mears State Park
45 Ludington State Park
46 Orchard Beach State Park
47 Port Crescent State Park
48 Sanilac Historic Site

49 Albert E. Sleeper State Park
50 Bay City State Recreation Area
51 Tawas Point State Park
52 Rifle River Recreation Area
53 Harrisville State Park
54 Negwegon State Park
55 Thompson's Harbor State Park
56 P. H. Hoeft State Park
57 Cheboygan State Park
58 Onaway State Park
59 Clear Lake State Park
60 South Higgins Lake State Park
61 North Higgins Lake State Park
62 Interlochen State Park
63 Traverse City State Park
64 Leelanau State Park
65 Young State Park
66 Fisherman's Island State Park
67 Petoskey State Park
68 Hartwick Pines State Park
69 Otsego Lake State Park
70 Burt Lake State Park
71 Aloha State Park
72 Wilderness State Park
73 Colonial Michilimackinac State Park
74 Mill Creek State Park
75 Mackinac Island State Park
76 Straits State Park
77 Brimley State Park
78 Tahquamenon Falls State Park
79 Muskallonge Lake State Park
80 Wagner Falls Scenic Site
81 Laughing Whitefish Falls Scenic
    Site
82 Indian Lake State Park
83 Palms Book State Park
84 Fayette State Park
85 J. W. Wells State Park
86 Porcupine Mountains Wilderness
    State Park
87 Twin Lakes State Park
88 F. J. McLain State Park
89 Fort Wilkins State Park
90 Baraga State Park
91 Lake Gogebic State Park
92 Bewabic State Park
93 Van Riper State Park
94 Craig Lake State Park

Foreword

One of the reasons I was so excited about becoming Director of the Michigan Department of Natural Resources was that I could "spread the word" about Michigan's truly wonderful state park system. Without exaggeration, there is no better system in the entire country. Michigan is blessed with a rich bounty of natural resources, the finest examples of which are preserved and protected in our state parks. Over 100 state parks offer visitors to Michigan and our own citizens miles of beaches, virgin forest stands, abundant wildlife, unique historical areas, excellent camping facilities, working farms, and quiet places. . .something for everyone to enjoy. Let me give you just a flavor of what is in store for you here in Michigan by describing four state parks which are special to me.

Tucked away in a forest in the Upper Peninsula near Manistique is a beautiful spring that the Native Americans call Kitch-Iti-Kipi or "Big Spring." Palms Book State Park is the home of this spring—the largest in Michigan. A short walk down a meandering path takes you to a ferry which you or your children pull to cross to the spring. A glass-enclosed frame allows you to look into the crystal clear spring at the bubbling sands and the huge trout which make the spring their home.

In southeast Michigan near the City of Northville, Maybury State Park is a living history farm. My favorite part of the farm is the matched set of Belgium work horses which are still called upon to plow, disk, and seed. I know you would also enjoy the bees in the glass-enclosed hive, the beautiful trails, a spooky Halloween hayride, or the old-fashioned farm gardens. I was raised on a farm and this is a great way to relive those wonderful memories.

Michigan sand dunes are very special places . . . P. J. Hoffmaster State Park has within its 1,000 acres some impressive examples and an outstanding interpretive center to better understand the unique characteristics of the dunes. But Hoffmaster is not just a place to learn about dunes, for it has long stretches of beautiful sand beaches where one can sit and absorb the beauty of Lake Michigan and our golden summers.

Last, but by no means least, is an underutilized treasure on Lake Huron named P. H. Hoeft State Park. If your idea of paradise is long uncrowded white beaches, quiet forests, and great fishing...then this is your kind of place. This is the "sunrise" side of the state, and my wife and I enjoy sitting on the beach every morning, watching the birds and listening to the quiet.

The four parks I described are special but not unique. Twenty-five million state park visitors all can describe their own special place—from the crowded beaches on the west side of the state to the quiet solitude of the Porcupine Mountains. Michigan state parks are our crown jewels and we most proudly flaunt them. Jim has captured these precious gems in the pages you are about to read. So come join us in exploring the spectacular shorelines, forests, beaches, scenic trails, unique natural areas, and the glorious four seasons of Michigan.

—Dr. Gordon Guyer
Former Director, Michigan
Department of Natural Resources

Acknowledgments

There's something special about coming home.

After experiencing and writing books on such far away places as Alaska's Glacier Bay and New Zealand's Fiordland, I turned my attention to where I grew up and have spent most of my life.

Michigan is a wonderful place to call home. And in the last two summers, I rediscovered the jewels in its crown: the sand dunes along Lake Michigan, bass raising on a wilderness lake, a crystal clear, gurgling trout stream bordered by stately pines.

The outdoor adventures were excellent, the scenery priceless, but it is the people of Michigan, my neighbors, which I cherish most. Midwest folks are neither superficial nor egotistic. They have good hearts, helping hands and a strong belief that the price of preservation is a small one to pay for the everlasting enjoyment of Michigan's natural wonders.

I am deeply indebted to Dr. Gordon Guyer, former director of Michigan Department of Natural Resources, and Ron Nagel of the Parks Division Visitors Services for their encouragement and assistance to this project. I enjoyed working with every DNR employee I came in contact with but, most of all, with park managers who gave me insights into their special areas of Michigan.

I was provided with assistance from the Michigan Tourism Bureau, The Mackinac Island Historic Parks Commission and Tom Frigens of the Michigan Iron Museum who straightened me out—historically.

Finally, thanks go to my many camping, hiking, and fishing partners who explored these wonderful parks with me, especially Steve Davis and my brother Rick, who shared his adventurous jaunt into Craig Lake State Park. Sometimes the best Michigan has to offer is only a short portage away.

Introduction

It's only natural.

Michigan, one of the most scenic regions of the country, possesses one of the most extensive state park systems. A few other states have greater acreage or a larger number of units, but for sheer beauty it's hard to surpass the nearly 100 state parks and recreation areas in Michigan. They showcase natural wonders found nowhere else in the Midwest or, in many cases, nowhere else in the United States.

The best of Michigan lies in its state parks.

They feature stretches of the country's longest freshwater shoreline, which extends 3,200 miles along four of the five Great Lakes. Parks protect a large portion of the 11,000 inland lakes and give access to the 36,000 miles of streams and rivers found in Michigan, a state where you are never more than 6 miles from water. Within these state parks you'll find the most extensive set of freshwater sand dunes in the world, the only "mountains" in the Midwest, and hundreds of waterfalls, including the third largest cascade east of the Mississippi River.

The 260,000 acres within the state park system not only protect the natural beauty of Michigan but provide opportunities to hike, ski, fish, mountain bike, swim, and camp. With more than 14,000 campsites, the Michigan park system ranks

Fishing in Craig Lake State Park

first among all states for total number of sites and overnight attendance. Most important, however, the parks are close at hand. Nowhere in Michigan are you more than an hour's drive from a state park.

Preserving parks was such a natural thing for Michigan residents that they created their first one, Mackinac Island State Park, in 1895, only twenty-three years after Yellowstone National Park was established. In 1917, 200 acres of virgin pine forest that escaped the lumberman's axe were turned into Interlochen State Park by the state legislature. The popularity of it and the arrival of the era of automobile vacations led the politicians and Governor Albert E. Sleeper to create the Michigan State Park Commission.

The commission's job was to set up the present park system with an eye on "preservation of natural beauty or historic association." The people of Michigan immediately swamped the ten-man commission with numerous parcels of land they wanted to donate as future state parks, and twenty-two units were added in two years. In 1921, the duties of the commission became a function of the newly organized Department of Conservation which later was reorganized into the present Department of Natural Resources (DNR). The first Superintendent of State Parks was P. J. Hoffmaster. With the volunteer efforts of his friend, renowned conservationist Genevieve Gillette, the Michigan park system quickly grew into one of the largest in the country. When Hoffmaster was promoted to Director of the Department of Conservation in 1934, Michigan had seventy-two state parks with 9 million visitors annually.

Today the parks system is administered by the Parks Division of the DNR and consists of state parks, which generally preserve outstanding natural features, large recreation areas, state historic parks, and the smaller scenic and historic sites. Together the units draw almost 25 million visitors a year, of which more than 5 million are campers.

Some parks are heavily used in the summer, especially several along Lake Michigan that draw more than a million visitors annually. Some are hardly used at all. The purpose of this book is to look at the outdoor activities each park offers and encourage people to explore the Michigan state park system. If you've been vacationing in the same park for years, break away and discover a new one. Experience the annual camping or fishing trip in a different scenic setting this summer. Chances are the new surroundings will be just as enjoyable.

It's only natural.

Park Season and Entry

The traditional season and busiest time of year for most parks is from Memorial Day to Labor Day, when the warm Michigan summer encourages people to swim, picnic, camp, fish, or struggle up a sand dune. But the parks are open year-round, and for many people the best time to visit them is the off-season, when there are no crowds, bugs, or long lines of cars waiting for an open site at a campground.

Autumn colors bring people in on foot, bicycle, horseback, or by canoe. Spring is the time for birders, morel mushroom hunters, and walks in the woods to view wildflowers. The parks are the site of many winter activities as well. Perhaps the most popular one is Nordic skiing. Ice fishing is also very popular, and Porcupine Mountains features one of the best and most affordable downhill skiing facilities in the Midwest. Many families feel there's not a better way to spend a "traditional Christmas" than by renting one of the wood-heated, candle-lit frontier cabins.

A motor vehicle permit is required for entry into all state parks and recreation areas. A daily permit can be obtained at the contact station located at the entrance of each unit and allows one vehicle into the park on the date it's issued. An annual permit can also be purchased and allows the vehicle on which it is posted unlimited access to all parks. There is a special annual permit for senior citizens, while the historic parks of Mackinac Island, Colonial Michilimackinac, and Historic Mill Creek have separate per-person entry fees.

Annual state park permits are available at all parks or by writing to the DNR Parks and Recreation Division, P.O. Box 30257, Lansing, MI 48909; or by calling (517) 373-9900.

Camping, Rent-a-Tents, and Cabins

There are campgrounds in more than seventy units of the state park system that combine for 14,000 campsites across Michigan. Modern campgrounds offer electric hookups at each site and heated restrooms with flush toilets and showers. The exception is Hartwick Pines State Park, whose modern sites are equipped with both electricity and water, the only state park facility that offers full hookups. Semi-modern facilities lack either electricity or modern restrooms, while rustic campgrounds have no on-site hookups and usually feature vault toilets and hand pumps for water. There is a separate fee for camping, which varies depending on whether the site is modern, semi-modern, or rustic. Permits are purchased and fees collected at the contact station of each campground.

The popular camping season is from May 15 to September 15, and during this time a visitor may not occupy a site for more than 15 consecutive days. Camping is a year-round activity at some state parks, such as William Mitchell State Park near Cadillac, which keeps its restrooms in service throughout the winter. But most parks turn off and winterize their water systems after October 15.

At a number of parks the DNR offers Rent-a-Tent Programs, designed for visitors and families with little or no camping experience. Most of the large wall tents are set up on wooden platforms within campgrounds and are equipped with folding cots, foam pads, and a picnic table. At many parks you can also rent propane stoves, lanterns, and ice chests. The tents are limited to individual families or groups of four, and allow persons to try camping before making a sizable investment in a tent and other equipment. A special feature at some parks is the Rent-a-Tipi Program, where families can try authentic tribal replicas for a different experience and setting in camping. All parks that offer the programs are described in the text.

A step up from sleeping in a tent is to rent a mini-cabin, of which there are more than fifty available in almost forty parks. A mini-cabin is a small shelter furnished with four bunk beds, a table, and electricity, and is usually located near a restroom with showers in a modern campground. Outside each features a large picnic table and a fire ring.

More secluded and very popular are the sixty rustic cabins available for rent in the state park system. They vary in size and are located in quiet wooded settings. Many overlook streams, inland lakes, or isolated stretches of the Great Lakes. Some cabins are a short walk from parking; others require a half-day hike or a portage and paddle across a lake. All cabins are described under the park they are located in and usually feature bunks with mattresses, a table, chairs, and woodstoves for heat. At some sites two or more cabins are near each other and can accommodate large groups. With the exception of the Porcupine Mountains and Craig Lake, cabins are rented year-round and make for an enjoyable base for cross-country ski trips, ice fishing, or snowmobiling, as well as fishing and hiking outings in the summer.

Whether you rent a tent, mini-cabin, or cabin, you need to pack along your own bedding such as sleeping bags, cookware and tableware, lanterns or flashlights, and other camp supplies, depending on the situation and time of year.

Also available for rent at many parks are picnic shelters and family group camping areas that feature a minimum of ten sites and allow large groups to camp together. At Proud Lake, Waterloo, and Yankee Springs Recreation Areas in southern Michigan there are outdoor centers available, which include dining hall, kitchen, bathhouse, and bunkrooms that sleep from thirty to 120 campers.

Reservations

In the mid-1990s, the Parks Division instituted its Central Reservation System with an "eleven-month rolling window" for reserving campsites in the Michigan state parks. The system, which links all the state parks via computer, allows campers to book a site in any state park campground with a single toll-free phone call. Operators instantly know which campgrounds are full, what weekends are open, and the nearest park that still has available sites.

To make a campsite reservation call (800) 44-PARKS (800-447-2757). Calls are accepted from 8:00 A.M. to 8:00 P.M. on weekdays, and from 9:00 A.M. to 5:00 P.M. on weekends, and reservations can be made up to eleven months in advance of when you want the site. When making a reservation, be ready to provide name, address, telephone number, and type of camping equipment (recreational vehicle or tent), and have either a Mastercard or Visa credit card handy.

At many parks, especially those along Lake Michigan, campground reservations are strongly recommended. Generally 80 percent of the sites in state parks are reserved in advance, while the rest often go to campers who are already there and want to extend their stay. Thus a popular park like Grand Haven may be off-limits to anybody without a reservation in July or early August.

There is a minimum two-night booking requirement for camping reservations for units in the Lower Peninsula, and there is a small reservation fee along with your nightly campground fee for any state park. When booking a reservation, it's good to have alternative campgrounds or dates in mind in case your first choice is not available. Before making a reservation, you can call the Parks Division at (517) 373-9900 and request its guide to Michigan State Parks, a brochure that describes the units and their features in more detail.

Keep in mind that at most parks, except those as noted in the text, it's usually possible to obtain a modern campsite in the middle of the week, while chances are pretty good that you'll get a site on weekends in most Upper Peninsula units. But at many popular Lower Peninsula parks, all modern sites might be booked for the weekend by Friday morning or even Thursday night. There is far less demand for rustic sites even when the modern campgrounds are filled. On the holiday weekends of Memorial Day, Fourth of July, and Labor Day, arrive early, even for a rustic site, or obtain a reservation in advance.

Mini-cabins are also reserved in advance through the Central Reservation System (800-44-PARKS), while rent-a-tents, rustic cabins, and picnic shelters are booked directly with the park they are located in either by mail or phone or in person. Telephone and in-person reservations can be made at most park offices from 8:00 A.M. until noon and from 1:00 P.M. until 5:00 P.M. Monday through Friday.

Visitor Programs and Interpretive Centers

The natural world around you, or a slice of Michigan history, is best understood and appreciated by visiting any of the more than a dozen visitor centers, historical forts, and museums within the state parks. Each visitor center is dedicated to a natural treasure that is unique to Michigan, and explains it through exhibits, hands-on displays, and interpretive programs. Five of the centers are open year-round: Saginaw Bay Visitor Center in Bay City State Recreation Area, Michigan Forest

Visitor Center at Hartwick Pines State Park, Gillette Sand Dune Visitor Center at P. J. Hoffmaster State Park, Carl T. Johnson Hunting and Fishing Museum at William Mitchell State Park, and Eddy Geology Center at Waterloo Recreation Area.

During the summer Adventure Rangers lead hikes, pond explorations, insect hunts, fishing clinics, and campfire programs at more than forty state parks. The Adventure Program is a cooperative effort between the DNR Parks and Recreation Division and the Kalamazoo Nature Center to provide interpretive programs to state park visitors. The one-hour programs are held from Memorial Day to Labor Day and are open to anybody but are designed primarily for children and families. They are free beyond the vehicle entry fee into a state park.

Boating and Fishing

With all its water, it's easy to understand why there are more registered boats in Michigan than any other state in the country. State parks and recreation areas provide access and, in many cases, boat launches and ramps to a wide variety of inland waters and Great Lakes. There is no additional fee to launch a boat after a motor vehicle permit has been obtained. Many parks also have facilities where visitors can rent rowboats or canoes for use on inland lakes and rivers.

Fishing opportunities, from trolling for salmon in the Great Lakes to bobbing for bluegill in a small pond, abound in state parks. Many parks offer piers and docks especially designed for shoreline anglers, while others have fish-cleaning stations. The facilities and the type of fishing available is described in the text for each state park. All anglers must have a current Michigan fishing license to fish in any state park or recreation area.

Winter steelhead fishing

Hiking, Skiing, and Biking

Hiking opportunities abound in state parks. Many units maintain nature trails: short loops with numbered markers that match interpretive descriptions in brochures available from park offices or contact stations. Other trails are designed for day hikes through the parks and range from 2 to 8 miles in length. There are also opportunities for multiple-day hiking trips, with Porcupine Mountains Wilderness State Park and its 90-mile network of trails the most noted area for backpacking.

One of the fastest-growing activities in state parks in recent years has been mountain biking. The Michigan Mountain Bike Association (MMBA) has worked closely with the DNR to design trail systems in many state parks. Pinckney Recreation Area is the most popular mountain biking area in the state and possibly the Midwest, drawing cyclists from Ohio and Indiana almost every weekend in the summer. Other units with extensive trail systems for bikers include Yankee Springs and Fort Custer Recreation Areas. Keep in mind that not all state park trails are open to mountain biking, particularly those in the sand dune areas of Lake Michigan and the Porcupine Mountains. Trails that are not open to mountain biking are clearly posted for use by hikers only.

There are 260 miles of Nordic ski trails in the state park system. Some routes are groomed and tracked during the winter, and nine parks feature warming shelters for skiers. The most extensive trail system in the Lower Peninsula is at Hartwick Pines State Park, which has 16 miles of trails that merge into the trail system at

Cabin along Lake Superior Trail, Porcupine Mountains Wilderness State Park

Forbush Corner, one of the state's finest Nordic centers. In the Upper Peninsula, Porcupine Mountains Wilderness State Park has 26 miles of groomed trails that allow cross-country skiers to enjoy waterfalls, 300-year-old pines, and the Lake Superior shoreline. Porcupine Mountains also has the only downhill ski operation in the state park system.

Linear Parks

Michigan's newest parks are literally nothing but trails and views. In the Lower Peninsula are four linear state parks, or rail–trails, converted from abandoned railroad corridors: Hart–Montague and Kal–Haven Trail State Parks on the west side, Lakelands Trail State Park in the southeast, and White Pine State Park, which extends from Grand Rapids to Cadillac. The main activities in these parks is bicycling and hiking in the summer and skiing and snowmobiling in the winter. Linear parks require a special per-person entry fee to use.

Park Etiquette

Michigan state parks belong to the people, who have a responsibility to take care of them. Careless campers, hikers, and other users quickly degrade the state's most treasured resources. When visiting a state park, check the park's rules, listed in every contact station and throughout most campgrounds, and keep in mind the following:

- Unless otherwise noted, hours for day-use areas are from 8:00 A.M. until 10:00 P.M.
- Pets are allowed in most parks but must be kept on a 6-foot leash and never left unattended. Pets are not allowed on beaches or in the water. Out of consideration for others as well as for the safety of your pet, consider leaving your pet at home.
- Many parks have a ban on alcoholic beverages, especially during the summer.
- Be considerate of other campers. Leave radios and portable stereos at home, and be conscious that most people go camping to get away from man-made noises.
- Build fires only in grills and fire rings provided at campgrounds and picnic areas. Never cut live trees for firewood; use only dead and downed wood.
- Do not litter in the park or dump household trash in campground trash receptacles. Every summer parks become overwhelmed by the amount of trash produced by visitors.

A Note About Safety

Safety is an important concern in all outdoor activities. No guidebook can alert you to every hazard or anticipate the limitations of every reader. Therefore, the descriptions of roads, trails, routes, and natural features in this book are not representations that a particular place or excursion will be safe for your party. When you follow any of the routes described in this book, you assume responsibility for your own safety. Under normal conditions, such excursions require the usual attention to traffic, road and trail conditions, weather, terrain, the capabilities of your party, and other factors. Keeping informed on current conditions and exercising common sense are the keys to a safe, enjoyable outing.

—The Mountaineers

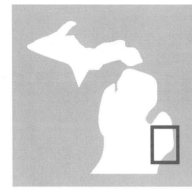

Southeast Michigan

Sterling State Park

▲ Sterling State Park is best known as the only Michigan park on Lake Erie, for its sandy beach, and as a popular departure point for walleye fishermen. But the park is dedicated to marshland and was named after William Sterling, a Monroe County resident who, by the mid-1800s, had already realized the value of wetlands to man as well as wildlife. Michigan had more than 70,000 acres of coastal wetlands when Sterling sought to protect those around Monroe, but since then, lakeshore development has dried up 70 percent of them throughout the state.

Sterling State Park, which was dedicated in 1935, protects a small portion of the once-extensive wetlands. It consists of four lagoons and the marshes that surround Sandy Creek Outlet. The 1,000-acre park, just north of the city limits of Monroe, offers excellent opportunities for birders during the spring and fall migrations, as the lagoons attract a variety of birds and waterfowl, including great blue herons, bluewing teals, mergansers, and large numbers of Canada geese, along with smaller shorebirds. Egrets are especially easy to spot here. The large, slender white birds, which stand more than 30 inches high, begin showing up at the park in late March and can be enjoyed until cold weather drives them south in mid-November. In late spring and early summer, it's possible to spot thirty to forty egrets at a time.

But more than birds, it's the beaches and fishing opportunities that draw more than 800,000 visitors to Sterling every year and make it one of the five most popular units in the system. Most of the usage occurs from spring to fall, as the park offers few winter activities.

Camping: Sterling features 288 modern sites in an open campground with little shade. The campground is located near the entrance of the park and a number of the sites are situated on Sandy Creek, which leads into Lake Erie. The campground is open year-round, but the modern restrooms are closed from November through April. During the summer, sites are usually available during midweek and most non-holiday weekends.

Mountain biker in Holly Recreation Area

Sandy beaches draw families to Sterling State Park.

Hiking: Marsh View Nature Trail is a 2.6-mile loop around a large impound-ment and features interpretive displays, an observation tower, and a viewing plat-form. It has been paved to make it a barrier-free trail and many visitors use bicycles on it. The trail is designed to be followed in a clockwise direction from the trailhead, and within a third of a mile you arrive at an outdoor interpretive display with pic-tures of the birds and waterfowl that frequent the park as well as a section on the importance of wetlands. The observation tower is reached within a mile and is an excellent place to search for birds.

Fishing: Lake Erie is renowned for its walleye fishery. The daily limit is ten fish rather than five as found throughout most of the state. The park operates a boat launch with four ramps and parking for 320 cars and trailers. Prime season for wall-eye is April through mid-July, and bait and tackle shops are located on Dixie High-way near the entrance of the park.

For the occasional fisherman, Sterling offers shore fishing opportunities on its two lagoons in the middle of the park. You can follow the banks or fish from one of four small piers that have been erected in the lagoons, where the main catch is crap-pie and catfish. It's also possible to rent rowboats, canoes, and paddleboats for use on the lagoon from the concession store on the beach. The rental boats are available daily from Memorial Day to Labor Day.

Day-Use Facilities: Sterling features more than a mile of beachfront along Lake Erie, with a shallow swimming area. Bordering the wide, sandy shoreline is an

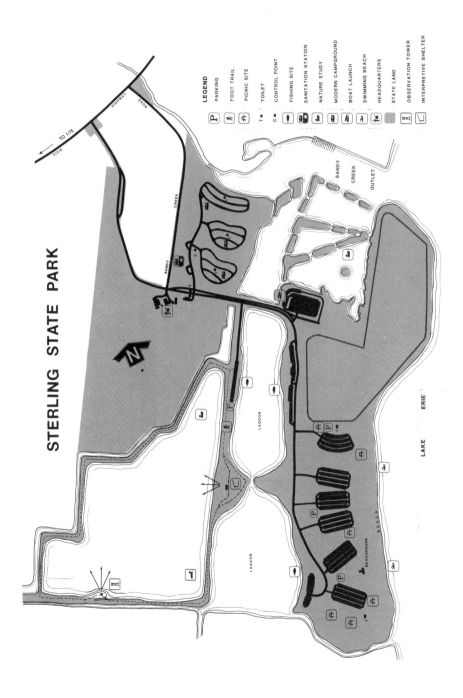

STERLING STATE PARK

open, grassy picnic area and three parking lots for almost 1,800 cars, attesting to the popularity of this Lake Erie beach. There is also a store, bathhouse, toilets, and a designated swimming area.

Access and Information: The park is reached from I-75 by exiting on Dixie Highway and heading east for a mile to its signposted entrance. For information or reservations, contact Sterling State Park, 2800 State Park Road, Monroe, MI 48161; or call (734) 289-2715.

Maybury State Park

In 1975 the DNR established Maybury State Park, the only unit in Wayne County, in an area that included a sanitarium with a working farm. It was an unusual place to establish a state park, but Maybury is a unique park. The buildings of the sanitarium were completely removed and today there's not a clue that the facility existed. But park officials kept the farm. The idea was to preserve a "living farm" close to the city, so that residents, especially children, who have never experienced the sights, sounds, and, yes, smells of a working farm would have the opportunity to do so nearby.

The 965-acre park also places a special emphasis on encouraging visitors to leave their cars and wander through the rolling terrain of forests and open meadows. By design, many of the park's facilities—picnic areas, shelters, and tot lot—can only be reached by a network of foot trails, bicycle paths, or bridle trails. The park draws more than 450,000 visitors annually with year-round activities, even though there are no facilities for swimming or camping—the main activities that draw visitors to other parks—other than an organization camp for youth groups (18 years and younger).

Interpretive Center: The Maybury Living Farm consists of several barns where visitors get a close, "hanging-on-the-fence" view of chickens, pigs, cows, sheep, and other typical farm animals. There is also a display of old farming equipment, but newer plows and harvesters are used by the staff to farm the 40 acres. Children not only get to feed animals but also view chicks in a brooder room, see modern tractors rumble along, and watch huge draft horses pull a plow through fields of corn, oats, beans, and other Michigan crops. The farm (248-349-0817) is open from 10:00 A.M. until 7:00 P.M. daily from June 1 until September 30, and from 10:00 A.M. until 5:00 P.M. the rest of the year.

Hiking: Six miles of foot trails begin at the Eight Mile Road parking lot and form two major loops south into the park through maple and beech forests and open meadows. It is also possible to hike from the Living Farm to the park headquarters on Beck Road.

Cycling: The park maintains 4 miles of paved bike paths that begin at the rental concession near the parking lot and loop south, while another segment heads east to the fishing pond and then ends in the southeast corner of the park. Situated along the paths are picnic tables, three rain shelters, toilets, and two picnic shelters that can be rented out by groups.

Mountain Biking: Maybury has a 4-mile, single-track loop that winds through a mix of woods and open fields and over numerous small hills. The loop does have several technical segments but generally is considered a beginning to intermediate trail. Mountain bikers park at the horse-staging area reached from the entrance off Beck Road and then follow a paved bike path a half mile south to the posted start of the mountain bike trail.

Visitors exploring the living farm at Maybury State Park

Equestrian Facilities: Eleven miles of bridle paths as well as a staging area for equestrians are located at the end of the access road just beyond the park head-quarters off Beck Road. Near the staging area is Maybury Riding Stable (248-347-1088), which offers horseback riding for both novice and experienced riders, and also offers hayrides. The stable is open daily from 9:00 A.M. until 6:00 P.M. from April through November; it is closed Mondays.

Fishing: Opportunities for anglers are limited in Maybury, but the park does maintain a large pond with fishing piers and docks where it's possible to catch bass and panfish. The pond is reached by taking the bicycle path, which begins a short distance from the Beck Road entrance.

Winter Activities: During the winter the park grooms and tracks 9.3 miles of ski trails, combining the foot trails, bicycle paths, and a portion of the bridle trails. The concession operator (248-348-1190) near the parking lot off of Eight Mile Road rents ski equipment and offers lessons as well as maintains a half-mile lighted trail for night skiing. There is also an excellent sledding hill a short walk in from the Eight Mile Road parking lot. Snowmobiles and all other off-road vehicles (ORVs) are prohibited in the park.

Day-Use Facilities: The park has a major picnic area, accessible by foot along a paved path that begins at the Eight Mile Road parking lot, with tables, shelters that can be rented, and a tot lot. Other picnic tables and shelters are scattered throughout

MAYBURY STATE PARK

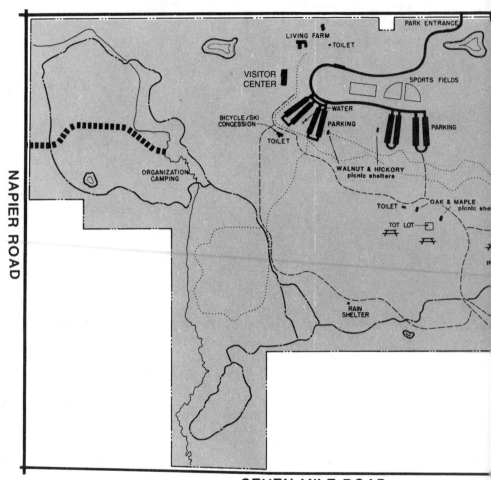

PARK ENTRANCE

LIVING FARM
TOILET

VISITOR
CENTER

SPORTS FIELDS

BICYCLE/SKI
CONCESSION

WATER

PARKING

PARKING

TOILET

ORGANIZATION
CAMPING

WALNUT & HICKORY
picnic shelters

TOILET

OAK & MAPLE
picnic she

TOT LOT

RAIN
SHELTER

NAPIER ROAD

SEVEN MILE ROAD

LEGEND

—··— AREA BOUNDARY	—·— HORSE TRAIL	
·········· FOOT TRAIL	PICNIC SITES	
— — — PAVED BIKE TRAIL	▮▮▮▮▮ OCG ENTRANCE	
···B··· MOUNTAIN BIKE TRAIL		

OPEN APRIL 15 TO DECEMBER 15 ONLY

STATE LAND

I-275 5 miles ⟶

EIGHT MILE ROAD

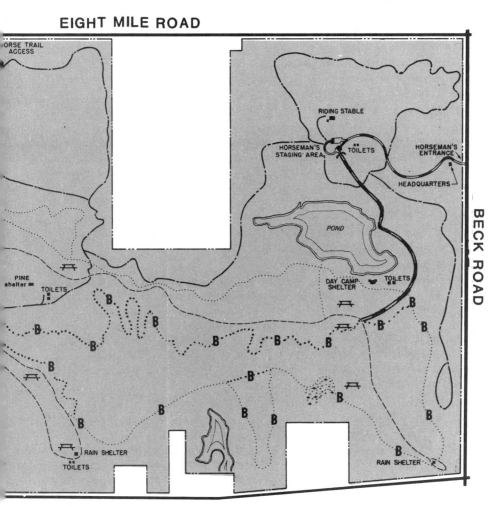

HORSE TRAIL
ACCESS

RIDING STABLE

HORSEMAN'S
STAGING AREA

TOILETS

HORSEMAN'S
ENTRANCE

HEADQUARTERS

BECK ROAD

POND

PINE
shelter

TOILETS

DAY CAMP
SHELTER

TOILETS

B

RAIN SHELTER
TOILETS

RAIN SHELTER

SCALE IN FEET

0   600

300   900

north

the park, while on the south side of the fishing pond is a day-use camp that is rented out to groups for natural resource education programs.

Access and Information: The main entrance to the park is on Eight Mile Road, 5 miles west of I-275. The horseman's entrance, parking area for mountain bikers, and park headquarters are located on an access road off Beck Road just south of Eight Mile Road. For more information, contact Maybury State Park, 20145 Beck Road, Northville, MI 48167; or call (248) 349-8390.

Island Lake Recreation Area

▲ Island Lake Recreation Area is a 3,466-acre park in Livingston County that is almost perfectly divided in half by the Huron River. At the northeast corner of the park is the lower half of Kent Lake and Kensington Dam, the reason for the huge man-made body of water. From here the Huron River, in its natural state, winds 7 miles through a rolling terrain of open meadows and old farm fields, mature woodlots of oak and maple, and small wetlands and marshes before departing from the park's southwest corner.

The recreation area was set up in 1927 with a 50-acre donation from the Dodge brothers, famous Detroit auto magnates, and today offers an incredible variety of activities from canoeing and mountain biking to hot-air ballooning. Island Lake draws around 375,000 visitors a year, with the bulk of them arriving between Memorial Day and Labor Day. From the main entrance off Kensington Road, a scenic park drive winds 6.5 miles along the south side of the Huron River before crossing it to end at Island Lake.

Camping: Island Lake no longer maintains a campground for individuals or families, only an organization campground for youth groups and a pair of canoe-in campsites on the Huron River.

Canoeing: Canoeing the Huron River might be the best way to view the recreation area. Heavner Canoe Rental (248-437-9406 or 248-685-2379), located at the day-use area on Kent Lake, is open during the summer from Wednesday through Sunday. Most people rent a canoe just to paddle around the lake, which is a shame, since perhaps the most scenic stretch of the river runs through Island Lake. This part of the Huron is undeveloped and designated "country scenic" under the Natural Rivers Act. Canoeists should plan on 1.5 hours to paddle from Kent Lake to Riverbend Picnic Area, 2.5 to 3 hours to paddle to Placeway Picnic Area, and 4 to 5 hours to paddle the entire park to US 23. Pick-ups and a return to Kent Lake can be arranged through Heavner Canoe Rental from either spot.

The canoe-in campsites are posted along the river halfway between Riverbend and Placeway picnic areas and each consists of a hand pump, tables, and fire rings in an open field.

Hiking: In the early 1990s, the park's hiking trails were redesigned to incorporate a mountain biking system. You can still walk the trails, but keep in mind the heavy bicycle usage the trails receive on weekends and in the evening during the summer.

Mountain Biking: Island Lake has a 13-mile, single-track trail system that was built in 1992 by a chapter of the Michigan Mountain Bikers Association. Divided into two loops, the West Loop is an 8-mile ride that is generally level and can be managed by most beginners. The 5-mile East Loop, rated as intermediate, involves steeper slopes but also includes a scenic stretch along the Huron River.

Both loops begin at a trailhead at the mountain biker's parking area in what used

Huron River

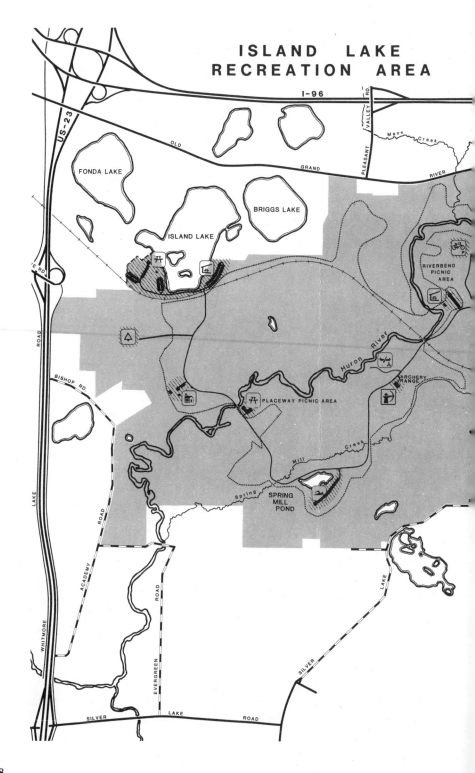

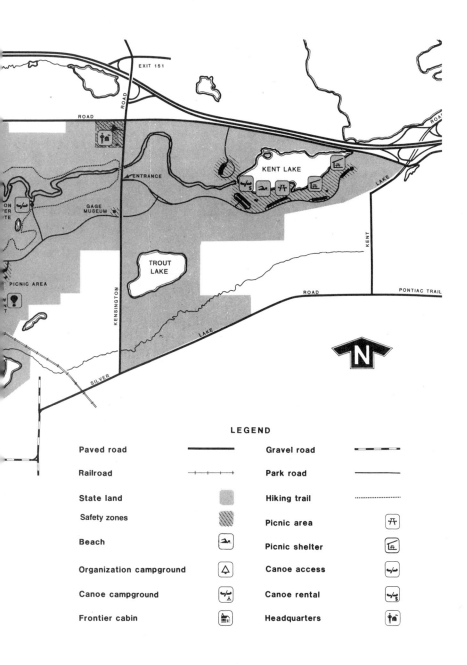

LEGEND

Paved road	——————	Gravel road	▬ ▭ ▬ ▭
Railroad	＋—＋—＋—＋	Park road	——————
State land	▓	Hiking trail	··········
Safety zones	▨	Picnic area	🌲
Beach	🏊	Picnic shelter	🏠
Organization campground	△	Canoe access	🛶
Canoe campground	🛶	Canoe rental	🛶$
Frontier cabin	🏚	Headquarters	👫

to be the organization campground. Just before reaching Riverbend Picnic Area, turn north on a dirt road and follow it to the bike staging area at the end of the road.

Fishing: Spring Mill Pond is stocked each spring with full-size rainbow trout, and a special catch-and-release season is held from April 1 to the last Saturday of that month. Only artificial lures can be used, and all trout must be returned to the water. The regular season begins on the last Saturday of April, when anglers can use live bait and keep the fish. The trout fishing tapers off by mid-May. There are panfish and some bass in Island and Kent Lakes and good bass fishing in the Huron River. Anglers often fish the river by floating a portion in a canoe or wading it.

Cabins: Island Lake has two frontier, twenty-bunk cabins for rent, located about 100 yards from each other at the west end of the park. You can drive to the cabins, which are situated in a wooded area of the park on the north side of the Huron River. Although they are popular with scout troops and other groups during the winter, they are often rented in the summer by families.

Balloon Port: In 1987, Island Park opened Meadow Balloon Port, the first permanent hot-air-balloon port in the state park system. Eventually, DNR officials estimate, spectators will be able to observe some twenty-five flights weekly during the May-through-September flying season. But for now, it's best to call the park ahead of time for dates of scheduled take-offs.

Day-Use Facilities: Day-use facilities, including sandy beaches, designated swimming areas, picnic tables, and grills, are located at Island Lake and Kent Lake, where there is a boat rental concession. There are also picnic areas at Riverbend, Placeway, where the park drive crosses the Huron River, and Meadow Balloon Port, and there is swimming at Spring Mill Pond. The park has three picnic shelters for rent, at Riverbend, Kent Lake, and the balloon port.

Winter Use: The cabins are rented year-round, and the park draws snowmobilers throughout the winter. They can use the entire park, with the exception of plowed roads and an area 400 feet on either side of the Huron River. There is little Nordic skiing at Island Lake during the winter.

Access and Information: The park entrance is on Kensington Road, a half mile south of Grand River Road. From I-96 head south on Kensington Road (exit 151). For information or cabin reservations, contact Island Lake Recreation Area, 12950 East Grand River Road, Brighton, MI 48116; or call (810) 229-7067.

Brighton Recreation Area

▲ Glacial activity blessed several southeast Michigan counties with rolling terrain and numerous lakes, examples of which can be seen at Brighton Recreation Area, 50 miles northwest of Detroit in Livingston County. Scattered throughout the 4,947-acre park are moraines, outwash deposits, kettles, and other typical features of the Pleistocene Epoch, the glacial era that ended 25,000 years ago.

Brighton's ten lakes were the result of retreating glaciers. The rolling terrain left by the glaciers is today covered by oak-hickory woodlands, along with the open fields of abandoned farms originally built in the 1820s. Brighton Recreation Area was established in 1944 and has increased its acreage over the years, but it is still broken up by privately owned lots. Its largest section lies east of Chilson Road and contains most of Bishop, Appleton, Reed, and Murray Lakes, whose campgrounds, foot trails, and beaches attract the most visitors.

The park draws 40,000 visitors annually, and the use is spread throughout the year. The interesting topography and the variety of wildlife, including whitetail

Riders on the trail at Brighton Recreation Area (Photo courtesy Michigan DNR)

deer, fox, and pheasant, make the recreation area a popular destination year-round for outdoor enthusiasts including hikers, skiers, and equestrians. In October it's an excellent area to view fall colors, and in the spring it becomes a favorite hunting ground for morel mushroom pickers.

Camping: On the shores of the largest lake in the park is Bishop Lake Campground, which contains 149 modern sites in a mostly open area of young trees. None of the sites are on the water, and there is very little shade. The campground has its own beach, and the boat launch for Bishop Lake is located here. More wooded settings are found at two rustic campgrounds, each with 25 sites. Appleton Lake Campground is posted on Bishop Lake Road and features picnic tables, fire rings, and access to the water. Murray Lake Campground is off Bauer Road.

The modern campground tends to be filled most weekends during the summer and often is more than half full during the week. It's generally easier to get a site at the rustic facilities, even on the weekends. An organization camp is located on the south side of Bishop Lake.

Hiking: The park has 7 miles of maintained foot trails with two main loops, located east of Chilson Road. The Penosha Trail is a 5-mile loop that wanders through wooded hills and planked wetlands and takes about 2.5 hours to walk. In the middle of this large loop is the Kahchin Trail, a 2-mile circular walk that passes abandoned farm fields with the original stone fences that were built in the 1800s.

BRIGHTON RECREATION AREA

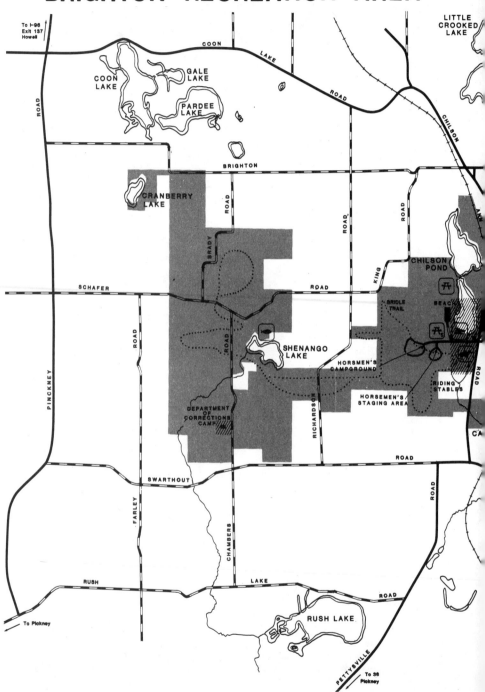

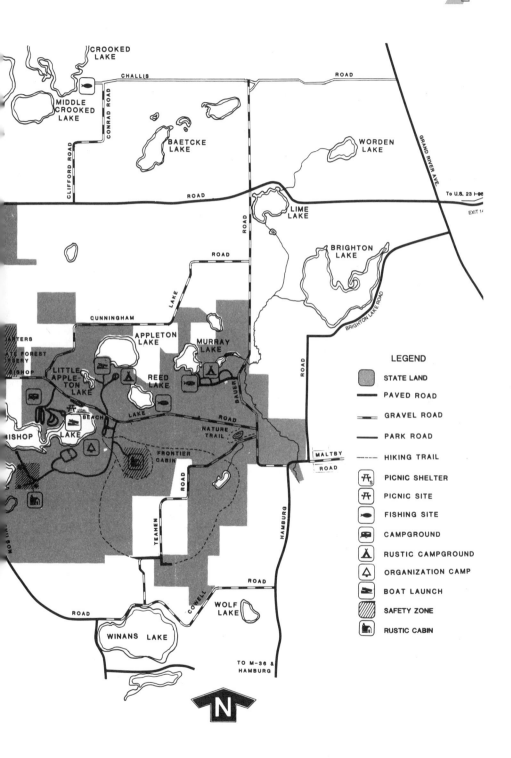

LEGEND

STATE LAND

——— PAVED ROAD

GRAVEL ROAD

PARK ROAD

- - - - HIKING TRAIL

PICNIC SHELTER

PICNIC SITE

FISHING SITE

CAMPGROUND

RUSTIC CAMPGROUND

ORGANIZATION CAMP

BOAT LAUNCH

SAFETY ZONE

RUSTIC CABIN

Both trails begin at a parking lot at the corner of Bishop Lake Road and Rolison Trail, just east of the day-use area on the large lake.

Mountain Biking: Mountain biking is allowed on the hiking trails, but in 1997, volunteers from the Michigan Mountain Biking Association began construction of a new bike trail. Designed exclusively for mountain biking, the new trail system is expected to be 10 to 15 miles in length and will wind through the same terrain as the hiking paths. Once it is completely finished, Penosha Trail and Kahchin Trail will be open only to hikers.

Fishing: Anglers have access to seven of the ten lakes found within the recreation area. Boat launches are found on Chilson Pond and Bishop and Appleton Lakes. Murray Lake has an unimproved launch. Chilson Pond allows electric but not gasoline motors, and Bishop Lake has a no-wake regulation.

Bishop Lake receives the most usage by anglers in search of bass, while Appleton and Murray Lakes are stocked annually with rainbow trout. There are no special seasons or regulations for the trout lakes, though most fishing for the rainbows takes place in April and May. Shenango Lake, reached from Chambers Road, used to be stocked with rainbow trout, but now most anglers enter it to catch bluegill and other panfish. Reed Lake also has an access site, reached from Bishop Lake Road, while Caroga Lake can be reached by foot from an old campground road along Chilson Road.

Day-Use Facilities: Brighton maintains a day-use area on the east side of Bishop Lake that includes a sandy beach, picnic area, and bathhouse. There is also a boat-rental concession that rents canoes, rowboats, and paddleboats daily throughout the summer. There is a day-use area on Chilson Pond with a smaller beach, picnic tables, grills, and three shelters. The shelters can be rented and are often reserved on weekends from June to September.

Cabins: Brighton Recreation Area has four rustic cabins built and designed for family use. Two of the eight-bunk cabins are located near Caroga Lake; another is a bit further from the lake, and it is a short walk from the fourth cabin to the south side of Bishop Lake. Each cabin has a hand pump and a vault toilet as well as a fire ring and a picnic table outside.

There are also three larger cabins located in a small clearing east of Bishop Lake. The twenty-bunk, sixteen-bunk, and twelve-bunk cabins are close to each other and are heavily used by scout troops and other youth groups. The white-frame structures have wood-burning stoves and are situated about halfway along the Kahchin Trail. A locked access road leads to the cabins from Bishop Lake Road.

Winter Activities: Nordic skiing is a popular activity in the park during the winter, with skiers using both the hiking trails and bridle paths. The hiking trails, which pass through a mixture of woods and open fields, make for easier runs than do the horse trails, which are heavily wooded and very hilly. The trails are not groomed, and there is no ski rental concession in the park. Other winter activities include snowmobiling, ice fishing, and sled rides that are arranged through the horse stable.

Equestrian Facilities: On the west side of Chilson Road, just past the park headquarters, there is a horseman's staging area, and an equestrian campground with twenty rustic sites, each equipped with a tie post. Brighton maintains 18 miles of bridle paths, and within the park on Chilson Road is a concession-operated riding stable. Brighton Riding Stables (810-220-6294) is open year-round daily and offers 1- and 2-hour rides as well as trail lessons. Fall is the busiest time of year for the stables, the equestrian campground, and the staging area.

Access and Information: From I-96 just west of US 23, head south on Grand River Road (exit 145) and turn west onto Brighton Road in downtown Brighton. The park is 3 miles southwest of the town and is reached by turning south onto Chilson Road from Brighton Road. For more information or cabin reservations, contact Brighton Recreation Area, 6360 Chilson Road, Route 3, Howell, MI 48843; or call (810) 229-6566.

Proud Lake Recreation Area

Proud Lake, in western Oakland County, is a 4,000-acre recreation area whose rolling terrain includes dense forests, wetlands, two lakes, and a stretch of the Huron River. It draws more than 536,000 visitors annually, but unlike most parks, its usage is evenly divided throughout the year. Camping, canoeing, and swimming are the main activities of the summer, but in the winter Proud Lake is a popular haven for cross-country skiers, and in the spring fly fishermen try their luck in the Huron River.

The park extends from Proud Lake west along the Huron River valley to Old Plank Road. It is split in half from north to south by Wixom Road, from which a dirt access road heads east into the heart of the recreation area, providing access to the headquarters, parking lot, and the Huron River Outdoor Center at the end of the road. Proud Lake Recreation Area also includes a separate parcel of land, which contains no visitor facilities or trails, at the corner of Carroll Lake and Commerce Roads.

Camping: The park has 130 modern sites situated on an open bluff, from which there is a good view of Proud Lake. Facilities include two mini-cabins for rent and a

Part of the Huron River is set aside for fly fishing only

35

MICHIGAN STATE PARKS

LEGEND

GRAVEL ROAD

PAVED ROAD

PARK ROAD

BIKING & BRIDLE TRAIL

PICNIC SITE

BOAT LAUNCH

ORGANIZATION CAMPGROUND

CANOE RENTAL

STATE LAND

NATURAL AREA

PICNIC SHELTER

HIKING TRAIL

HORSEMEN'S STAGING AREA

BEACH

CAMPGROUND

OUTDOOR CENTER

HEADQUARTERS

AREA CLOSED TO HUNTING

NATURE CENTER

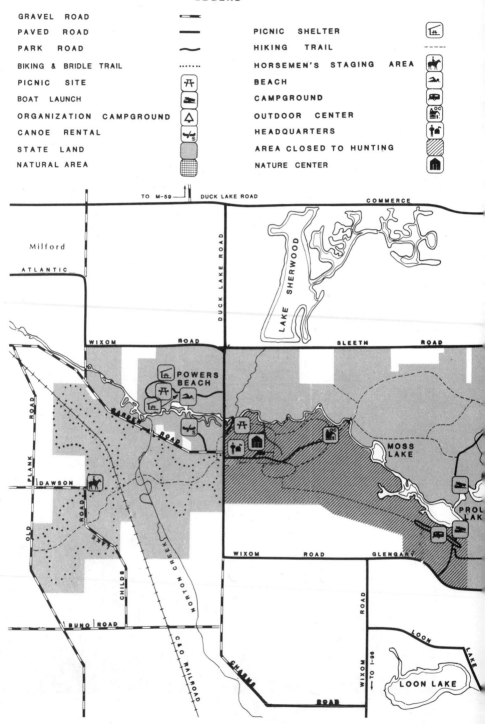

36

PROUD LAKE RECREATION AREA

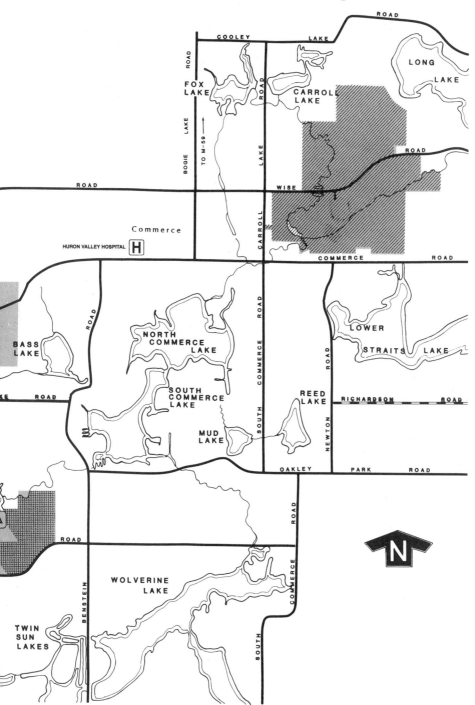

separate beach and boat launch for campers. Because it's close to metropolitan Detroit, the campground is filled most weekends from early May through mid-September when the weather is good. The campground is reached east from Wixom Road on Glengary Road and is well posted. There are no rustic sites at Proud Lake Recreation Area, but there is an organization camp.

Hiking: There are 11 miles of maintained trails, with most of them beginning at the nature center parking lot. South of the parking lot is the Marsh Trail, a 1.25-mile walk around a wetland area. Departing east is the Main Ski Loop, which winds 2 miles through stands of towering red pine and hardwoods before returning to the parking lot. From this trail a footbridge crosses Huron River and gives access to two longer loops. The trail with blue markers is a total of 3 miles beginning at the parking lot; the red trail is 2.5 miles.

Winter Activities: Proud Lake Recreation Area has an 8-mile trail system for cross-country skiers, who can expect sufficient snow on a handful of weekends in January and February. The trails are accessible from the nature center and wind through forests of gentle, rolling terrain that can be handled by most novice skiers. Experienced skiers often follow the 10 miles of bridle trails on the west side of Duck Lake Road to attempt steeper hills for more challenging runs.

None of the trails are groomed and there is no warming shelter, but skis can be rented from Heavner Canoe Rental (248-685-2379), located near the park headquarters at 2775 Garden Road. Heavner is also the best place to call for a snow report.

Canoeing: Canoeing is a popular activity during the summer along the Huron River, with many canoeists paddling from Powers Beach to the Kensington Dam on Kent Lake in Island Lake Recreation Area, a 6-hour trip. Portage around the dam and utilize the canoe campsites at Island Lake and you can turn the paddle into an overnight trip to a pick-up point on US 23.

Heavner Canoe Rental (248-685-2379) operates a canoe concession daily in the park across from Powers Beach and accessed by Garden Road, which heads west from Wixom Road. The long-time canoe concession also rents boats on Kent Lake in Island Lake Recreation Area, and provides a pick-up service to a number of locations along the river, including US 23.

Fishing: The Huron River is stocked every spring with full-size rainbow and brown trout through a program to introduce anglers to fly fishing. From April 1 to the last Saturday of the month, there are catch-and-release, flies-only regulations on the river from Moss Lake to 100 yards below Wixom Road. Regular trout fishing regulations begin on the last Saturday of April until the season closes on September 20. Most trout fishing takes place in April and early May. After that, anglers generally concentrate on panfish and bass in Huron River and Proud Lake, which has two boat launches.

Day-Use Facilities: West of Wixom Road and north of the headquarters is Powers Beach, a small sandy beach and pond that was made by impounding the Huron River. There are two picnic areas, one near Powers Beach and the other on the shore of Huron River on the east side of Wixom Road.

Equestrian Facilities: Proud Lake Recreation Area has a horseman's staging area that is reached from Dawson and Childs Lake Roads and serves as the starting point for 10 miles of bridle trails through a hilly section of the park. There are no riding stables within the recreation area.

Outdoor Center: Beyond the park headquarters at the end of the access road is the Huron River Outdoor Center, a modern facility with several cabins and a dining hall. The entire facility, not individual cabins, is rented out and can sleep up to 128 persons.

Access and Information: The recreation area is just east of Milford or 12 miles southwest of Pontiac and is reached from I-96 by taking the Wixom Road exit and heading north, or from M-59 by turning south on Duck Lake Road. For reservations, contact Proud Lake Recreation Area, 3500 Wixom Road, Milford, MI 48382; or call (248) 685-2433.

Highland Recreation Area

Highland Recreation Area's rolling terrain, the result of glacial moraines, was originally the country estate of Edsel and Eleanor Ford, and included a magnificent lodge and even farm buildings. In 1926, Ford dammed a small stream to convert what was then a marshy pond into a waterfowl sanctuary that he named Haven Hill Lake. Twenty years later the state purchased the 2,400-acre retreat: lake, lodge, and hills. It became Dodge State Park No.10 in the 1940s, and eventually was expanded into Highland Recreation Area, which preserves a large segment of the hill country in western Oakland County. The lodge, though boarded up, is still an impressive sight, but what really is impressive is the second-growth forest that has been left undisturbed for almost a century. The trees are so large and the species so diverse that 546 acres around the lake was designated a protected natural area in 1954.

Most of the 5,800-acre park extends south of M-59, 17 miles west of Pontiac, and contains a network of scenic roads that wind through the rolling, mostly forested terrain. Come fall these roads, particularly Beaumont Road and the park drive through the Haven Hill Natural Area, become popular destinations for those enchanted by the brilliant autumn colors of sumacs, oaks, birches, and other trees.

The park draws 180,000 visitors year-round, with most of them attracted to Haven Hill or the mountain bike trail, one of most challenging systems in southeast Michigan. Other activities include horseback riding, Nordic skiing, and fishing.

Camping: Highland Recreation Area offers only rustic camping in a former equestrian campground and an organization campground. The rustic campground's thirty sites are situated on the east side of the Haven Hill Natural Area and are open to all campers, with or without horses.

Hiking: Most of the foot trails are in the Haven Hill Natural Area in the northeast corner of the recreation area.

The trailhead for Haven Hill is located on the south side of the lake in Goose Meadow Picnic Area near the dam. The 2-mile network of trails is a pair of loops that pass through the forested rolling hills and low-lying wet areas. The White Loop takes you further into the natural area, over several hills, and across two footbridges through what remains of the original marsh before returning along the lakeshore.

Mountain Biking: Highland Recreation Area features one of the newest and most challenging mountain bike trail systems in southern Michigan. The 16-mile network is composed of four loops and is accessed from a trailhead on Livingston Road south of M-59 via Duck Lake Road. The 3.8-mile A Loop is the easiest ride, but is still a hilly course with many steep climbs and drops. The 5.9-mile B Loop is very hilly with longer climbs, off-camber runs, and logs and rocks. Loops C and D are rated very technical and for advanced riders only. Loop D is often called the "hardest 4 miles of mountain biking in Michigan," and includes climbing 1,140-foot Mount Omich.

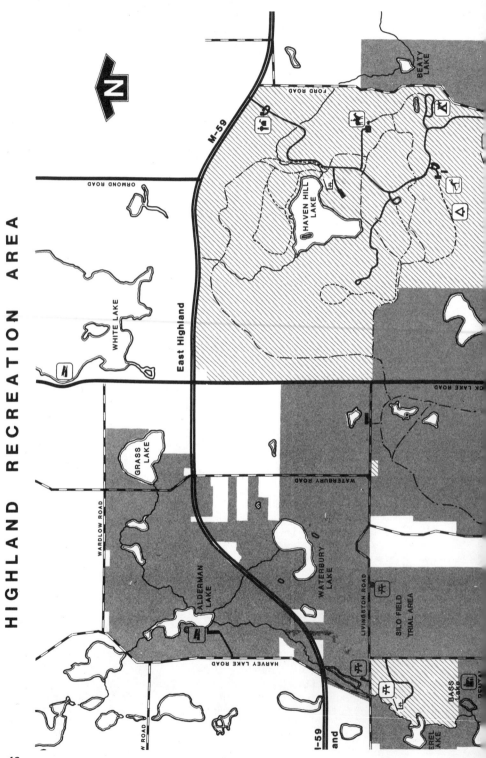

HIGHLAND RECREATION AREA

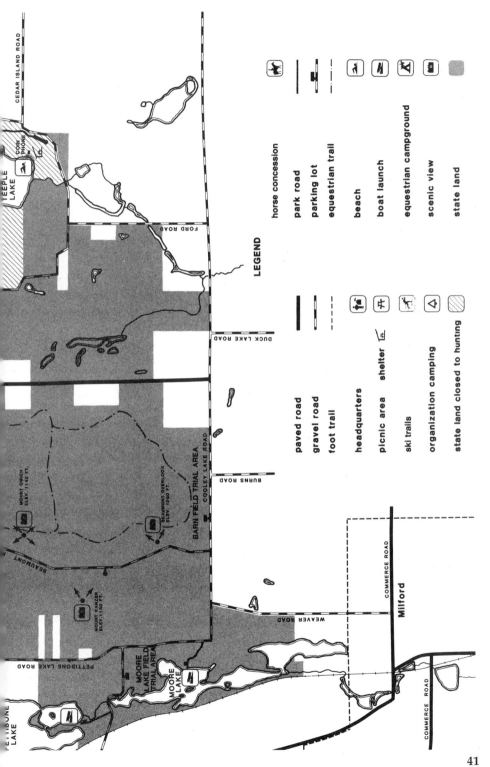

The mountain bike system lies within an area open to horseback riders, but bikers are not allowed to ride on the equestrian trails.

Winter Activities: Nordic skiing is popular in the Haven Hill area, where snowmobilers are prohibited. The trailhead is located at a parking area halfway along the park drive between Haven Hill and Teeple Lake. From here skiers can depart on a 12-mile network of three loops that range from 2.1 miles to 5.3 miles. The skiing is considered moderately challenging due to the terrain of rolling hills. There is no warming shelter nor are the ski trails groomed. Snowmobiling is also allowed in the park but must take place west of Duck Lake Road.

Fishing: There are boat launches on four lakes—Moore, Lower Pettibone, Alderman, and Teeple—and there is access on several others. Many of the lakes are shallow and become weedy during the summer. Perhaps the most popular lake with anglers is Lower Pettibone, which features good populations of northern pike and perch. All the lakes are open for ice fishing during the winter.

Day-Use Facilities: The day-use area at Teeple Lake features a beach and designated swimming area, boat launch on the lake, picnic area, and a rental shelter. At Goose Meadow, on the shores of Haven Hill Lake, there is a picnic area with a shelter as well as trails into the nature study area. Scattered throughout the old pine plantation of Dodge Park No.10 are picnic tables and a shelter. This day-use area is a picturesque spot overlooking Pickerel Lake.

Cabin: The park maintains a six-bunk frontier cabin on Bass Lake just south of Dodge Park No.10. The cabin can be reached by car and features an electric stove and refrigerator.

Equestrian Facilities: Horseback riding is a popular activity here, and the park features 16 miles of equestrian trails and the Highland Recreation Area Riding Stable (248-887-4349). The stable is open year-round daily from spring through fall and offers trail riding, lessons, and sleigh rides in the winter.

Access and Information: The park drive through Haven Hill Natural Area to Teeple Lake and Goose Meadow is reached from M-59 (Highland Road) 15 miles west of Pontiac. Also providing access into the recreation area, further west along M-59 is Duck Lake Road, from which Lower Pettibone and Beaumont Roads are reached by turning west onto Livingston Road. For more information or reservations, contact Highland Recreation Area, 5200 East Highland Road, Milford, MI 48363; or call (248) 685-2433.

Dodge No. 4 State Park

⚓ At 139 acres, Dodge No. 4 State Park is the smallest unit in southeast Michigan but one of the most popular. The park, on Cass Lake in Oakland County, draws 600,000 visitors a year with the vast majority of them arriving between Memorial Day and Labor Day. There is a lightly wooded hill in the middle of the park that makes for a pleasant picnic area, but undoubtedly the main attraction of Dodge No. 4 is its sandy beach and swimming area. There are no camping sites or hiking trails in the park and very little use during the winter.

Day-Use Facilities: The park has parking for 1,000 vehicles, but on most Sunday afternoons in June and July the lot fills up and rangers are forced to turn away additional visitors. The swimming area has picnic tables and grills, a large bathhouse, a store, and a boat rental concession. Canoes, rowboats, and paddleboats

Cass Lake, Dodge No. 4 State Park

are rented from late May to early September with hours varying according to the weather and demand. The park also has a picnic shelter on Gerundegut Bay that can be rented.

Fishing: At 1,280 acres, Cass Lake is the largest body of water in Oakland County and is unquestionably one of the busiest during the summer. Heavy competition from jet skis, water skis, and sailboats make most fishing activity impossible in the middle of the day. Anglers head out early in the morning or after dusk to fish for the lake's renowned populations of largemouth and smallmouth bass.

Shore fishermen at Dodge No. 4 catch mostly panfish and concentrate around Gerundegut Bay. The no-wake bay is also the best location for northern pike and largemouth bass. During the winter anglers venture out onto the bay to fish for pike and bluegill through the ice. The state park maintains a boat launch on Gerundegut Bay with parking for seventy-six vehicles and trailers.

Access and Information: The park is 6 miles southwest of Pontiac and is reached from M-59 by turning south on Cass Lake Road and then west on Cass-Elizabeth Road. Opposite of Mitch's Restaurant turn onto Parkway Drive. For information, contact Dodge No. 4 State Park, 4250 Parkway Drive, Waterford, MI 48328; or call (248) 666-1020.

Pontiac Lake Recreation Area

Although it contains four lakes, by far the most noted one in Pontiac Lake Recreation Area is its namesake, a 585-acre body of water created when the Huron River was dammed in the 1930s. It is known by anglers as a superb bass lake, but on a hot day it attracts hundreds of day visitors who want to lie out on its sandy beaches or dive into the lake's cool water to escape the heat of the city.

North of Pontiac Lake lies the rest of the 3,800-acre recreation area, which is situated in the heart of Oakland County. The middle of the park is a ridge of wooded moraine hills of oak, maple, and aspen, while nearby open fields are remnants of the farms that once occupied the area before the state took it over in 1944. The Huron River flows through the western end of the park, a low-lying wetland area.

Thanks in part to a mountain biking trail system that was built in the early 1990s, Pontiac Lake now attracts more than 700,000 visitors year-round. Surprisingly, although the park is on the edge of metropolitan Detroit, its campground is rarely filled in the summer, even on the weekends.

Camping: There are 176 sites in Pontiac Lake Recreation Area's modern campground, situated in the heart of the park and reached by driving north on Teggerdine Road from Pontiac Lake Road and then turning east on Maceday Road. The area, a former apple orchard, is mostly rolling fields with many of the sites set back in the bordering woods. There are also rent-a-tipi units available. The campground fills on holiday weekends and during special events such as historical encampments, mountain bike races, and Halloween Campout weekend. But during the rest of the summer a site can usually be obtained without advance reservations, even on weekends. Pontiac Lake also has an organization camp on Maceday Road and a horseman's campground at the east end of it.

Hiking: The only official foot trail is a 1.8-mile path from Orchard Hill Campground to the beach on Pontiac Lake. Halfway, the trail climbs an old ski club hill from where good views are obtained of the park to as far away as the Silverdome Stadium in Pontiac.

Mountain Biking: Pontiac Lake is home to one of the most popular mountain biking trail systems in southeast Michigan, so popular that on the weekends it is often packed with bike traffic by midmorning. The 11.5-mile system begins at a trailhead at the day-use area parking lot and then crosses Gale Road and winds through the wooded hills and fields in the heart of the park. The outside loop of the system is a 10.5-mile ride along a winding single track that includes several scenic overlooks and steep downhill runs. Although not as challenging as the Potawatomi Trail in the Pinckney Recreation Area or the Highland Recreation Area trail, Pontiac Lake is still recommended for intermediate to advanced mountain bikers.

Fishing: Pontiac Lake is regarded as a good bass lake and is the site of several bass tournaments each summer. The other popular species is northern pike, and during the winter the lake is a shantytown of anglers who spear pike through the ice. The lake is also fished for channel catfish, black crappie, bluegill, and yellow perch.

Although the lake reaches depths of 30 feet, more than 80 percent of it is less than 5 feet deep. Also keep in mind that Pontiac Lake is heavily used during the summer by water skiers, tubers, and jet skiers. The park has a barrier-free fishing pier and boat launch at the east end of the lake that is reached by the beach entrance off Gale Road.

Equestrian Facilities: Along with 17 miles of bridle trails, the park has a horseman's staging area and campground at the end of Maceday Road. Nearby is the Pontiac Lake Riding Stable. The concession-operated stable (248-625-3410) rents horses and offers hayrides, sunset rides, and lessons daily in the summer and from Tuesday through Sunday in the spring and fall.

Day-Use Facilities: The park maintains a large beach at the east end of the lake, reached by exiting north off of M-59 onto Williams Lake Road and then turning

Canada geese

PONTIAC LAKE RECREAT

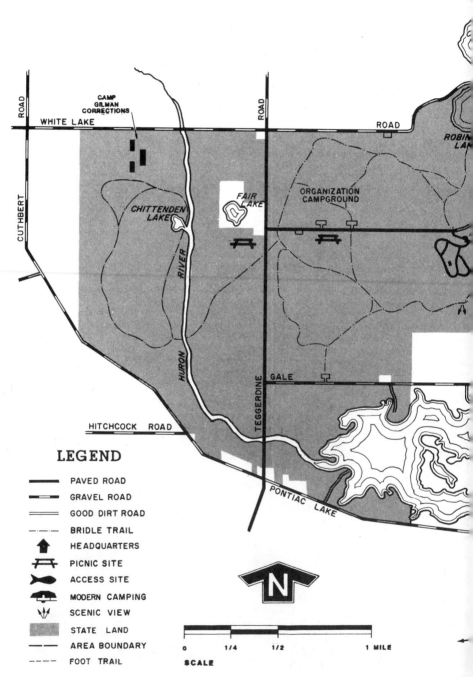

CAMP
GILMAN
CORRECTIONS

WHITE LAKE

ROAD

ROAD

ROAD

ROBIN
LA

ROAD

CUTHBERT

CHITTENDEN
LAKE

FAIR
LAKE

ORGANIZATION
CAMPGROUND

RIVER

HURON

GALE

TEGGERDINE

HITCHCOCK   ROAD

PONTIAC   LAKE

LEGEND

————	PAVED ROAD
—·—·—	GRAVEL ROAD
═══	GOOD DIRT ROAD
─··─··─	BRIDLE TRAIL
⬆	HEADQUARTERS
⛱	PICNIC SITE
🐟	ACCESS SITE
⛺	MODERN CAMPING
⚜	SCENIC VIEW
▓	STATE LAND
— —	AREA BOUNDARY
----	FOOT TRAIL

N

SCALE

0   1/4   1/2   1 MILE

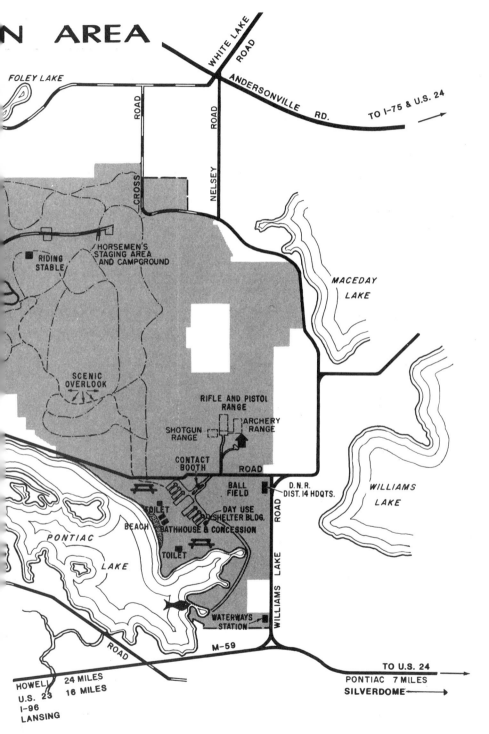

N AREA

FOLEY LAKE

WHITE LAKE ROAD

ANDERSONVILLE RD.

TO I-75 & U.S. 24

ROAD

NELSEY ROAD

CROSS ROAD

RIDING STABLE

HORSEMEN'S STAGING AREA AND CAMPGROUND

MACEDAY LAKE

SCENIC OVERLOOK

RIFLE AND PISTOL RANGE

SHOTGUN RANGE

ARCHERY RANGE

CONTACT BOOTH

ROAD

BALL FIELD

D.N.R. DIST. 14 HDQTS.

WILLIAMS LAKE

TOILET

BEACH

DAY USE SHELTER BLDG.

BATHHOUSE & CONCESSION

WILLIAMS LAKE ROAD

TOILET

PONTIAC LAKE

WATERWAYS STATION

ROAD

M-59

HOWELL 24 MILES
16 MILES
U.S. 23
I-96
LANSING

TO U.S. 24
PONTIAC 7 MILES
SILVERDOME

west on Gale Road. The day-use area includes picnic tables, a bathhouse, a day shelter, volleyball courts, and a concession store. On the north side of Gale Road, opposite the beach entrance, are practice ranges for shotgun, rifle and pistol, and archery. The park provides sandbags, a staple gun for targets, and ear protection, but no other equipment or ammunition. The ranges are extremely busy from Labor Day to December, when they are used by more than 26,000 shooters preparing for the upcoming hunting seasons.

Winter Activities: Park use after December is limited for the most part to ice fishermen and snowmobilers. There is very little Nordic skiing at Pontiac Lake Recreation Area, as most skiers choose to go to nearby Highland Recreation Area, where a large section of the park is closed off to snowmobiling.

Access and Information: Most visitors reach the park from M-59 (Highland Road), exiting at Williams Lake Road to reach the day-use areas or Pontiac Road for the campground. The park is 16 miles east of US 23 and 7 miles west of Pontiac. For information or reservations, contact Pontiac Lake Recreation Area, 7800 Gale Road, Waterford, MI 48327; or call (248) 666-1020.

Seven Lakes State Park

Big Seven Lake, with its many arms and islands ringed by rolling hills, occupies the heart of Seven Lakes State Park and is the destination of most visitors. But the 1,600-acre park in northern Oakland County features six other lakes, and all but two of them can be reached by vehicle or on foot. A relatively new park, Seven Lakes opened in 1977 after the farmland and wooded rolling hills that make up the park were purchased from a development group, whose plans fell through.

The park drive provides a good overview of the area. Several times the road passes high points, including one posted as Overlook Parking, which has a good view of Big Seven, Little Seven, and Dickinson Lakes.

The park draws almost 100,000 visitors annually, with most usage taking place during the summer on Big Seven Lake, which draws swimmers, anglers, and families looking for a scenic place to picnic.

Camping: Seven Lakes State Park features a seventy-one-site modern campground that overlooks Sand Lake in the southeast corner of the park. Sand Lake used to be a gravel pit, so the campground is in an open, grassy area in a partially wooded bowl. There's a small swimming area on the lake, and a trail that connects the campground to Spring Lake, a walk-in lake that can be fished for bluegill and bass.

The campground fills up on holiday weekends, but the rest of the summer it's easy to obtain a site, even on the weekends.

Hiking: The park maintains a 6.5-mile trail system that is open to hikers. Trails start at the beach and day-use area on Big Seven Lake, go past Little Seven, Dickinson, and Spring Lakes, and end at the campground. The paths wind over mostly wooded hills but pass open fields and wetlands near Little Seven Lake. Nature Trail Loop is a 0.7-mile-long interpretive path that begins at the campground and swings past Spring Lake. The main trailhead and a display of the routes are located at the picnic area overlooking Big Seven Lake, but you can connect up with the trails at several places throughout the park, including Overlook Parking and the Dickinson Lake boat launch.

Mountain Biking: Mountain bikers are allowed on a 3.5-mile segment of the park's trail system, which begins at Overlook Parking and extends to Dickinson

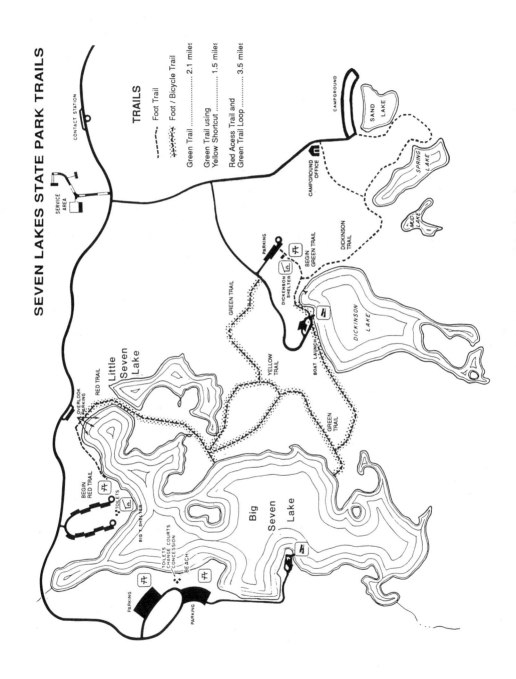

SEVEN LAKES STATE PARK TRAILS

TRAILS

- – – – Foot Trail
- ······· Foot / Bicycle Trail

Green Trail .... 2.1 miles

Green Trail using
Yellow Shortcut .... 1.5 miles

Red Acess Trail and
Green Trail Loop .... 3.5 miles

CONTACT STATION

SERVICE AREA

CAMPGROUND

CAMPGROUND OFFICE

SAND LAKE

SPRING LAKE

MUD LAKE

DICKINSON TRAIL

PARKING

BEGIN GREEN TRAIL

DICKENSON SHELTER

GREEN TRAIL

DICKINSON LAKE

BOAT LAUNCH

YELLOW TRAIL

GREEN TRAIL

Little Seven Lake

RED TRAIL

OVERLOOK PARKING

BEGIN RED TRAIL

TOILETS

BIG SHELTER

TOILETS CHANGE COURTS CONCESSION

BEACH

Big Seven Lake

PARKING

PARKING

Lake. The mountain bike trails, marked as red, green, and yellow trails, cover a rolling terrain that can be handled by most intermediate mountain bikers.

Fishing: Of the seven lakes in the park, Big Seven Lake attracts the most anglers. Many fish its inlets and around the islands for largemouth bass, or search the deeper sections with leadhead jigs or crankbaits for walleye, which were stocked by the DNR Fisheries Division for a number of years. The 170-acre lake also offers opportunities to land both panfish and perch. The second largest lake, at 44 acres, is Dickinson Lake, a deep, clear body of water that features muskie along with panfish and bass. Spring Lake, a quarter-mile walk from the campground, is best fished in float tubes for bass and panfish.

Wood duck

There are boat launches on both lakes, and there is an electric-motor-only regulation on both lakes as well. Anglers without a boat can rent one from a concessionaire at the day-use area. Dickinson Lake also has a floating pier for anglers.

Day-Use Facilities: On the west side of Big Seven Lake, the park maintains a beach and picnic area, which includes a bathhouse, a designated swimming area, tables, and grills. There is also a boat rental concession open daily during the summer. Boats for rent include canoes, rowboats, and paddleboats. On the north end of Big Seven Lake there is a picnic area with tables, grills, and two shelters on a hill with an excellent view of most of the lake. There is a picnic area off the park road to Dickinson Road with a shelter that can be rented.

Winter Activities: A small number of Nordic skiers use the trails in the winter, though the trails are neither tracked nor groomed and there is no ski rental concession in the park.

Access and Information: The park is a mile west of Holly, with an entrance off Fish Lake Road, just north of Grange Hall Road. From I-75, take exit 101 and head west on Grange Hall Road. For more information or reservations, contact Seven Lakes State Park, 2220 Tinsman Road, Fenton, MI 48430; or call (248) 634-7271.

Holly Recreation Area

Holly Recreation Area is an 8,000-acre park in northern Oakland County that contains a diversity of terrain in six different sections on both sides of I-75. The sections of the park on the west side of I-75 consist of fairly flat wooded lots, reverted orchards, tamarack swamp, and marsh bog. Areas east of the highway feature heavily forested hills, second-growth forests, more wetlands, and open fields that at one time were farmed. Throw in seventeen lakes and a handful of creeks, and you have a park that not only offers a variety of activities but also draws an incredible diversity of birdlife.

Holly offers excellent opportunities for birders and wildlife photographers, as 105 species of birds nest in the recreation area and an additional 87 species stop here during migration. Of the 209 species that may be spotted in the park, five are listed as threatened or endangered in the state of Michigan, including ospreys, loggerhead shrikes, and Kirtland's warblers. Other rare birds not commonly seen in this part of the state but sometimes spotted in the park are northern harriers, common loons, and caspian terns.

The largest, most developed and heavily used area of the park contains McGinnis Lake, north of McGinnis Road, and Heron, Valley, and Wildwood Lakes south of it. The majority of the 297,000 visitors that annually enter the park are drawn to this section, and the bulk of them arrive during the traditional summer season.

Camping: McGinnis Lake Campground offers 144 modern sites with electricity and fifteen rustic sites that fill only on weekends and holidays. The sites are spread out along five loops, offering quite a bit of privacy though not much shade, as the campground is set up on open hills near McGinnis Lake. There is no swimming area or boat launch on the lake. Within the campground is a rent-a-tipi that sleeps four and is popular with families, and two mini-cabins. On the south side of the lake the park maintains an organization camp that is available to scout troops and other nonprofit groups.

Hiking: Looping through the units east of I-75 are 10 miles of foot trails that are lightly used and at times may be hard to follow. The longest walk is the Wilderness

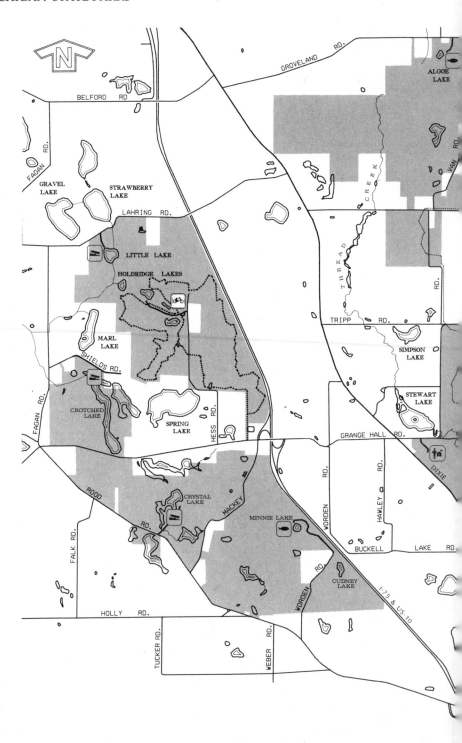

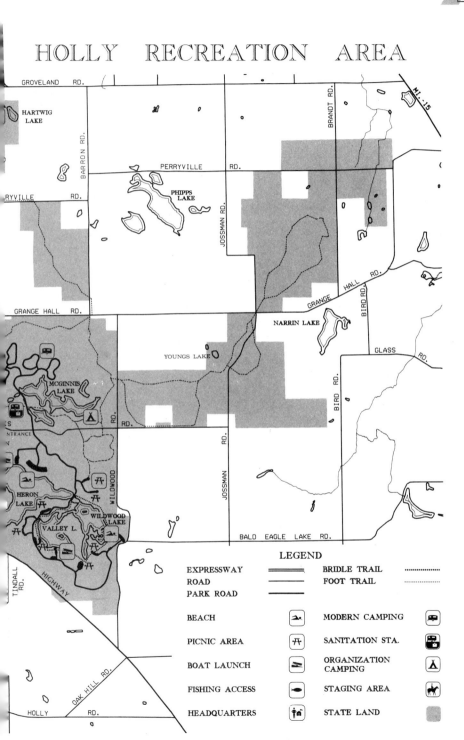

HOLLY RECREATION AREA

LEGEND

EXPRESSWAY

ROAD

PARK ROAD

BEACH

PICNIC AREA

BOAT LAUNCH

FISHING ACCESS

HEADQUARTERS

BRIDLE TRAIL

FOOT TRAIL

MODERN CAMPING

SANITATION STA.

ORGANIZATION CAMPING

STAGING AREA

STATE LAND

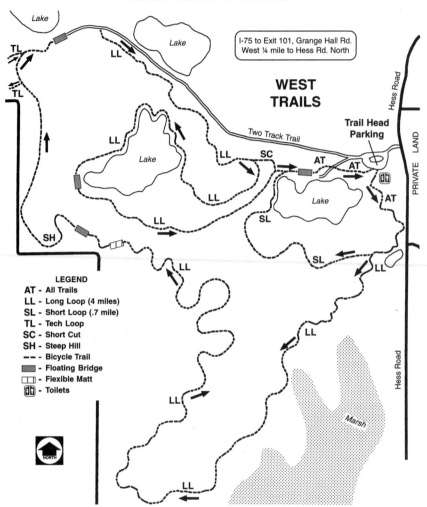

HOLDRIDGE LAKES
MOUNTAIN BICYCLE AREA
HOLLY RECREATION AREA

I-75 to Exit 101, Grange Hall Rd.
West ¼ mile to Hess Rd. North

WEST TRAILS

Two Track Trail

Trail Head Parking

PRIVATE LAND

Hess Road

LEGEND

AT - All Trails
LL - Long Loop (4 miles)
SL - Short Loop (.7 mile)
TL - Tech Loop
SC - Short Cut
SH - Steep Hill
- - - - Bicycle Trail
- Floating Bridge
- Flexible Matt
- Toilets

Marsh

Trail, which can be picked up from Wildwood or McGinnis Roads and followed as it extends several miles past Young Lake to a section north of Grange Road. The Saginaw Trail begins near the campground and loops north along Perryville Road before returning to McGinnis Lake. There is also a short loop that has a trailhead at Overlook Picnic Area near Wildwood Lake.

Mountain Biking: In 1994, volunteers from the Michigan Mountain Bike Association designed and constructed the Holdridge Lakes Mountain Area in a section of the park on the west side of I-75. The 7-mile trail system has five loops through a terrain of rolling woods, lakes, and marshes. Most of the system is single track that can be handled by beginners. The Long Loop is the most impressive ride, a 4-mile trail that winds past three marshy lakes and features a steep hill on its back side.

Frontier cabin, Holly Recreation Area

To reach the area from I-75, take exit 101 and head west on Grange Hall Road. Within a quarter mile turn north on Hess Road and in 1.4 miles you will reach the posted trailhead and parking area.

Day-Use Areas: Small beaches are maintained on Heron and Wildwood Lakes and there are picnic tables, grills, and a bathhouse at each. Heron Lake also has a boat rental concession that varies its hours throughout the summer. The day-use area, reached from a park entrance off McGinnis Road, contains five separate picnic areas, many with fine views of the water and shelters available for rent.

Fishing: Most fishing activity takes place on Heron, Valley, and Wildwood Lakes, where anglers catch predominantly bluegill and largemouth bass. The lakes have an electric-motor-only regulation on boats, which can be launched from ramps on Heron or Valley. At the northern edge of the park are Algoe and Hartwig Lakes, two small lakes off Groveland Road that have fishing access sites and occasionally attract anglers. On the west side of I-75, Crystal, Crotched, and Little Lakes have small boat launches, but these lakes are extremely shallow in places and the roads in to them are rough.

Cabin: Within the recreation area is Rolston Cabin, an extremely scenic log structure situated on a small pond just off McGinnis Road. The six-bunk cabin has a hand pump for water and pit toilets, but electric lights, stove, and refrigerator. The popular cabin, which can be reached by car, is heavily booked on weekends almost year-round.

Winter Activities: The park road in the Heron and Wildwood Lakes day-use area is not plowed in the winter and when there is sufficient snow, the road becomes a fun and scenic place to cross-country ski. It is a 6-mile round trip from the park entrance that traverses several hills, including an especially long downhill run from Overlook Picnic Area to Heron and Wildwood Lakes.

Access and Information: Holly Recreation Area, located 12 miles north of Pontiac, can be reached from I-75 by turning east onto Grange Hall Road (exit 101). To the east just past Dixie Highway is the park headquarters. From here Grange Hall Road curves sharply to the north. Continuing east is McGinnis Road, which passes the entrances to the campground and the day-use areas on Heron and Valley Lakes. For information or reservations, contact Holly Recreation Area, 8100 Grange Hall Road, Holly, MI 48442; or call (248) 634-8811.

Ortonville Recreation Area

Straddling the border of Oakland and Lapeer Counties is Ortonville Recreation Area, a lightly used unit of 5,400 acres. The park features a hilly contour, including one of the highest points in southeast Michigan at almost 1,200 feet, along with nineteen lakes and a vast acreage of forests. Most of the park, in fact, is heavily wooded, while open fields, regenerating farmlands, and wetlands north of Tody Lake constitute the rest of the terrain.

Ortonville draws about 90,000 visitors a year, of which 75 percent arrive during the traditional summer season to enjoy the day-use facilities at Big Fish Lake. The rest of the park offers interesting terrain and a variety of activities, from camping and hiking to mountain biking, Nordic skiing, and horseback riding, with virtually no crowds to contend with.

Camping: Algoe Lake Campground is a rustic facility of twenty-five sites with vault toilets located off Sawmill Road. It is rarely filled, even on the weekends.

Fishing: Opportunities for anglers abound throughout the recreation area. The most popular spot is Big Fish Lake, where there is a boat launch and fishermen do well for bluegill and bass. The lake is also stocked annually with brown trout. Most are caught during the fall by wading fly fishermen using wet flies, or during the winter by ice fishermen. There are fishing access sites on Algoe Lake, a small bass lake that is catch-and-release only, and on Tody Lake, and Davison Lake, which is posted off Fox Lake Road and known primarily for panfish and northern pike.

For more adventurous anglers, Ortonville offers two walk-in lakes. Round Lake is a half-mile hike from a signpost on Fox Lake Road and popular with ice fishermen searching for bluegill in the winter. Mud Lake is also a half-mile walk from a posted trailhead near the west end of Brauer Road and supports a population of northern pike.

Hiking and Mountain Biking: Part of the recreation area, located off State Park Road between Hornert and Sands Roads, is the original Bloomer No. 3 State Park, with its impressive stand of white pine, that was donated to the state in 1922. Located here is the trailhead and parking area for a 5-mile trail system that includes a loop for hikers and mountain bikers.

Canada geese, Ortonville Recreation Area

This 3-mile foot/bike loop is a lightly used trail through a rolling wooded terrain, broken up by semi-open fields and featuring a few steep descents at one end. The route is not well posted and passes several unmarked spurs that lead to nearby roads.

More trails, some of them old two-tracks, are also intermingled with the bridle trail in the northwest corner of the park near Tody Lake. The trails are used by both hikers and equestrians and are accessible either from Jasmond, Tody, or Hegel Roads or from the equestrian campground. One of the paths winds near Pinnacle Point, a high point with a view of much of the park.

Equestrian Facilities: The recreation area maintains an equestrian campground off Fox Lake Road, which includes the trailhead for a 6.5-mile system of bridle trails.

Winter Activities: Within the foot/bike trail in Bloomer No. 3 State Park and sharing the same trailhead and parking area is a 1.5-mile loop for cross-country skiing. The forested loop features several hills but is not groomed on a regular basis.

Cabins: The park has a pair of large rustic cabins for rent in the Bloomer No.3 unit. The Cedar Cabin sleeps twenty-four people and has electricity and propane heat but outdoor toilet facilities. The single-room Pines Cabin sleeps twenty people in triple-high bunks, does not have electricity, and is a 75-yard walk from the parking area. Both cabins have a two-night minimum stay on weekends.

Day-Use Facilities: The most popular section of Ortonville is the day-use area of Big Fish Lake. With an entrance off Hadley Road, the lakeside facilities include a sandy beach with a designated swimming area, a picnic area with grills, a boat launch, a bathhouse, and a concession store. The park also maintains a rifle and trap range off Sawmill Lake Road, with targets at 100, 50, and 25 yards and four trap platforms. No other equipment is provided. Check the park headquarters for the exact schedule, but the ranges are usually open weekdays Labor Day through

ORTONVILLE
RECREATION AREA

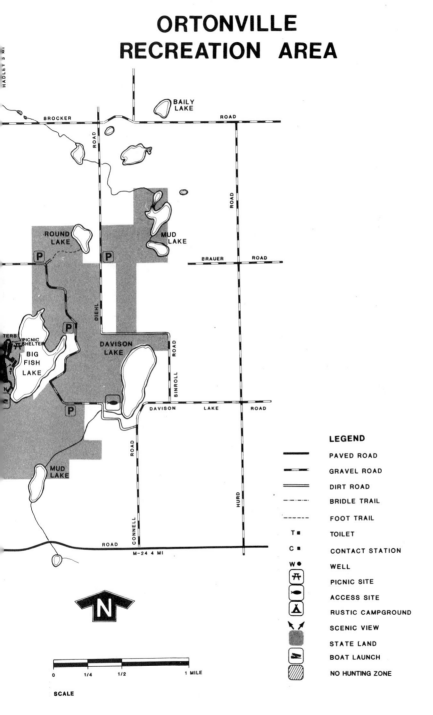

LEGEND

━━━━	PAVED ROAD
━ ━ ━	GRAVEL ROAD
═══	DIRT ROAD
─·─·─	BRIDLE TRAIL
─ ─ ─	FOOT TRAIL
T ■	TOILET
C ■	CONTACT STATION
W ●	WELL
🛦	PICNIC SITE
	ACCESS SITE
🏕	RUSTIC CAMPGROUND
	SCENIC VIEW
	STATE LAND
	BOAT LAUNCH
	NO HUNTING ZONE

mid-October and then daily during deer season until mid-December. The facility is then open 2 days a week from March through Memorial Day.

Access and Information: Ortonville Recreation Area is spread out with many roads providing access. To reach the park headquarters and Big Fish Lake from the village of Ortonville on M-15, follow Oakwood Road east and then turn north on Hadley Road. For more information, contact Ortonville Recreation Area, 5779 Hadley Road, Route 2, Ortonville, MI 48462; or call (248) 627-3828.

Metamora–Hadley Recreation Area

In the middle of Metamora–Hadley Recreation Area, the heart of this 723-acre park in Lapeer County is Lake Minnawanna. The 80-acre lake and the rolling, wooded terrain around it were purchased and dedicated by the state in 1946. The park experiences only moderate use with an average of 225,000 visitors a year, most of them arriving from late spring through the summer. The majority are day users, as the lake is a popular area for swimmers, fishermen, and canoeists.

Camping: Metamora–Hadley Recreation Area features one of the most delightful state park campgrounds in southeast Michigan. The modern facility has 198 lightly shaded sites on two loops along the west side of the lake. A number of sites along the first loop are right on the shoreline and are usually the first to be selected by campers. Equally scenic, however, is the second loop, where many sites are on

Footpath, Metamora-Hadley Recreation Area

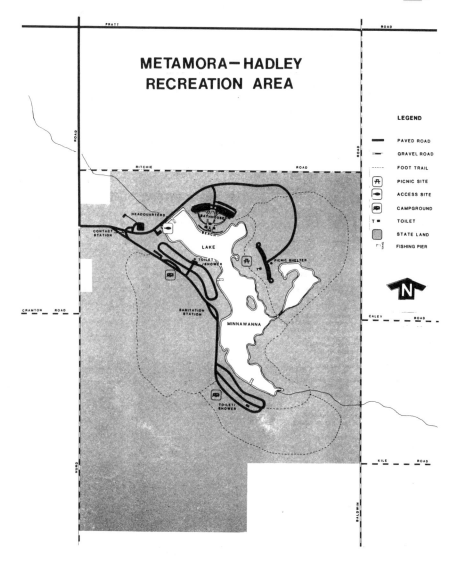

a bluff overlooking the lake. Along with modern bathroom and shower facilities in each loop and a sanitation station for recreational vehicles between them, the campground also has two mini-cabins available for rent. Metamora–Hadley fills most weekends during the summer as well as two or three nights preceding major holidays.

Day-Use Facilities: At the north end of the lake is a beach with a marked swimming area, a bathhouse, picnic tables, and a concession building that rents canoes, rowboats, and paddleboats daily from May through mid-September. On the east side of the lake in a wooded setting is the park's picnic area with a picnic shelter that can be rented.

Fishing: Several species of fish can be caught in Lake Minnawanna, but it is best known as a bass lake. Anglers do best working standard bass baits and lures in the south half of the lake and around the small island on the east side. Other species sought after include bluegill, perch, and crappie. There is both a boat launch and three fishing piers along the west shore for anglers to use.

Hiking: There are 6 miles of trails, forming a mostly forested loop that runs from the campground around the lake to the beach area on the north shore. The segment between the two loops of the campground is a mile-long, self-guided nature trail that corresponds to an interpretive brochure available at the contact station. One of the most scenic spots of the system is where the trail crosses the South Branch of Farmers Creek in the southeast corner of the park.

Winter Activities: Snowmobiling is the most popular winter activity here, and 450 acres are open for snowmobilers, although there are no marked trails. A number of ice fishermen set up on Lake Minnawanna for perch and panfish, and the park trails attract a small number of Nordic skiers.

Access and Information: The entrance to the park is off Hurd Road, which is reached by taking Pratt Road 1.5 miles west of M-24 or 2 miles from the village of Metamora. For more information, contact Metamora–Hadley Recreation Area, 3871 Hurd Road, Metamora, MI 48455; or call (810) 797-4439.

Bald Mountain Recreation Area

There is no longer a Bald Mountain. The high point, which at one time was the site of a ski club, eventually became part of a landfill and met its fate at the front end of a bulldozer. But the so-called mountain is remembered 2 miles to the north in Bald Mountain Recreation Area, whose 4,637 acres preserve some of the steepest hills and most rugged terrain in southeast Michigan.

The park is three separate units located south and east of the community of Lake Orion. The unit west of M-24 is mostly old farmland with no developed facilities. The units east of M-24 are the rugged areas of Bald Mountain with a terrain of both open fields and forests of hardwoods and conifers. There are seventeen lakes in these units, two trout streams, and a topography that offers some interesting opportunities for hikers, mountain bikers, cross-country skiers, and fishermen.

Despite the rapid development of the farmland around the park, Bald Mountain Recreation Area still abounds with wildlife. The Oakland Audubon Society has compiled a list of 176 species of songbirds, upland birds, and waterfowl that have been sighted in the park while hikers spot deer, weasels, red fox, beavers, and even an occasional badger.

There is no camping in the recreation area other than an organization camp for groups only. Despite the lack of a campground, Bald Mountain Recreation Area still draws around 450,000 visitors annually that arrive almost year-round.

Hiking: The park has a total of 15 miles of maintained trails in both units east of M-24. In the south unit, the Red Loop is a 4.8-mile circular trail that passes several ponds and marsh areas and crosses Spring Creek. It can be entered at a car park on Greenshield Road or off of Kern Road, and crossover spurs allow you to shorten the walk or to begin it near the park headquarters on Greenshield Road. In the north unit there are 8 miles of trails. The White Loop is a 2.1-mile walk past several small lakes west of Harmon Road. East of Harmon Road the Orange Loop is a 3.6-mile hike around six lakes, including East and West Graham Lakes and over several high points. There are several parking lots for trail users with the main one for the White Loop at the junction of Harmon and Predmore Roads and another for the Orange Loop at the corner of Harmon and Miller Roads.

Hikers need to keep in mind that the trail system is heavily used by mountain bikers on the weekends. The best time to avoid bikers is in the middle of the week or in April when the trails are too wet to withstand the impact of bicycles. April can be a particularly pleasant time to walk the trails, as you will encounter a variety of wildflowers, including trillium, marsh marigold, bloodroot, and jack-in-the-pulpit.

A small portion of the Paint Creek Rail–Trail also passes through Bald Mountain Recreation Area and can be picked up where Clarkston Road crosses the creek. Paint Creek was Michigan's first rail–trail, and today it's probably the most popular one, used by hikers, joggers, mountain bikers, and equestrians. The trail spans 8 miles from downtown Rochester to Lake Orion.

Mountain Biking: Both the north unit and south unit loops are open to mountain bikers, a popular activity in the park. Most cyclists prefer the north unit trails, especially the 3.6-mile Orange Loop as it features more challenging downhill runs and climbs. Some mountain bikers combine the south unit trail with a portion of the Paint Creek Rail–Trail for an interesting ride. Where the rail–trail crosses Clarkston Road, bikers can depart south on Kern Road and in a quarter mile reach the park's organization campground where there is a trailhead to the south unit's Red Loop.

Winter Activities: Snowmobiles are prohibited in the north unit, where the 8 miles of trails are groomed for skiers during the winter. There is no ski rental concession in the park, and all trails are rated challenging due to the hilly terrain. Also in the north unit is a sledding hill, one of the best and most scenic in southeast Michigan, as it overlooks Carpenter and Chamberlain Lakes. A small parking area for the sledders is on Stoney Creek Road west of Adams Road, and from there it's a short quarter-mile walk into the park to the hill. Snowmobiling is allowed in the south unit, and most users follow the 7.1 miles of trails through the area.

Fishing: The Graham Lakes in the north unit draw the most fishing activity in the recreation area. A boat launch on East Graham is reached from Predmore Road,

Whitetail buck

BALD MOUNTAIN RECREATION AREA

NORTH AND SOUTH UNITS

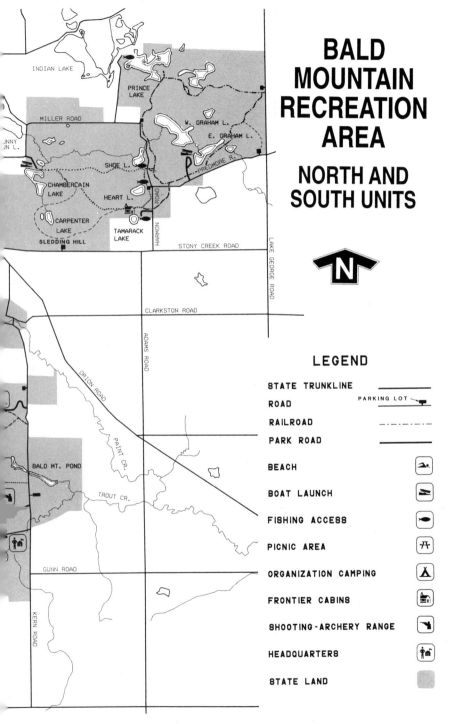

LEGEND

STATE TRUNKLINE	———
ROAD	PARKING LOT ⌐
RAILROAD	– ·· – ·· –
PARK ROAD	———
BEACH	🏊
BOAT LAUNCH	🚤
FISHING ACCESS	🐟
PICNIC AREA	🍴
ORGANIZATION CAMPING	⛺
FRONTIER CABINS	🏠
SHOOTING-ARCHERY RANGE	🔫
HEADQUARTERS	👫
STATE LAND	▨

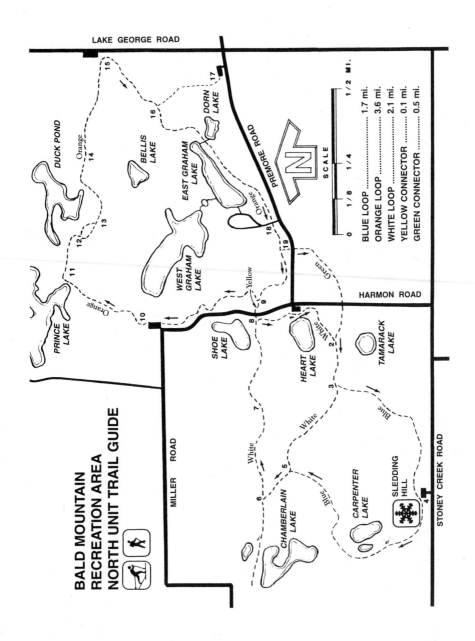

BALD MOUNTAIN
RECREATION AREA
NORTH UNIT TRAIL GUIDE

LAKE GEORGE ROAD

HARMON ROAD

SCALE

BLUE LOOP	1.7 mi.
ORANGE LOOP	3.6 mi.
WHITE LOOP	2.1 mi.
YELLOW CONNECTOR	0.1 mi.
GREEN CONNECTOR	0.5 mi.

0   1/8   1/4   1/2 MI.

DUCK POND

PRINCE LAKE

BELLIS LAKE

EAST GRAHAM LAKE

WEST GRAHAM LAKE

DORN LAKE

PREMORE ROAD

SHOE LAKE

HEART LAKE

TAMARACK LAKE

CARPENTER LAKE

CHAMBERLAIN LAKE

SLEDDING HILL

MILLER ROAD

STONEY CREEK ROAD

Orange
Yellow
Green
White
Blue

Hiker in Bald Mountain State Park

and a channel connects the lake to West Graham. Many anglers head straight to West Graham, where they fish for bass and panfish. There are also boat launches on Prince Lake and Chamberlain Lake posted along Miller Road in the north unit as well as in the day-use area on Lower Trout Lake. There is good bass fishing in Lower Trout Lake and a fishing pier for shore anglers.

Both Paint Creek and Trout Creek are stocked with brown trout. Both streams were flies-only at one time but now draw mostly bait fishermen who wade in. Trout Creek, which flows from Lower Trout Lake into Paint Creek, is accessible from Kern and Adams Roads. Best time to go is late August through September, when the fish are good-sized and actively feeding at night.

Day-Use Facilities: Roughly 50 percent of visitors are drawn to the picnic and swimming facilities around Lower and Upper Trout Lakes. The day-use area is reached from M-24 and contains a beach, bathhouse, and picnic area on Lower Trout Lake and additional picnic tables and grills, and shelters that can be rented on Upper Trout Lake.

Bald Mountain also has the most developed gun range in the state park system. The facility includes two skeet, two trap, and one combination field that are all mechanically operated. A concession operator (248-814-9193) runs the range and a lounge area and charges a fee for the use of the trap and skeet fields. Shooters can also purchase ammunition, targets, and other shooting supplies at the concession. The range is open year-round on Saturday and Sunday from 10:00 A.M. until 6:00 P.M., and Wednesday from 10:00 A.M. until sunset. It is also open Monday and Tuesday during the summer from noon until sunset, and daily for a short period before deer season. The entrance to the gun range is posted off Kern Road north of Greenshield Road.

Cabins: The park features a pair of twenty-bunk rustic cabins in the north unit reached from Harmon Road. The cabins, a short walk from the parking area, are within 100 yards of each other in a wooded area overlooking Tamarack Lake. Nearby is the White Loop trail. Although designed for youth groups and still heavily used by scout groups from January through April, the cabins are being rented by an increasing number of families. If planning a weekend at one, book it three to four weeks ahead.

Access and Information: Bald Mountain Recreation Area is 7 miles north of Pontiac and can be reached from I-75 by exiting north on M-24 (exit 81). Turn east onto Greenshield Road to reach the park headquarters. For more information or reservations, contact Bald Mountain Recreation Area, 1330 Greenshield Road, Route 1, Lake Orion, MI 48360; or call (248) 693-6767.

Wetzel State Park

▲ Wetzel State Park is an undeveloped area of 844 acres in the center of Macomb County. The park was formed in 1969 after the land was purchased by the DNR from the Wetzel family. Most of the land was farmed at one time and today consists of open areas and wet lowlands where the East Branch of the Coon Creek winds through the middle of the park. There is very little standing timber.

The only facility is a series of rough parking areas, the most commonly used one at the end of Twenty-Seven Mile Road off Werderman Road. The main activity in Wetzel State Park is hunting, primarily for rabbit, and snowmobiling and cross-country skiing in the winter, although there are no maintained trails. Camping is not allowed in the area.

Access and Information: Head west on Twenty-Six Mile Road from I-94 (exit 248) or east from M-53; then turn north onto Werderman Road to Twenty-Seven Mile Road. For more information, contact the DNR Field Office, 28681 Old North River, Harrison Township, MI 48045; or call (248) 465-2160.

Algonac State Park

▲ The only unit on the St. Clair River is Algonac State Park, which was established in 1937 and has since been enlarged to 1,411 acres. More than 300,000 visitors annually are attracted to its frontage and campground overlooking the international waterway, although there is no swimming due to dangerous currents and heavy boat traffic. But the river is renowned for its walleye fishery, while many visitors enjoy strolling along the breakwall for the close-up views of the large freighters and iron-ore carriers that make up the Great Lakes shipping traffic. During the peak of the shipping season in midsummer, a freighter will pass through almost every hour.

M-29 separates Riverfront Campground from the river, while the back section of the park is the Prairie and Savanna Natural Area, which includes low ridges of climax oak forests, wetlands, and small remnants of the original open prairie that once covered much of southern Michigan.

The state park is the site of several special events throughout the year, with the most popular one being the St. Clair Flats Historical Encampment, held on the second weekend of September. The encampment focuses on the life of the Native Americans and early French settlers of the Great Lakes during the mid-1700s, with period-dressed participants tanning deer hides, sewing with porcupine quills, making candles, telling stories, and displaying other crafts.

Camping: Algonac State Park contains two modern campgrounds. Riverfront Campground has 220 sites in an open area along M-29, with twenty of them featuring a good view of the river and its boat traffic. This facility, which also contains restrooms, showers, and a sanitation station, is by far the most popular among visitors. In the center of the park is Wagonwheel Campground, with 76 modern sites in a much more wooded and private setting. The camping season opens up in early May at Algonac, and from Memorial Day to Labor Day, the park is 90 percent filled and almost always filled on weekends and during its special events.

Fishing: The park features a boat launch facility, as the St. Clair River supports a strong walleye fishery that anglers enjoy from the spring opener through the summer and fall. The most productive method for catching walleye is to troll the river with a boat. Shore fishermen, trying their luck off the breakwall, usually concentrate on perch and rough fish.

Hiking: There are two nature trails in the park. Opposite the archery range is a quarter-mile trail that loops through a lake plain prairie, dominated by such species as tall goldenrod, iron weed, prairie lustrife, black-eye susan, and Michigan lily. Just east of the archery range is the trailhead for a 2-mile trail that loops through an

A Great Lakes freighter sails past Algonac State Park

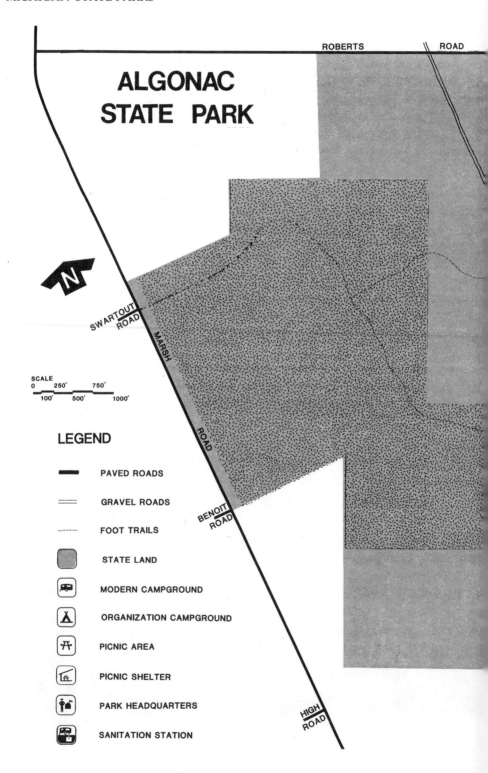

ALGONAC
STATE PARK

ROBERTS   ROAD

SWARTOUT ROAD

MARSH ROAD

BENOIT ROAD

HIGH ROAD

SCALE
0   250'   750'
  100'   500'   1000'

LEGEND

▬▬ PAVED ROADS

═ GRAVEL ROADS

------ FOOT TRAILS

STATE LAND

MODERN CAMPGROUND

ORGANIZATION CAMPGROUND

PICNIC AREA

PICNIC SHELTER

PARK HEADQUARTERS

SANITATION STATION

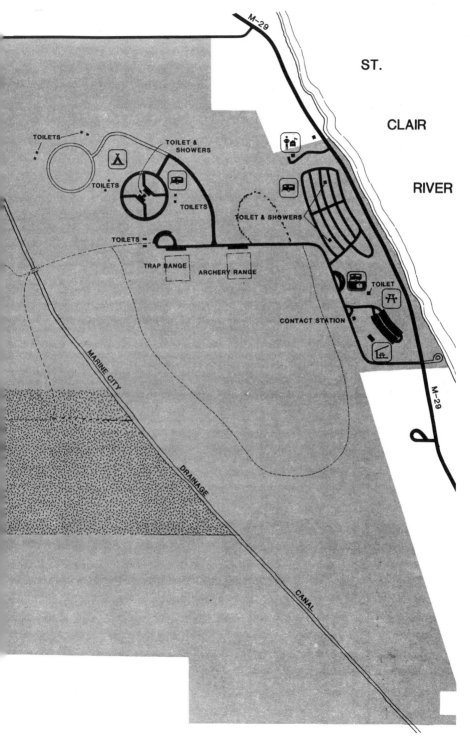

Campers along the St. Clair River, Algonac State Park

oak savannah. This trail can also be picked up at the end of the road to the trap range where it crosses Marine City Drainage Canal. At one point the trail passes through the largest remnant of prairie in the park, then continues through a stand of oaks more than 200 years old before looping back.

Cycling: The former Detroit-Urban Railroad is being paved as a bike path and presently connects the state park with the town of Algonac to the south. Eventually the plans call for a 50-mile bike path that would extend from Port Huron to the Metro Beach Metropark near Mount Clemens, providing cyclists with a multi-day ride in which a night could be spent at Algonac State Park.

Day-Use Facilities: The park has a trap and archery range (no equipment supplied) along with a picnic and play area next to Riverfront Campground, which includes volleyball courts and a baseball field.

Access and Information: The park's entrance is off M-29, 2 miles north of the town of Algonac. For more information, contact Algonac State Park, 8730 North River Road, Marine City, MI 48039; or call (810) 765-5605.

Lakeport State Park

The first state park preserving a segment of the Lake Huron shoreline is Lakeport State Park, a 565-acre unit situated at the south end of the Great Lake in St. Clair County. Established in 1936, the park is actually two separate units that lie on two sides of the small village of Lakeport. To the south is the Franklin Delano Roosevelt unit, the day-use area, while to the north is the park's campground.

Together the two units contain almost 1.5 miles of Lake Huron shoreline and make Lakeport the only state park on the lake south of Harrisville. The wide sandy beach is the main attraction, as the park has no trails or boat launch and has very little activity in the winter.

Camping: The unit north of Lakeport contains 315 modern sites in two separate loops. The sites are in a semi-open, lightly shaded area with a playground, a sanitation station, and a pair of mini-cabins for rent. No sites are on the water or within sight of Lake Huron, but the beach, a sand/pebble strip lined by bluffs, is only a short walk away. The campground is open from April to December and is extremely popular from June to mid-September. During the summer sites tend to fill by Friday afternoon for the weekend. There are usually open sites in midweek.

Also located in the north unit are two organization campgrounds and the park headquarters.

Day-Use Facilities: The Roosevelt unit south of Lakeport contains the best beach in the park, a mile of wide sandy shoreline bordered by low bluffs. M-25 cuts through the middle of the unit, and the entrance and parking lot is on the west side of the highway. Visitors use a pedestrian overpass to cross the road and enter the beach and lightly shaded picnic area on the east side of the road, an area where no cars are allowed. The parking lot holds 2,000 vehicles but is rarely, if ever, full. Due to the Port Huron city parks nearby, Lakeport's day-use area and beach is surprisingly uncrowded throughout the summer, an aspect of the park that is as attractive as its beach.

The west side of the Roosevelt unit has another picnic area and a shelter that can be rented.

Access and Information: Lakeport State Park is split by M-25 and is located 8 miles north of Port Huron. For more information, contact Lakeport State Park, 7605 Lakeshore Road, Lakeport, MI 48059; or call (810) 327-6224.

Lake Huron beach, Lakeport State Park

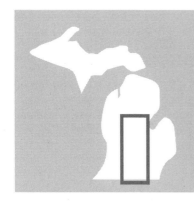

Heartland

Lake Hudson Recreation Area

The fact that you can see a barn off in the distance from the shores of Lake Hudson in the heart of Lenawee County is no coincidence. The large, 600-acre lake was created when Bear Creek was dammed, while the recreation area that now surrounds it was originally farm fields. The 2,700-acre park in the heart of Lenawee County became the southernmost unit in Michigan when it was established in 1979. Although facilities began to appear in the mid-1980s, use of the area is still extremely light with less than 90,000 people visiting it annually.

The reverted farmlands give Lake Hudson's rolling terrain an open appearance where it's possible to see the entire lake from several vantage points along the park road. In the fields are a few stands of trees here and there and patches of scrub and brush. Park usage is seasonal, limited almost entirely to fishing, boating, and camping in the summer and heavy hunting activity in the fall.

Because of its rural setting, Lake Hudson is Michigan's first Dark Sky Preserve. The park's isolation from any large towns or cities allows stargazing with minimal interference from other light sources. Stargazers are allowed to stay in the day-use area to study the night sky after 10:00 P.M. even if they are not camping overnight.

Camping: Camping was added to the recreation area in 1987 when the DNR opened a campground on the south side of the lake. The open campground has fifty semi-modern sites equipped with electricity, with some sites right on the water. Almost all are in view of the lake. There are vault toilets and a hand pump for water but little shade and no showers. The campground receives minimal use, and getting a site is rarely a problem even on most weekends.

Fishing: Lake Hudson supports a variety of fish but is best known for muskie. The DNR Fisheries Division has designated it a brood-stock lake for its muskie-rearing program and has imposed special regulations on it. Lake Hudson has a

Lake Hudson Recreation Area

no-wake zone, and the minimum size of muskie that can be kept is 38 inches. The minimum size throughout the rest of the state is only 30 inches. There is a boat launch on the east side of the park with a dock, toilets, and parking for thirty vehicles and rigs. The contact station also hands out contour maps with lake depths to assist anglers.

Located just northeast of Lake Hudson is a small, walk-in lake that can be reached from the picnic area and fished for bluegill and other panfish.

Day-Use Facilities: The recreation area features a beach and day-use area on the east end of the park with tables, grills, a picnic shelter, a volleyball court, and a separate parking area.

Access and Information: From the town of Hudson, head east on M-34 for 6 miles and then south on M-156 for 1.5 miles to the posted entrance. For information, contact Hayes State Park, 1220 Wampler's Lake Road, Onsted, MI 49265; or call (517) 467-7401.

Cambridge State Historic Park

▲ Cambridge State Historic Park is a 183-acre park located at the junction of US 12 and M-80 in Lenawee County, 25 miles southeast of Jackson. Originally Native American trails, the two roads became the state's earliest highways in the mid-1830s and played an important role in "Michigan Fever," an epidemic of cheap land sales that was spread when the federal government began selling parcels for $1.25 an acre.

US 12 was completed by 1833 as the Detroit–Chicago Road, and M-50 soon followed as the La Plaisance Turnpike. Together they were the heart of Michigan's stagecoach era. The coaches bumped and rumbled over the rough dirt roads, traveling no more than 50 miles a day under the best conditions and needing 5 days to reach Chicago from Detroit. The key to frontier-era travel was a string of inns and taverns that supplied crude lodging at twenty-five cents a night, plus offered homecooked meals and nightcaps. The most popular stop, whose table fare was known as the "best west of Detroit," was Walker Tavern, which today is a restored historical complex at the state park.

Cambridge State Historic Park also has a picnic area but no camping facilities. The park is open daily from 10:00 A.M. until 5:00 P.M. from June until Labor Day but is closed during the winter.

Interpretive Center: A 90-minute, self-guided tour begins in the visitor center, where an audiovisual program and museum galleries provide background information on the settling of Michigan and the stagecoach era. Interpretive plaques then lead visitors across the grounds, past the Heritage Garden, to the saltbox tavern that was built in the late 1830s.

Walker became a prominent innkeeper because his tavern was on the main road junction, not only catching the traffic going east and west but also those travelers heading north and south along the La Plaisance Bay Turnpike that ran inland from Monroe on Lake Erie. The inn offered hot meals, a spot to lie down, and a barroom, the three necessities in stagecoach accommodations, but not necessarily a good night's rest.

There was drinking and pipe smoking in the barroom, a wood-burning stove in the parlor, somebody clanging pots in the kitchen. All that noise and mixed aromas easily drifted through the warped floors upstairs where travelers were trying to sleep on mattresses stuffed with straw.

The self-guided tour concludes at the wheelwright barn, which contains a covered wagon, carriages, and the tools that were needed to repair and build fragile wood-spoke wheels.

Access and Information: The entrance to the park is on M-50, a quarter mile north of the junction with US 12 in Irish Hills. For more information, write to the Michigan Historical Museum, 717 West Allegan, Lansing, Ml 48918; or call (517) 373-1979. During the summer you can call the park at (517) 467-4414.

W. J. Hayes State Park

A small portion of the green, rolling terrain of the Irish Hills is preserved within W. J. Hayes State Park, a 654-acre unit that was established in 1920 and touches the corners of Jackson, Lenawee, and Washtenaw Counties. This region of the state, a popular tourist destination during the summer, got its name when it reminded early Irish settlers of their homeland. The gentle hills are featured in the southern half of the park, but the northern portion is the shoreline of two lakes, Round and Wampler's.

M-124 divides the park in half, separating the day-use area on Wampler's Lake from the campground on Round Lake. Both are heavily used, as Hayes draws 326,000 visitors annually with the vast majority arriving from May through October.

Camping: W. J. Hayes State Park maintains a modern campground on the south side of Round Lake. There are 183 sites along with modern bathrooms and showers and a sanitation station for recreational vehicles. There are no sites directly on the lake; most of them are in a semi-open and lightly shaded setting well away from the water. Within the campground are also a pair of mini-cabins for rent and a campers-only boat launch and access site to Round Lake.

The campground is open from April to December and during the summer is filled almost every weekend by Friday afternoon or even earlier if there is an event at the nearby Michigan International Speedway. Sites are usually available without reservations from Sunday through Thursday.

Fishing: There are opportunities on both lakes for anglers to catch bass, bluegill, and northern pike. Wampler's Lake is considered one of the best smallmouth bass lakes in southern Michigan and is generally the more productive of the two park lakes for anglers. But the 780-acre lake, the site for several bass tournaments each summer, is heavily used by both anglers and recreational boaters, including jet skiers. The 67-acre Round Lake has a no-wake speed regulation for a more serene setting for anglers.

A boat launch on Wampler's Lake in the day-use area includes parking for 100 vehicles and trailers. A boat rental concession on the lake rents canoes, rowboats, and paddleboats daily from May through September. Although the launch on Round Lake is for campers only, boaters can put in on Wampler's Lake and then follow a canal into the smaller lake. There is also a fishing pier for anglers in the campground.

Day-Use Facilities: Hayes features a 1,000-foot-long sandy beach in its day-use area that is bordered by a grassy picnic area. There is also a bathhouse, concession stand, volleyball court, and parking for 900 vehicles. Still, the lot becomes filled just about every Sunday afternoon from mid-June through July and additional vehicles are turned away.

Winter Activities: There is considerable ice fishing activity on the weekend on

Wampler's Lake with locals often riding their snowmobiles through the park to reach their favorite spots on the lake.

Access and Information: Hayes is located 9 miles west of Clinton at the junction of US 12 and M-124. For more information, contact W. J. Hayes State Park, 1220 Wampler's Road, Onsted, MI 49265; or call (517) 467-7401.

Waterloo Recreation Area

▲ Michigan topography was carved by retreating glaciers 10,000 years ago, and in ⊥ the Waterloo Recreation Area of Jackson County, they left a hilly terrain of moraines, potholes, bogs, and small lakes. They also left a topsoil of predominantly sand and gravel that hindered the efforts of farmers beginning with the first settlers in the early 1800s. During the Great Depression in the 1930s, desperate families needing assistance turned to the federal government, which purchased their farms and moved them to more productive land as part of a relocation relief measure.

Here the government acquired 12,000 acres and turned it over to the National Park Service, which designated it the Waterloo Recreation and Demonstration Area. In 1943 it was handed over to Michigan, which used the land to create one of eleven recreation areas that were added to its state park system in 1943–44. Today Waterloo consists of almost 20,000 acres of hilly terrain, hardwood forests of oak, hickory, and maple, eighteen lakes, and old farm fields that have become prime habitat for whitetail deer.

Waterloo Recreation Area draws 626,000 visitors year-round with activities that range from camping, fishing, and skiing to touring fall colors and multi-day backpacking trips. The park, the largest recreation area in the state park system, has a parcel-by-parcel appearance that stretches from M-52 west to within 6 miles of Jackson.

Camping: Waterloo has five different campgrounds, including two modern units bordering its largest lakes. Portage Lake Campground features 114 sites in a lightly shaded area of rolling terrain. The campground is near the lake and an easy walk to the beach, but none of the sites are directly on the water. Also within the area is the Dry Marsh Nature Trail, while nearby is an organization camp. Access to Portage Lake Campground is off Seymour Road, reached from I-94 by taking exit 150 and heading north on Mount Hope Road.

Sugarloaf Lake Campground has 170 modern sites in an open, grassy area near the large lake, but not on it. Within the campground there is a boat launch, small swimming beach, boat rental concession, and the Woodland Nature Trail. Sugarloaf is off Loveland Road and can be reached from I-94 by taking exit 156 and heading north on Kalmbach Road and then west on Cavanaugh Lake Road. At the peak of the summer, July to early August, both campgrounds are usually filled on weekends and often more than 50 percent filled Sunday through Thursday.

Waterloo Recreation Area maintains two rustic campgrounds, where sites can usually be obtained throughout the summer. Green Lake Campground has twenty-five wooded sites on a hill overlooking the lake and is reached from M-52. There is a posted horseman's campground with twenty-five sites well spread out in a pleasant wooded setting reached just before the entrance to Sugarloaf Lake on Lovelace Road. This rustic campground is open to anyone with or without horses.

Hiking: The park's longest trail is the 23-mile portion of the Waterloo–Pinckney Trail that winds from Big Portage Lake to M-52 (see Backpacking in this section). But there are also nine nature trails that are considerably shorter scattered throughout the park. Six of them—Lowland, Spring Pond, Old Field, Lakeview, Oak

Fishing at Waterloo Recreation Area

Woods, and Floating Bog—are short loops that combine for almost 9 miles of foot-paths beginning outside the Gerald Eddy Geology Center. Each loop is a 20- to 30-minute easy walk with interpretive signs along the way that identify plants or natural features. The longest hike is the Lakeview Trail, a round trip of 3.6 miles from the interpretive center to the west side of Mill Lake. One of the most interesting walks is the 1.5-mile Floating Bog Trail that ends at a boardwalk spanning a bog.

Near the park headquarters on McClure Road is the Hickory Hills Trail, a 1-mile loop that traverses oak-hickory forested hills. It becomes a 5.3-mile hike if you start at the Geology Center. At Portage Lake Campground is the Dry Marsh Trail, a 20-minute walk that begins near the sanitation station and circles a series of marshes that were once a small lake. At Sugarloaf Lake is the Woodland Trail, a 1-mile loop that takes 30 minutes to cover.

Pamphlets are available for Hickory Hills, Dry Marsh, and Woodland Trails at the park headquarters or the contact station at the campgrounds.

Backpacking: In 1984, the DNR purchased property and obtained rights to build

WATERLOO RECREATION AREA

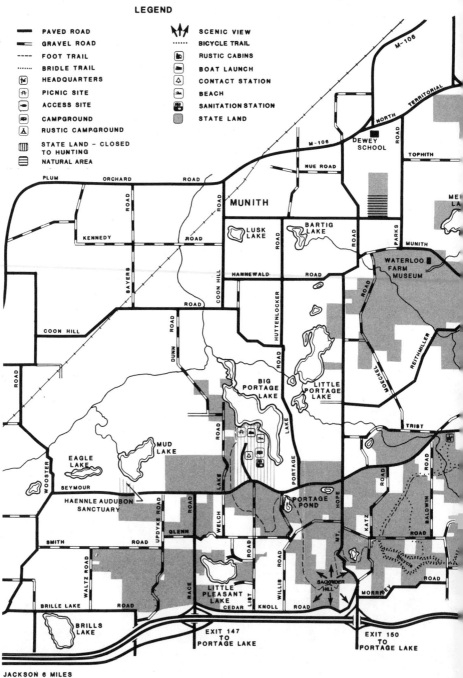

LEGEND

▬▬	PAVED ROAD	🔱	SCENIC VIEW
▬▬	GRAVEL ROAD	⋯⋯	BICYCLE TRAIL
----	FOOT TRAIL	🏠	RUSTIC CABINS
⋯⋯	BRIDLE TRAIL	🚤	BOAT LAUNCH
🅗	HEADQUARTERS	△	CONTACT STATION
🅟	PICNIC SITE	🏖	BEACH
🅞	ACCESS SITE	🚽	SANITATION STATION
🅟	CAMPGROUND		STATE LAND
🅐	RUSTIC CAMPGROUND		
▥	STATE LAND – CLOSED TO HUNTING		
⬛	NATURAL AREA		

JACKSON 6 MILES

80

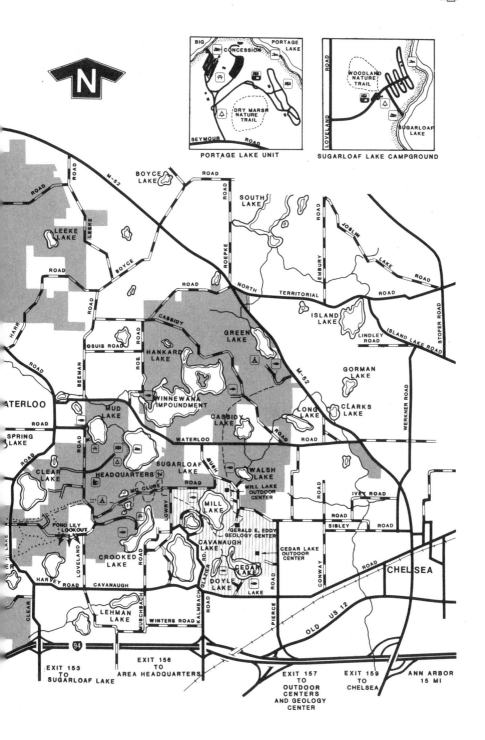

PORTAGE LAKE UNIT

SUGARLOAF LAKE CAMPGROUND

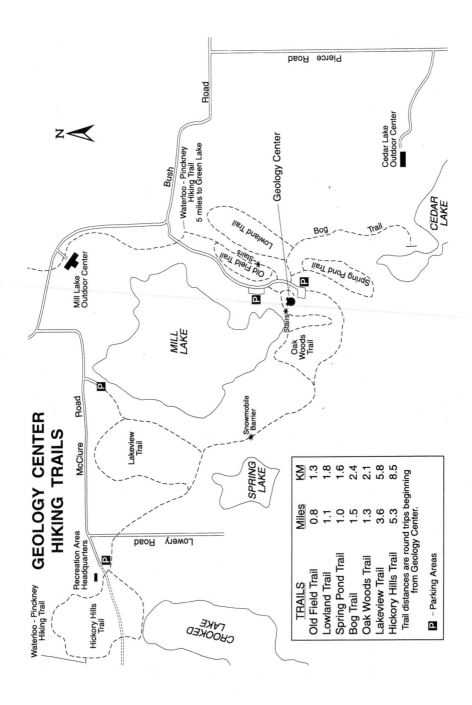

GEOLOGY CENTER HIKING TRAILS

TRAILS	Miles	KM
Old Field Trail	0.8	1.3
Lowland Trail	1.1	1.8
Spring Pond Trail	1.0	1.6
Bog Trail	1.5	2.4
Oak Woods Trail	1.3	2.1
Lakeview Trail	3.6	5.8
Hickory Hills Trail	5.3	8.5

Trail distances are round trips beginning from Geology Center.

P - Parking Areas

a 2-mile trail that linked longer footpaths in the Waterloo and Pinckney Recreation Areas. The 46-mile-long Waterloo–Pinckney Trail was finished and dedicated two years later as the longest hiking trail in southern Michigan. It is a rare backpacking opportunity that lies within an hour's drive of most of metropolitan Detroit. The trail begins in the day-use area on Portage Lake in Waterloo Recreation Area and winds east over undulating moraine countryside and through pine plantations, deciduous forests, open fields, and wetlands before it ends at the day-use area of Silver Lake in Pinckney Recreation Area.

Hikers in good shape can cover the route in 2 days, spending the night at Green Lake Campground, approximately the halfway point. Most hikers cover the route in 3 days, staying at Waterloo's horseman's campground or at Sugarloaf Lake Campground, and spending the second night at a backpacker's campground on Blind Lake in Pinckney. Hikers can also camp at Pinckney's Crooked Lake and Glenbrook Campgrounds, while in the winter skiers can rent a cabin at Mill Lake Outdoor Center. Both recreation areas have maps of the entire trail system. Keep in mind that in the Waterloo Recreation Area the trail merges with bridle paths and at times requires a little searching to find it. The segment in the Pinckney Recreation Area is part of the Potawatomi Trail, a popular mountain bike route.

Mountain Biking: Waterloo has a 5-mile loop designated for mountain bike use that can be picked up at a trailhead on Glenn Road just east of Katz Road. It's important to remember the trail is also part of the equestrian system and the hoof marks of horses can make the riding jarring at times.

Interpretive Center: Waterloo opened up the Gerald Eddy Geology Center in 1989 in memory of the former state geologist and DNR director. The center contains exhibits, displays, and video and slide programs that examine rocks, minerals, and oil resources in Michigan as well as its glacial and geologic history. Outside is the Michigan Geology Walkway, a barrier-free path lined with numerous boulders, each featuring its own geological story. The center (734-475-3170) is open year-round from 9:00 A.M. to 5:00 P.M. daily. From I-94, take exit 157 and head north on Pierce Road and then west on Bush Road, where the entrance is posted.

Within the recreation area, but not administered by the DNR or park staff, is the Waterloo Area Farm Museum, an 1844 farm complex that includes seven restored buildings and other structures. The museum is open June through August on Tuesday through Sunday from 1:00 P.M. to 4:00 P.M., and Saturday and Sunday in September from 1:00 P.M. to 4:00 P.M. There is a separate admission fee to enter the complex, which is located off Munith Road.

Fishing: Waterloo provides access to seventeen lakes with most of them featuring bass and panfish fisheries. There is a developed boat ramp on Big Portage Lake and a campers-only launch on Sugarloaf Lake. Big Portage is the largest lake in the park at 360 acres and produces largemouth bass in the one-to-three-pound range regularly, and occasionally a few over four pounds. In the winter, it is a favorite spot of ice anglers in pursuit of panfish.

Unimproved launches are located on Cassidy, Crooked, Cedar, Green, Hankard, Mill, Mud, Portage Pond, Sylvan Pond, Walsh, and Winnewana Lakes. Walk-in access is available for Doyle, Clear, and Little Portage Lakes. Merkle Lake, an excellent bluegill lake in June, is accessed by a half-mile trail located across from the Waterloo Farm Museum. The most popular lake for fishing is Crooked Lake, where anglers catch bluegill, sunfish, and bass, while Sugarloaf also features northern pike.

Day-Use Facilities: On the south side of Big Portage Lake is a day-use area with a sandy beach, a designated swimming area, and an extensive picnic area on a lightly wooded hill overlooking the lake. The area includes a shelter and a bath-house on the beach. The day-use area shares the entrance with Portage Lake Campground.

Cabins: In the heart of Waterloo are the Burns Cabins, two frontier cabins lo-cated next to the horseman's campground off Lovelace Road. The twenty-bunk structures are located across from each other in an open, grassy meadow that is hemmed in by woods. The cabins are rustic in nature, with wood-burning stoves, but can be reached by car. The park also rents out eight semi-rustic cabins located in its Cedar Lake Outdoor Center. They feature electric stoves and lights, but the bath-rooms are outside. Cedar Lake Outdoor Center is reached from Pierce Road, exit 157 from I-94, and is situated in a wooded setting on the edge of the lake. To the north on Bush Road is the Mill Lake Outdoor Center. All cabins can be rented year-round by either families or groups.

Equestrian Facilities: Within the park is the Waterloo Riding Stable and Dude Ranch (517-522-8920), which offers trail riding, hay rides, and overnight riding ad-ventures. The recreation area also maintains a horseman's campground off Lovelace Road, which serves as a staging area for a 12-mile network of bridle paths. The campground is open year-round, with much of the riding activity taking place during the fall.

Winter Activities: During the winter, the Geology Center serves as the trailhead for Waterloo's cross-country ski area. The center's trails become a 7.5-mile system of loops for Nordic skiers with most of them rated "easy" in difficulty. There are a few short hills along the Oakwoods Trail, however. The trails are not groomed or track set, nor is there a ski rental concession, but the center serves as a warming shelter. The park also draws snowmobilers and ice fishermen during the winter.

Scenic Viewpoints: An overall view in the park is obtained from Sackrider Hill, which is crossed by the Waterloo–Pinckney Trail. Along Mount Hope Road, exit 150 from I-94, there is a small parking lot on the west side where the trail crosses. From here it's a 5-minute climb to the top of the hill. The high point is marked by a large observation platform with a view of the rolling farm country to the south-west of the park. Equally scenic is Pond Lily Lookout, located on McClure Road just west of its junction with Loveland Road. Look for a small parking area on the north side of the road, then follow the trail through the ORV barricades to the scenic view of the small pond and surrounding fields.

Access and Information: There are six exits along I-94, between Ann Arbor and Jackson, that lead north into the recreation area: M-52 (exit 159) to Green Lake Campground, Pierce Road (exit 157) to the outdoor and geology centers, Kalmbach Road (exit 156) to the park headquarters, Clear Lake Road (exit 153) to Sugarloaf Lake, and Mount Hope Road (exit 150) and Race Road (exit 147) to Big Portage Lake. For more information, contact Waterloo Recreation Area, 16345 McClure Road, Route 1, Chelsea, MI 48118; or call (734) 475-8307.

Pinckney Recreation Area

▲ The Inland Waterway in northern Michigan is a popular chain of lakes and └ channels that extends from Cheboygan to Petoskey. Although not as well known as the Inland Waterway, southern Michigan has its own Chain-of-Lakes, which makes up the heart of the Pinckney Recreation Area. The cluster of seven lakes, connected by streams and short channels, is set in rolling hills forested pri-marily by oak. The small lakes not only create a picturesque scene but also offer a

Children swim among beached boats, Pinckney Recreation Area

wide variety of outdoor activities, including excellent opportunities for bass fishing, canoeing, and swimming.

Pinckney's numerous named lakes, ponds, and marshes and its hills and ridges are all typical remnants of the glacial activity that took place in this region of the state. The 10,201-acre unit was created in 1944 as one of a number of recreation areas in southern Michigan. The park is spread out, and within the boundaries of the park are parcels of private land with cottages and homes that dot the shores along the larger lakes.

Pinckney draws more than 850,000 visitors annually, due primarily to mountain biking and the park's proximity to Ann Arbor and metropolitan Detroit. When the sport of mountain biking arrived in Michigan in the mid-1980s, Pinckney was one of the first parks to welcome off-road cyclists on its trail system. Now the recreation area is something of a mecca for mountain bikers, attracting more than 100,000 riders a year from as far away as Ohio, Indiana, and even Illinois.

Pinckney stretches from M-52 near its southwest border northeast to M-36, with a number of county roads bisecting it. Come autumn, the winding roads are scenic avenues of fall colors reflected off small lakes.

Camping: The park has both a modern and a rustic campground. Bruin Lake Campground is located on the northwest corner of the lake and features 180 modern sites, some near the water, in a partially wooded setting. Located just east of the small village of Unadilla off Kaiser Road, the campground also has a beach, swimming area, and boat launch. Crooked Lake Campground has 25 rustic sites and is situated north of the Silver Lake day-use area on Silver Hill Road. The sites are on a

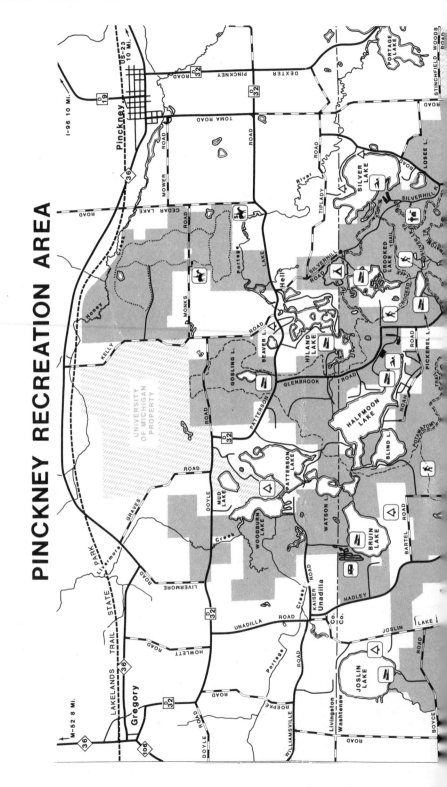

PINCKNEY RECREATION AREA

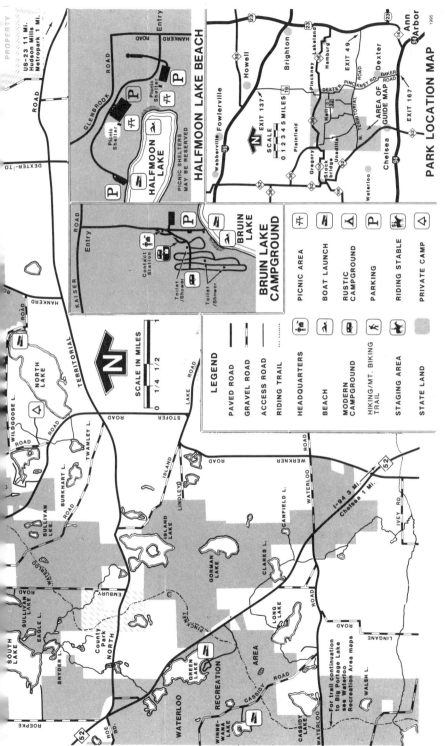

HALFMOON LAKE BEACH

PICNIC SHELTERS
MAY BE RESERVED

PARK LOCATION MAP

US-23 11 MI.
Hudson Mills
Metropark 1 MI.

PROPERTY

GLENBROOK ROAD

HANKERD ROAD

Entry

Picnic Shelter

Picnic Shelter

HALFMOON LAKE

DEXTER-TO

ROAD

Ann Arbor

1995

Howell

Brighton

Fowlerville

Webberville

Plainfield

Lakeland

Hamburg

Pinckney

Dexter

Baker ROAD

PINCKNEY RD.

DEXTER

N. TERRITORIAL

EXIT 49

EXIT 167

AREA OF
GUIDE MAP

Gregory

Stock
bridge

Unadilla

Hell

Chelsea

Waterloo

EXIT 137

SCALE
0 1 2 3 4 5 MILES

BRUIN LAKE CAMPGROUND

BRUIN LAKE

KAISER ROAD

Entry

Contact
Station

Toilet
/Shower

Toilet
/Shower

HANKERD ROAD

TERRITORIAL

NORTH LAKE

WILDGOOSE L.

STOFER ROAD

LAKE ROAD

SCALE IN MILES

0   1/4   1/2

N

TWAMLEY L.

BURKHART L.

SULLIVAN LKS.

ISLAND ROAD

LINDLEY

ISLAND LAKE

GORMAN LAKE

CLARKS L.

CANFIELD L.

WATERLOO ROAD

WERKNER ROAD

52

I-94 3 MI.
Chelsea 1 MI.

IVEY RD.

LINGANE ROAD

WALSH L.

LONG LAKE

GREEN LAKE

PINCKNEY

County Park NORTH

EMBURY ROAD

SULLIVAN LAKE

EAGLE L.

SNYDER L.

SOUTH LAKE

WATERLOO ROAD

WATERLOO

RECREATION

AREA

CASSIDY ROAD

CASSIDY LAKE

WINNE-WANA LAKE

ROE RD.

ROEPKE

52

For trail continuation
to Big Portage Lake
see Waterloo
Recreation Area maps

LEGEND

PAVED ROAD

GRAVEL ROAD

ACCESS ROAD

RIDING TRAIL

HEADQUARTERS

BEACH

MODERN
CAMPGROUND

HIKING/MT. BIKING
TRAIL

STAGING AREA

STATE LAND

PICNIC AREA

BOAT LAUNCH

RUSTIC
CAMPGROUND

PARKING

RIDING STABLE

PRIVATE CAMP

87

semi-open hillside overlooking the scenic lake, with a few sites quite near the water. There is a boat launch, but Crooked Lake is not part of the Chain-of-Lakes. Bruin Lake Campground is filled virtually every weekend during the summer and it's almost impossible to get a site without a reservation. Crooked Lake also fills up many weekends despite being a rustic facility.

Mountain Biking: Pinckney is generally regarded as the most popular mountain biking area in Michigan. On any nice weekend from spring through fall the trailhead parking lot at the Silver Lake day-use area is filled with cyclists coming or going.

The park features three single tracks: the 2-mile Silver Lake Trail, the 5-mile Crooked Lake Trail, and the 17.3-mile Potawatomi Trail, one of the toughest rides in the state. To avoid conflicts among users, directional flows have been established with bikers following the trails in a clockwise direction, and hikers counter-clockwise.

With the exception of the Silver Lake Trail, Pinckney is considered a challenging and technical place to ride for advanced bikers, with numerous hills and ridges to negotiate. This is particularly true of the Potawatomi Trail, where every summer a number of biking accidents occur. For trail conditions, call the park headquarters or the Potawatomi Chapter of MMBA at (734) 663-9940.

Hiking: Winding throughout the recreation area are 40 miles of trails, including the northern half of the Waterloo–Pinckney Trail. All trails begin at the Silver Lake day-use area, where there is a large trail sign displaying the routes and distances. Keep in mind that Silver Lake, Crooked Lake, and Potawatomi Trails are so popular with mountain bikers that it may be best to avoid hiking these trails on the weekends.

To accommodate hikers, the park recently built the Losee Lake Trail, a 3.3-mile loop open to foot traffic only. The trail also begins at the Silver Lake day-use area and skirts several interesting marshes and swamps as well as the southern shore of Losee Lake. Crossover spurs allow you to shorten the hike to 1.5 or 2.5 miles.

Backpacking: Pinckney offers multi-day backpacking trips, rare opportunities in southeast Michigan. The Waterloo–Pinckney Trail is a 3-day hike that is described earlier in the Waterloo Recreation Area section. Pinckney also has the Potawatomi Trail, a 17.3-mile route that is a popular mountain biking ride. Most backpackers need at least 9 hours to cover the trail, but often break up the trek with a night at the walk-in campground on Blind Lake, the halfway point.

Canoeing: The Chain-of-Lakes is an interesting area to spend a day canoeing. The lakes are easy to cross, and all of them can be paddled within a day by experienced canoeists. A canoe rental concession rents boats daily during the summer at the day-use area of Halfmoon Lake. From there paddlers head west to reach Blind, Bruin, Watson, Patterson, and Woodburn Lakes. At the northeast corner of Halfmoon, canoeists can follow Portage Creek into Hiland Lake and even extend their trip further by following Portage River out of the park to Portage Lake. At the Bruin Lake Campground, Hell Creek Ranch (734-878-3632) rents canoes that can be paddled one-way to their riding stables just outside the park on Portage River, a 4-hour trip. Paddlers meet at the horse ranch on Cedar Lake Road and then are transported to Bruin Lake. The canoe service is available daily from May through October. Canoes are also rented out on Silver Lake, but the large body of water is isolated from the Chain-of-Lakes.

Fishing: Most anglers head for the Chain-of-Lakes, where they can fish a number of different lakes on one trip. Boat launches into the chain are located at Bruin Lake Campground and at the Halfmoon Lake day-use area. The species most anglers seek is bass, but the lakes also provide good panfish opportunities as well as

88

northern pike and crappie. Accessible from Hankerd Road is a boat launch to Pickerel Lake, which is stocked every spring with rainbow trout. Other lakes with ramps include Joslin and South Lakes off Joslin Lake Road, Gosling Lake off Patterson Lake Road, Crooked Lake at Crooked Lake Campground, and North Lake from North Lake Road just west of Hankerd Road.

On Silver Lake there is a fish pier in the day-use area. Although there is no boat launch on this lake, a canoe or belly boat can be easily launched and would be ideal in May and June to fish for spawning bluegill along the west shoreline.

Day-Use Facilities: The park has two day-use areas, including one on the west side of Silver Lake reached from Dexter–Townhall Road by exiting onto Silver Hill Road. Here the shoreline is an open grassy area with tables, grills, a store, and a boat rental concession that rents out canoes, rowboats, and paddleboats. In the center of the park is Halfmoon Lake with a day-use area reached from Hankerd Road. Along with a beach and swimming area, the day-use area offers a large shelter that can be rented, located on a hill overlooking the lake, a boat launch, and rental canoes.

Winter Activities: Designated ski trails begin at the Silver Lake day-use area, but they are not groomed and rental equipment is not available. The loops primarily follow the hiking trails but are renamed the Alpha Ski Trail, a 2-mile trip, and the Bravo Ski Trail, a 4-mile circuit. Both trails include some hilly terrain but can be handled by most intermediate skiers. Snowmobiling is also allowed in some areas of the park, and, as might be expected, there is a considerable amount of ice fishing in the winter for bluegill and crappie.

Equestrian Facilities: In a northeast section of the park there are 8 miles of bridle trails along with a staging area off Monk Road between Kelly and Cedar Lake Roads. The trail system is a series of loops connected to Lakelands Trail State Park, which is also open to equestrians. Hell Creek Ranch (734-878-3632) runs a stable just outside the park on Cedar Lake Road but uses the Pinckney bridle trails. The stable is open daily from April through October and, depending on the weather, on the weekends in the winter.

Access and Information: From I-94 take exit 159 and head north on M-52 for 6 miles to North Territorial Road. The headquarters can be reached by turning north onto Dexter–Townhall Road and then left onto Silver Hill Road and driving for a half mile. Dexter–Townhall Road can also be reached north of Ann Arbor from US 23 by going west on North Territorial Road (exit 49) for 12 miles. For information, contact Pinckney Recreation Area, 8555 Silver Hill Road, Pinckney, MI 48169-8901; or call (734) 426-4913.

Lakelands Trail State Park

Abandoned by the railroad in 1978, Lakelands Trail State Park was established as Michigan's third linear state park in 1989 when the rail corridor was transferred to the DNR Parks Division. Plans call for LakeLands to eventually be a 40-mile corridor stretching across four counties and open year-round to hikers, cyclists, equestrians, and cross-country skiers. The park will be divided into two sections. The West Unit is slated to be a 31-mile route that begins north of Jackson and ends in Hamburg. The East Unit will be a 9-mile stretch from South Lyon to Wixom in Oakland County.

As of this writing, a 12.7-mile segment of the park that extends from Stockbridge to Pinckney has been completed and dedicated. The trail departs Stockbridge as a

89

A cyclist checks his gears in Lakelands Trail State Park

graded pathway of crushed slag and enters a country setting. The scenery then alternates between farm fields and patches of marsh, small ponds, and stands of hardwoods. You cross only three roads before you arrive at Gregory, 5.5 miles from Stockbridge.

Another scenic stretch enters the Pinckney Recreation Area, 2.5 miles west of the town of Pinckney. The route here passes through open woods and marshland and four times crosses small bridges over Honey Creek before arriving at the old red train depot on the north side of Pinckney.

The next seven miles to Hamburg are open but should be attempted only by hikers or mountain bikers until the trail is upgraded with crushed slag. In this stretch you cross long railroad trestles over Hay Creek and then the Huron River and in between skirt the north shore of Zukey Lake.

Staging Areas: Once completed, the West Unit of the Lakelands Trail will begin at a staging area on Hawkins Road, five miles north of Jackson, and extend to another on Hamburg Road in Hamburg. The East Unit will have staging areas on Eleven Mile Road in South Lyon and near Old Plank Road in Wixom.

90

Currently you can park a car and pick up the trail at a park-and-ride lot off of M-106 in Stockbridge or another carpool lot off County Road D-19 in Pinckney.

Access and Information: A special trail pass is needed to use the Lakelands Trail. Individual or family passes can be purchased at the Pinckney Recreation Area headquarters or the Village Cyclery Shop in Pinckney. For more information, contact Pinckney Recreation Area, 8555 Silver Hill Road, Pinckney, MI 48169-8901; or call (734) 426-4913.

Yankee Springs Recreation Area

In 1836, "Yankee Bill" Lewis departed from New York and didn't stop until he reached the hilly country south of Grand Rapids. Intrigued by the many lakes and the dense forests of the area, Yankee Bill settled here and built an odd assortment of log cabins, which soon became one of the most noted inns west of Detroit. Located between Grand Rapids and Kalamazoo, Yankee Springs Inn was known to accomodate up to 100 travelers in a night while stabling sixty teams of stagecoach horses.

The inn and surrounding village went the way of the stagecoaches, and what remains today is Yankee Springs Recreation Area, which still attracts a large number of travelers but for different reasons. The 5,017-acre park borders the 13,000-acre Barry State Game Area, and together they preserve a highly scenic region of hills and lowlands, well wooded with more than seventy species of native trees and interspersed with lakes, bogs, and marshes. Within the recreation area are nine lakes, while Gun Lake, a 2,680-acre body of water, makes up a good portion of the park.

Yankee Springs Recreation Area draws 790,000 visitors annually, making it one of the five most popular units in the state park system. The reasons for its popularity are obvious. Along with a variety of year-round activities, the park is blessed with several scenic areas and overlooks that encourage people to visit the park if for no other reason than to drive through it.

Camping: Yankee Springs Recreation Area has three campgrounds and an organization camp. Its largest and most heavily used facility is Gun Lake Campground, located off Gun Lake Road at the base of Murphy's Point Peninsula. The campground has 200 modern sites that are close together with little privacy, but the area is well shaded and features its own beach and boat launch. A row of modern sites are located on a small canal off Gun Lake, where it's possible to tie up a boat just outside your tent or trailer. The campground is extremely popular, filling up most nights with the exception of Sunday from mid-June to late August. Gun Lake is open year-round, but the modern restrooms are closed from November through March.

On the east side of the park off Yankee Springs Road is Deep Lake Campground with 120 rustic sites. The area is a mix of large wooded sites and open fields with a few sites situated on a bluff overlooking the lake. There is a small boat launch on the lake but no official beach or swimming area. Deep Lake Campground is usually filled most holiday weekends and on Saturday for the majority of the summer. Yankee Springs also maintains a horseman's campground of 25 sites for equestrian use only and an organization camp opposite the park headquarters on Gun Lake Road.

Hiking: There are 17 miles of hiking trails in the recreation area, including a segment of the North Country Trail, a national trail that extends from North Dakota to

New York, passing through the length of Michigan. The shortest walk is the half-mile Sassafras Nature Trail, which begins near the Gun Lake Campground contact station and includes a series of interpretive signs. A brochure for the walk is available at the campground office or the park headquarters. Departing from Chief Noonday Road is Chief Noonday Trail, a 4-mile trek to Devil's Soup Bowl and then back along much of the same path. Along with the Soup Bowl, other scenic attractions of the hike include an overview of McDonald Lake.

Connecting these two footpaths is Long Lake Trail, a 5-mile return trip that follows a portion of the Chief Noonday Trail. Long Lake can also be picked up on Gun Lake Road, where it is posted just north of the park headquarters. From this trailhead it quickly enters an interesting bog area and at one point crosses the wetlands on an extensive boardwalk. It also follows an old wagon road to Graves Hill and then connects with Chief Noonday Trail at Devil's Soup Bowl.

At the east side of the park is Deep Lake Trail, a 4-mile loop that begins in the rustic campground and passes old homesteads, bogs, and a junction with Chief Noonday Trail at Devil's Soup Bowl. Keep in mind that a good portion of this trail is also used by mountain bikers. Hall Lake Trail begins across from the entrance to Long Lake Outdoor Center and forms a 2-mile loop, passing the shoreline of the lake and continuing on to Graves Hill before returning. The North Country Trail passes through the park by following existing trails and a segment of a bridle path on the south side of Gun Lake Road.

Since just about all the trails pass through the Graves Hill–Devil's Soupbowl area, they are color-coded for hikers. Long Lake is marked in yellow, Chief Noonday in orange, Deep Lake in ivory, and Hall Lake in blue.

Mountain Biking: The Deep Lake Mountain Bike Trail at Yankee Springs is arguably the most popular system in western Michigan. The 13-mile trail system begins at a staging area near the Deep Lake Campground and consists of two single-track segments: a 2-mile loop north of the parking lot for beginners, and an 11-mile Expert Loop south of it.

The 11-mile route is recommended for intermediate and advanced riders, as it winds through some of the most rugged hills in the park. Along with steep climbs and rocket descents, the loop includes a number of sand pockets. Although the trail swings near Devil's Soup Bowl, mountain bikers are not allowed into the natural depression. Every spring the MMBA chapters and bike shops host a series of races at Yankee Springs to raise funds for trail maintenance.

Fishing: There are access sites on eight lakes within the park, but by far the most popular fishing spot is Gun Lake. The 3.5-mile-wide body of water is an exceptional warmwater fishery and is southwest Michigan's most consistent producer of walleyes. The 2,680-acre lake is basically two large basins that are divided in the middle by Murphy's Point Peninsula, with the eastern half consistently producing a larger yield of walleye, bluegill, and perch. Yankee Springs maintains a boat launch in its day-use area on the peninsula and a barrier-free fishing pier.

Other access sites, where hand-carried boats can be launched, are on Hall, Deep, Long, Payne, Chief Noonday, Baker, and McDonald Lakes.

Cabins: Yankee Springs has twenty-seven cabins or bunkhouses for rent that sleep four to twenty-four persons at a time. Half of them are at Chief Noonday Outdoor Center, located in the northern half of the park off Chief Noonday Road. These cabins are spread out in a wooded area with three of them right on Chief Noonday Lake. The other half of Yankee Springs cabins are at Long Lake Outdoor Center and are set up in units with six to eight cabins each. Long Lake Outdoor Center is located just off Gun Lake Road. The cabins are mainly rented to groups and scout

Park rangers patrol on mountain bikes in Yankee Springs Recreation Area

troops, but can be rented singly for family use. They are extremely popular, and interested persons should reserve them in advance by calling the park headquarters.

Scenic Viewpoints: Yankee Springs has several scenic areas that are easily reached by car. Graves Hill and Devil's Soup Bowl are north of Gun Lake Road off Norris Road, a rough dirt road. Take the first road that departs east (right) from Norris Road. Drive carefully; this one is even more rutted out than Norris Road. The posted road leads to two parking areas, the first for Graves Hill Overlook, an old moraine. The high point is a short walk uphill and provides a scenic view of Yankee Springs' wooded interior and Gun Lake. Nearby is Devil's Soup Bowl, a deep and very steep wooded depression that was a result of glacial activity. Back on Gun Lake Road, continue east and turn south on the first dirt road past Hall Lake. The road leads through Pines Scenic Area, an old pine tree plantation that was planted in the late 1920s.

Day-Use Facilities: Murphy's Point Peninsula is Yankee Springs' scenic day-use area. The mile-long peninsula extends halfway across Gun Lake and features three beaches and designated swimming areas, two on the west side and one on the east shoreline. But you can walk along the edge of the lake the entire length of Murphy's Point or take a refreshing dip any place along the way. There are also two bath-houses, picnic shelters that can be rented, parking for 2,000 cars, and a pair of concession buildings that rent out canoes and rowboats.

Winter Activities: Although there is no winter equipment rental concession in the park, cross-country skiing is a popular activity during the winter. A warming lodge is maintained on weekends and holidays at Long Lake Outdoor Center, and from there skiers can enjoy a 10-mile trail system of six loops that range from an

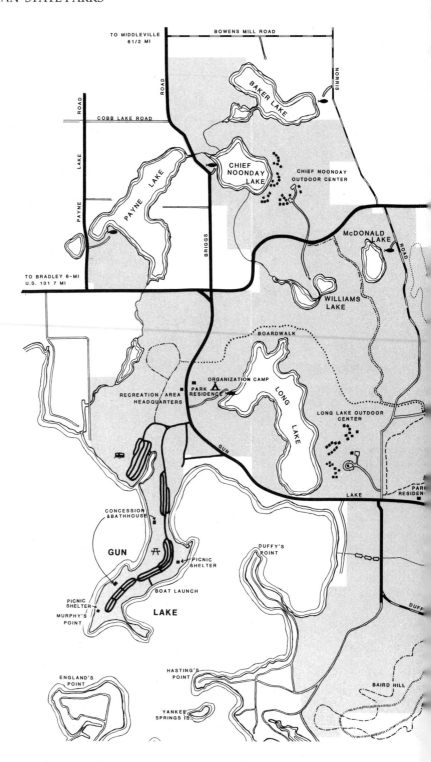

YANKEE SPRINGS
RECREATION AREA

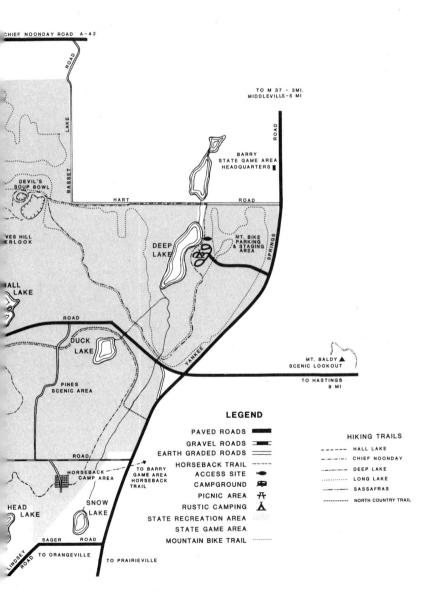

LEGEND

PAVED ROADS
GRAVEL ROADS
EARTH GRADED ROADS
HORSEBACK TRAIL
ACCESS SITE
CAMPGROUND
PICNIC AREA
RUSTIC CAMPING
STATE RECREATION AREA
STATE GAME AREA
MOUNTAIN BIKE TRAIL

HIKING TRAILS

HALL LAKE
CHIEF NOONDAY
DEEP LAKE
LONG LAKE
SASSAFRAS
NORTH COUNTRY TRAIL

95

easy ski of less than a mile to a 5.3-mile circuit of rolling terrain rated "most difficult." The tracks are set and groomed periodically throughout the winter. The park
also has designated snowmobiling trails, and fishermen do a considerable amount
of ice fishing during the winter, especially on Gun Lake for perch and walleye.

Equestrian Facilities: The park has a horseman's campground off Duffy Road
and a 4-mile bridle loop for riders. A trail also leads east from the campground to
join the 10-mile network of bridle trails in Barry State Game Area.

Access and Information: From Hastings, head west on M-37; then turn onto
Gun Lake Road to reach the park in 10 miles. Yankee Springs Recreation Area can
also be reached from US 131 by taking exit 61 and following County Road A42 east
for 7 miles to its junction with Gun Lake Road. For more information, contact Yankee Springs Recreation Area, 2104 Gun Lake Road, Middleville, MI 49333; or call
(616) 795-9081.

Sleepy Hollow State Park

Sleepy Hollow State Park features one of only two state-administered campgrounds in a twelve-county mid-Michigan region. The modern facility opened
in 1988, providing Lansing residents with a weekend escape just 30 minutes from
the bustle of the city, and elevating Sleepy Hollow from a rather tranquil state park
to a more moderately used unit that draws 320,000 visitors annually.

Established in 1974, the park's name can be traced to Ichabod Crane, the main
character from "The Legend of Sleepy Hollow," a well-known short story written
by Washington Irving, because one of the landowners who sold his property to the
DNR was I. B. Crane. The centerpiece of the state park is Lake Ovid, a 410-acre body
of water that was created when Little Maple River was dammed in 1975. The rest of
the 2,678-acre unit is reverted farmlands consisting mostly of open meadows and
fields that are dotted with stands of hardwoods and patches of bush. Sleepy Hollow
offers year-round activities, with cross-country skiing and ice fishing being especially popular in the winter.

Camping: The modern campground offers 180 sites on four loops within a short
walk of the park's beach area. For the most part, the campground is in an open area
with little shade, although some sites are wooded and a few overlook the lake. The
campground is 75 percent filled from Sunday through Thursday throughout the
summer and is almost always full on the weekends.

Hiking: Sleepy Hollow maintains 16 miles of trails that are shared by hikers and
mountain bikers. The system completely encircles Lake Ovid and forms additional
loops at the north end of the park. The main trailhead is located at the end of the
gravel road past the organization campground. The system can also be accessed via
spurs from the campground, the beach parking lot, and the picnic areas on the west
side of the lake. The terrain is predominantly fields of prairie grasses, but also includes some stands of hardwood and pine forests.

Mountain Biking: The trail system at Sleepy Hollow makes for an easy 9-mile
ride around Lake Ovid for mountain bikers. Most of the terrain is flat, reclaimed
farm fields and wooded lots, but there are some bits of elevation where the trail
crosses the Little Maple River twice.

The southern half of the system can be quite wet and muddy in spring, with long
stretches of trail totally submerged in water. Delay mountain biking in the park
until May, or ride only in the northern half, where the higher ground makes it sub-
stantially drier.

Fishing: Lake Ovid is often referred to as the best fishery in mid-Michigan, a region of the state where there are few large lakes. For experienced anglers there are tiger muskies and northern pike to seek out, while not-so-serious anglers concentrate on largemouth bass and panfish, especially bluegill and crappie. The only motors allowed on the lake are electric motors of three horsepower or less. In the southwest corner of the lake is a boat launch and a concession store (517-651-5586) that rents canoes, rowboats, and pontoons, and sells live bait and tackle.

There are also many opportunities for shore fishermen, who are usually rigged with worms or wax worms for panfish. Lake Ovid is dotted with three islands, of which the largest is connected to the mainland by a bridge to the Island Picnic Area on the west side. Anglers often do well by fishing off the island's east side. There are also a pair of barrier-free fishing piers in the West Picnic Area and at the boat launch.

The park maintains a night fishing gate off Shepardsville Road that is open from 10:00 P.M. until 8:00 A.M., when the rest of the unit is closed. This gives anglers access to the boat launch and allows them to fish late evening or early morning, often the most productive time to catch fish.

Day-Use Facilities: There is a half-mile-long sandy beach and a designated swimming area at the north end of the lake. Bordering the beach is a grassy hillside with tables, a bathhouse, and a parking lot that holds 2,000 vehicles. The park has three picnic areas: East Picnic Area on the east side of the lake, and Island Picnic Area and West Picnic Area on the west side, each with tables and playground equipment, and day shelters that can be rented.

Winter Activities: Cross-country skiing is popular, as the park grooms and tracks 7.5 miles of easy trail. A small parking lot and ski trailhead is maintained

Sleepy Hollow State Park

SLEEPY HOLLOW STATE PARK

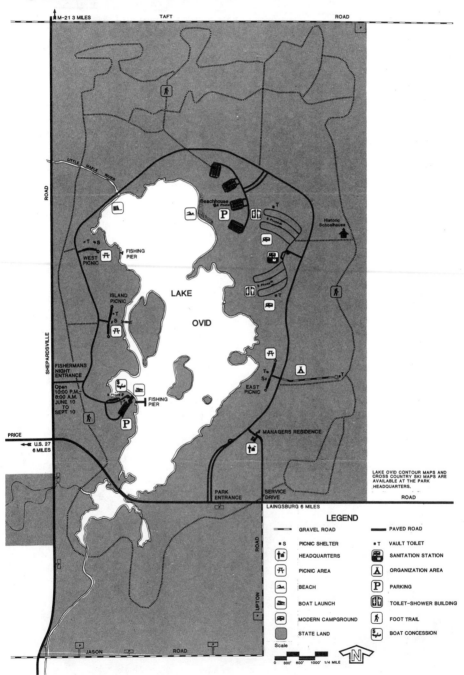

LEGEND

	GRAVEL ROAD		PAVED ROAD
■ S	PICNIC SHELTER	■ T	VAULT TOILET
	HEADQUARTERS		SANITATION STATION
	PICNIC AREA		ORGANIZATION AREA
	BEACH		PARKING
	BOAT LAUNCH		TOILET-SHOWER BUILDING
	MODERN CAMPGROUND		FOOT TRAIL
	STATE LAND		BOAT CONCESSION

Scale

0   300'   600'   1000'   1/4 MILE

N

LAKE OVID CONTOUR MAPS AND
CROSS COUNTRY SKI MAPS ARE
AVAILABLE AT THE PARK
HEADQUARTERS.

Boats for rent, Sleepy Hollow State Park

opposite the East Picnic Area, which serves as an overflow parking lot for skiers on the weekend. Loops range from 1.7 miles to a 7-mile ski through open uplands with views of the lake.

Snowmobilers are prohibited from entering the north or east sides of the park, but can pursue their activity in the rest of the unit. Ice fishing is also a popular winter activity, as anglers are allowed to set up shanties on the frozen lake and leave them there through the winter.

Access and Information: The park is 15 miles northeast of Lansing off US 27. From the highway, head east on Price Road for 7 miles to the park's main entrance. For more information, contact Sleepy Hollow State Park, 7835 Price Road, Lainsburg, MI 48848-9438; or call (517) 651-6217.

Fort Custer Recreation Area

Those looking for a fort at Fort Custer Recreation Area will be disappointed. Despite all the military activity that has taken place in the park, there has never been a stockade here. Originally the park was the site of Lawler, a small farming community that turned into a ghost town when it was deserted during the Great Depression. Today you can still see the town's crumbling remains—cisterns, wells, and stone foundations—along the mountain bike trails.

During World War II, the area became Camp Custer, an induction center for the Army, before the DNR acquired the site, located in Kalamazoo County, in 1971.

Today bordering the recreation area to the south is the Fort Custer Reserve Forces Training Site of the National Guard.

The park itself is 3,025 acres of nonmilitary activities, ranging from swimming, boating, and fishing to camping, mountain biking, and fall hunting. Most of the terrain is typical, flat southern Michigan farm country, but a quarter of the park, areas bordering the Kalamazoo River and at the south end of the park, are well-forested, gently rolling hills. The park also features four inland lakes and a 3-mile stretch of the Kalamazoo River. Annual attendance is 450,000, with much of a recent increase in visitors due to a mountain bike trail system that was completed in 1996.

Camping: Fort Custer has a 217-site modern campground, which includes a pair of mini-cabins, located on the north side of Jackson Lake. Although none of them are directly on the water, all are well separated in a lightly wooded area. There is direct access from one loop to Jackson Lake, but there is no boat launch. The campground is open year-round, but fills up only on weekends and holidays in the summer. There is also an organization campground in the park.

Hiking: The park has 2.25 miles of footpaths that form two loops around Jackson Lake, beginning near the picnic shelter of the Whitford Lake day-use area. A 1.5-mile loop circles Whitford and Lawler Lakes, while adjoining it is a spur that can be hiked as a 1-mile loop around Jackson Lake. The trails pass through the Jackson boat launch and the campground, and near the frontier cabins. There is some mountain biking activity on these trails, but most of the riding takes place on trail systems around Eagle Lake.

Mountain Biking: In 1993, members of the Michigan Mountain Biking Association (MMBA) began connecting the old roads of the abandoned township of Lawler with single-track trails to create a trail system on the south side of Eagle Lake. Within three years they had built a 15-mile system that has become one of the premier mountain biking areas in southwest Michigan.

The trailhead is located at a parking area off the park road between the entrance to the Jackson Lake Campground and the Eagle Lake day-use area at the end of the road. The trails have become so popular, it's now tough to find a place to park at the trailhead on any weekend that's not raining.

The heart of the Fort Custer mountain bike trail system is the Red Loop, an 8-mile route of single track and old roads that includes the biggest hills and most challenging terrain in the area, including the Trenches. Originally built by the military as training ditches, the Trenches is an area where bikers weave back and forth along the rounded sides of the narrow troughs.

Bikers will also encounter many other technical segments along the Red Loop, but the beauty of Lawler's abandoned streets is that they allow beginning and intermediate riders to easily bypass all the difficult stretches of the loop, which are clearly posted in advance.

In 1996, MMBA members unveiled the Green Loop, a 7-mile route designed to be an easier, more scenic ride. This loop winds completely around Eagle Lake and includes two shallow water crossings and even a small waterfall.

Fishing: All four lakes are accessible and have an electric-motor-only regulation on boats. There are boat ramps on Eagle, Jackson, and Whitford Lakes; Whitford is connected to Lawler Lake by a short channel. Eagle Lake is the largest and deepest of the four, up to 30 feet deep in some spots, and is fished for largemouth bass, bluegill, and crappie. The other lakes are shallow bodies of water and often weedy in the summer, when they are fished primarily for bass.

Cabins: The park has three rustic cabins for rent. Two of them are near each other and are located east of Whitford Lake in a wooded setting. Each holds 16 bunks and is at the end of a park road that is closed off to other visitors. The third

Mountain bikers in Fort Custer Recreation Area

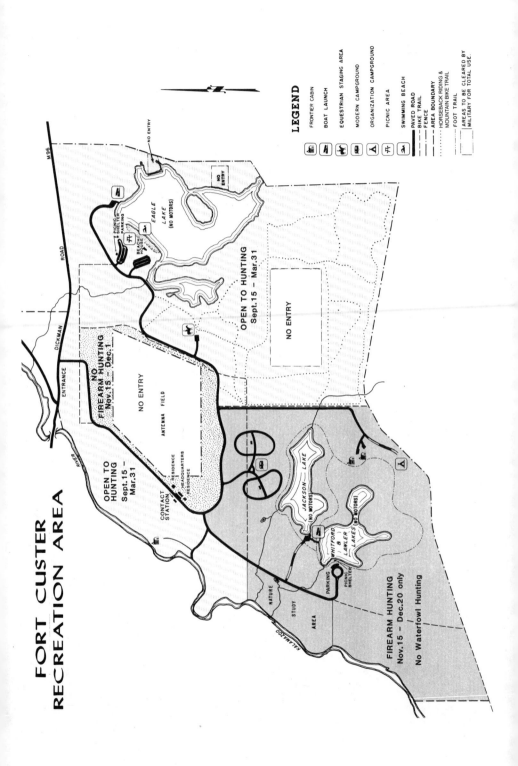

FORT CUSTER
RECREATION AREA

LEGEND

FRONTIER CABIN
BOAT LAUNCH
EQUESTRIAN STAGING AREA
MODERN CAMPGROUND
ORGANIZATION CAMPGROUND
PICNIC AREA
SWIMMING BEACH

PAVED ROAD
BIKE TRAIL
FENCE
AREA BOUNDARY
HORSEBACK RIDING &
MOUNTAIN BIKE TRAIL
FOOT TRAIL

AREAS TO BE CLEARED BY
MILITARY FOR TOTAL USE.

unit, Riverside Family Cabin, is a six-bunk, reconstructed log cabin on the banks of the Kalamazoo River. Dedicated in 1987, the structure is in a scenic location and is reached by a quarter-mile footpath opposite the park headquarters.

Day-Use Facilities: The park maintains a beach, a bathhouse, and picnic grounds with shelters in an open area on the north side of Eagle Lake. Also located here is a concessionaire that rents rowboats, canoes, and paddleboats daily during the summer.

Equestrian Facilities: Fort Custer has 18 miles of bridle paths located south of Eagle Lake, which equestrians share with mountain bikers. The staging area and parking lot for horseback riders is also the same one that cyclists use.

Winter Activities: Nordic skiers use the hiking paths for short and easy runs and the bridle trails for longer trips into the park. The trails are not groomed, nor is there a ski rental concession. Snowmobiling is allowed throughout the park except on ski trails, and ice fishing is also a popular activity in January and February.

Access and Information: Fort Custer is located 8 miles west of Battle Creek on M-96, and just across the Kalamazoo River from Augusta. For information, contact Fort Custer Recreation Area, 5163 West Fort Custer Drive, Augusta, MI 49012; or call (616) 731-4200.

Ionia Recreation Area

Ionia Recreation Area, a 4,018-acre unit in Ionia County, offers swimming, fishing, camping, mountain biking, and other outdoor activities traditionally associated with the Michigan state park system. But what Ionia is best known for is field dog trialing. The park has one of two upland pointing breed national championship courses in Michigan, and is the site of numerous trials during the year from mid-March through May and late August to November.

Michigan is only one of two states that allows dog trialing in state parks, and the Ionia trialing facility covers 2,000 acres of the park. State, regional, and national championships are held on the course, when up to 150 dogs will be worked and judged on their ability to locate game and hold points. The recreation area, a mixture of wooded, gently rolling hills, open fields, and wetlands, is also a noted hunting area for woodcock, rabbit, and especially whitetail deer, whose firearm opener often draws more than 300 vehicles to the park in November.

Ionia attracts 275,000 visitors annually, and because of a recently developed mountain bike trail system and day-use area along Sessions Lake, now draws 60 percent of its visitors during the summer.

Camping: The park maintains a 49-site rustic horseman's campground in a semi-open area east of Sessions Lake near the end of the park road, and has a group camping site nearby. Also located on the east side of the lake is a modern campground with 100 sites and a sanitation station.

Hiking: Within the recreation area are 3.5 miles of designated foot trails that traverse woods, meadows, streams, and lakeshore. The main trailhead is in the Beechwood Picnic Area, and from there two loops, including a mile-long trail for the visually-impaired, head along the south side of Sessions Lake to Point Picnic Area.

Mountain Biking: Ionia Recreation Area added off-road cycling to the many activities the park offers when the Chief Cob-Moo-Sa Mountain Bike Trail was completed in 1996.

Named after an Ottawa chief of the Flat River tribe who once had a camp along the river, the 9-mile trail system runs along a narrow band of park land between

IONIA RECREATION AREA

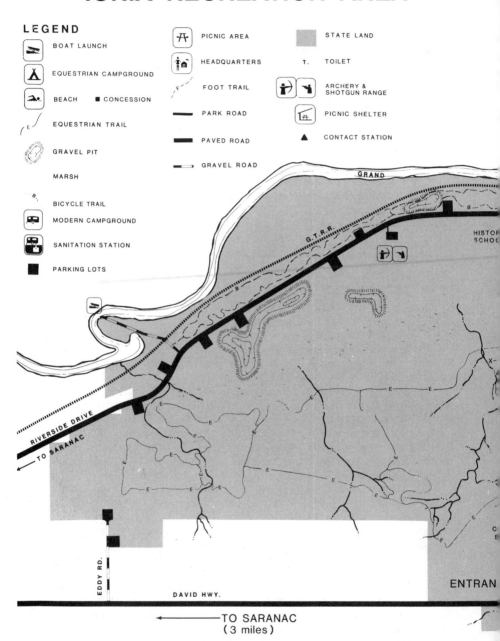

LEGEND

- BOAT LAUNCH
- EQUESTRIAN CAMPGROUND
- BEACH ■ CONCESSION
- EQUESTRIAN TRAIL
- GRAVEL PIT
- MARSH
- BICYCLE TRAIL
- MODERN CAMPGROUND
- SANITATION STATION
- PARKING LOTS

- PICNIC AREA
- HEADQUARTERS
- FOOT TRAIL
- PARK ROAD
- PAVED ROAD
- GRAVEL ROAD

- STATE LAND
- T. TOILET
- ARCHERY & SHOTGUN RANGE
- PICNIC SHELTER
- ▲ CONTACT STATION

GRAND

G.T.R.R.

HISTORIC SCHOO

RIVERSIDE DRIVE
TO SARANAC

EDDY RD.

DAVID HWY.

ENTRAN

TO SARANAC
(3 miles)

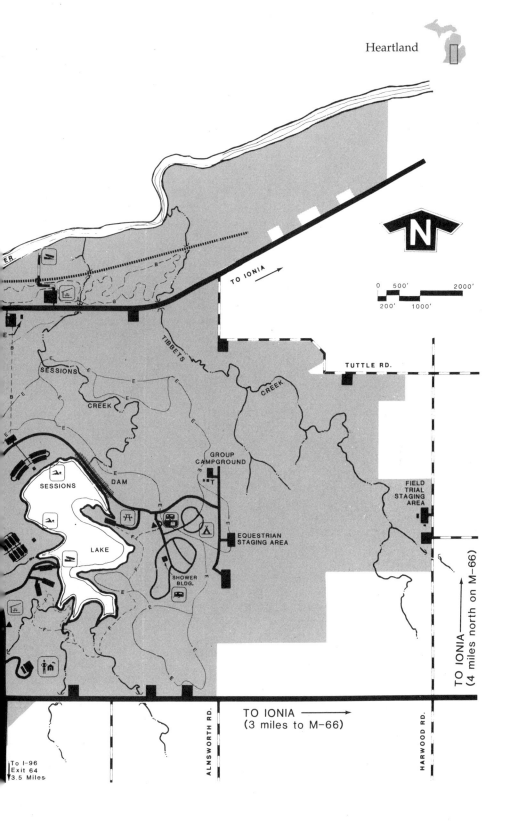

Riverside Drive and Grand River. The system includes a 5.8-mile loop for intermediate and advanced riders, a 2.5-mile beginner's loop, and a 0.7-mile spur that allows riders to reach the loops from the beach and day-use area.

The 5.8-mile loop is scenic but technical, as the single track weaves up and down the river bluffs for a series of sharp climbs and descents. Halfway along the loop there is a cross-spur that shortens the ride to 3.1 miles. The main trailhead for the trail system is the Riverside Picnic Area, and from there the intermediate loop is ridden in a counter-clockwise direction, and the beginner's loop, clockwise.

Fishing: Sessions Lake is a man-made body of water that was dammed in 1983. The 140-acre lake reaches depths of 55 feet and is stocked annually with several species of fish. It is best known for its largemouth bass, but in recent years the walleye fishery has begun to take hold. DNR surveys also have shown good populations of bluegill and crappies.

A boat launch is situated at the southwest corner of the lake and has parking for twenty-five cars and trailers. In the Point Picnic Area there is a barrier-free fishing pier situated near a steep drop-off in the lake where shore anglers have a reasonable chance of catching panfish or even an occasional bass.

Day-Use Facilities: The park has three picnic areas and a beach area. At the north end of the lake is a 1,600-foot beach, a bathhouse, and a boat rental concession. Beachwood Picnic Area is located on the southwest corner of the park, and along with tables, a shelter, and trail access, it also contains a boat launch. On the east side of the lake is Point Picnic Area, a very scenic spot with tables and grills on a small peninsula, while off Riverside Drive is Riverside Picnic Area with tables, a

Sessions Lake fishing pier, Ionia Recreation Area

shelter, and the trailhead for the mountain biking trails. Further west along River-side Drive is a shotgun and archery range that is open from daybreak to dusk year-round, but shooters must furnish all their own equipment and targets.

Equestrian Facilities: There are 15 miles of bridle trails in the park that begin at the horseman's staging area east of the horseman's campground and form loops to the southern and western edges of the park. There is also a forty-nine-site horseman's campground but no concession riding stable.

Winter Activities: The park turns 9 miles of bridle paths into ski trails during the winter. The trailhead and parking area for skiers is just north of the Beechwood Picnic Area, and from there a 1-mile beginner's loop heads north while a 2.5-mile intermediate loop and a 5.5-mile expert run heads west into the rolling terrain of woods, open fields, and small hills. The trails are not groomed, nor is there a warming center.

Access and Information: From the town of Ionia, head south on M-66 for 5 miles and then west on David Highway for 3 miles to the park entrance. From I-96 take exit 64 and head north on Jordan Lake Road for 3.5 miles. For more information, contact Ionia Recreation Area, 2880 West David Highway, Ionia, MI 48846; or call (616) 527-3750.

Wilson State Park

Located on the north end of Budd Lake in Clare County, Wilson State Park is one of the smallest units in the system, at 36 acres. It was originally a sawmill for the Wilson Brothers Lumber Company before it was deeded to the city of Harrison in 1900. The land was transferred to the state twenty-two years later, and in 1927, Wilson State Park was dedicated. The unit draws more than 100,000 visitors annually, the vast majority during the summer, as Wilson is mainly a campground and picnic facility with no trails, natural areas, or boat launch.

Camping: Wilson has 160 modern sites situated along two loops. The area is well shaded with pines and hardwood trees, and a few sites are within view of Budd Lake, but none of them are on the water. The campground has a sanitation station in each loop as well as a pair of mini-cabins and a rent-a-tipi. The authentic tribal tipi is very popular with families and should be reserved two or three weeks in advance. Sites are usually available Sunday through Thursday, but the campground fills up most weekends during the summer due to its close proximity to US 27. Located across the street from the Clare County Fairgrounds, the campground also fills up the entire week of the county fair, from the last Saturday in July to the first Saturday in August. The campground is open April to December.

Fishing: The 175-acre Budd Lake is well known for muskie fishing, as it has been stocked with the species since the mid-1950s. Both tiger and northern muskellunge are present, and fish up to 30 pounds have been caught in recent years. The average angler, however, is generally more concerned with the lake's other fish—perch, crappie, and largemouth bass—which can be found in good numbers and are considerably easier to catch. The only problem for many anglers is that Wilson does not have a boat launch, but the town of Harrison does maintain a public ramp at the south end of the lake. Shore fishing can also be difficult in the park due to the steep banks that border much of the lake.

Day-Use Facilities: The state park has a narrow but long picnic area overlooking the high banks of the lake, with tables, grills, and playground equipment. There is

Rent-a-Tipi in Wilson State Park

also a small beach that has been terraced to provide additional room. The designated swimming area is shallow and sandy.Overlooking the beach is a classic log structure, built by Civilian Conservation Corps (CCC) crews in 1939–41, that today serves as a shelter and bathhouse.

Access and Information: The park is located 1 mile north of Harrison right off Business US 27. For more information, contact Wilson State Park, 910 North First Street, Harrison, MI 48625; or call (517) 539-3021.

White Pine Trail State Park

Michigan's newest state park is also its longest. Dedicated in 1995, White Pine Trail is the fourth rail-to-trail state park and the longest trailway in the Lower Peninsula, stretching 92 miles from Cadillac to Comstock Park near Grand Rapids.

Converted from an abandoned Michigan Northern Railroad corridor, the White Pine features a flat surface of gravel and cinder that in the northern half extends through woodlands and farmland. One of the most scenic spots is a mile north of the Big Rapids staging area, where the 319-foot Whites Bridge crosses the Muskegon River. The White Pine also intersects the Pere Marquette Trail, another rail–trail, 13 miles north of Big Rapids. DNR officials are calling the new linear state park the "backbone of the Michigan Trailway System," because between the two rail–trails, you can travel in any direction across the Lower Peninsula.

Like all rail–trails, the White Pine is ideal for hybrid and mountain bikes, and is also open to hikers. The only motorized activity allowed on the trail is snow-mobiling in the winter. Camping is not allowed in the park, but there are more than a dozen commercial campgrounds within a mile of the trail.

Winter Activities: Cross-country skiing is allowed, but the main activity during the winter, especially on the northern half of the trail, is snowmobiling. There is so much snowmobiling activity between Cadillac and Big Rapids, in fact, that Nordic skiers would do well to skip the White Pine all together and search out another place to ski.

Staging Areas: Eventually, fourteen staging areas will be constructed, with the southern terminus on Lamoreaux Drive in Comstock Park. The northern trailhead is in Cadillac at a staging area on North 44 Road, a half-mile north of M-115. Exist-ing staging areas are also located at the railroad depot on Maple Street in Big Rap-ids, on Lake Street in Sand Lake on the Montcalm and Kent County border, between Edgerton and Williams Streets in Howard City, on First Street in Mortley, and be-tween Gilbert and Main Streets in Leroy.

Access and Information: Trail use requires an individual or family pass, which can be purchased at businesses of the various communities along the route or the District 6 DNR Headquarters in Cadillac. For more information on the White Pine Trail State Park, contact White Pine Trail State Park, 211 W. Upton Ave., Reed City, MI 49677; or call (231) 832-0794.

Mitchell State Park

Most people know Mitchell State Park as the busy campground that is ideally located between Lake Mitchell and Lake Cadillac in Wexford County. But the park is also home of the Heritage Nature Study Area, a 110-acre wetland marsh that provides an unusual opportunity to view a variety of wildlife on the outskirts of Cadillac.

The water source for the marsh is the Black River, which was originally used by lumbermen to move logs between the two large lakes. But it was a difficult task moving logs along the shallow and winding river, and in 1873 the loggers built the present canal between Lakes Cadillac and Mitchell. In 1973 the DNR constructed a dike around the Heritage area and for a few years used it as a pike-rearing pond before more cost-effective hatcheries were developed. Finally, in 1979, the wetlands were formally dedicated as a nature study area. They are a pleasant contrast to the often-busy state park campground.

Mitchell draws 175,000 visitors a year to its 265-acre unit, beginning in spring when morel mushroom pickers set up camp to invade state and national forests nearby to search out the fungus delicacy. The use continues year-round, as Mitchell's campground is one of the few modern ones that have heated restrooms in operation during the winter.

Camping: Mitchell State Park has 215 modern sites that are well shaded by hard-woods. The campground includes 24 pull-through sites specially designed for large recreational vehicles and a mini-cabin that overlooks Lake Cadillac. But the most popular sites are those that line the canal, where boats can be docked right next to tents or trailers. Also available to campers is a small sandy beach and the boat launch on Lake Cadillac. The campground is filled weekends from mid-April to mid-October and filled daily from July to mid-August.

Hiking: Following the dike along the perimeter of the Heritage Nature Study

MITCHELL STATE PARK

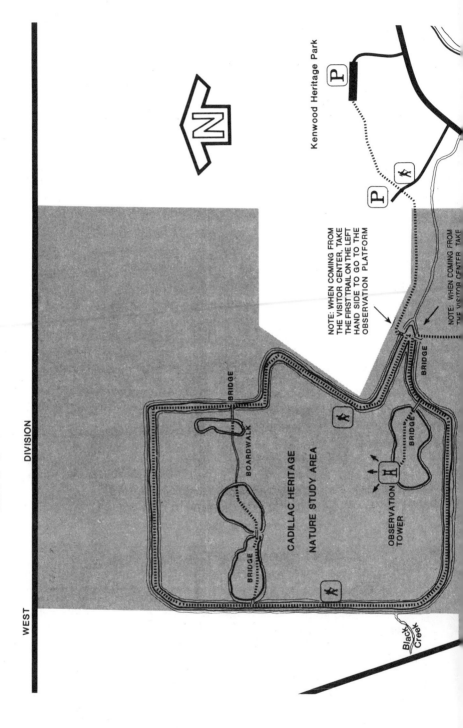

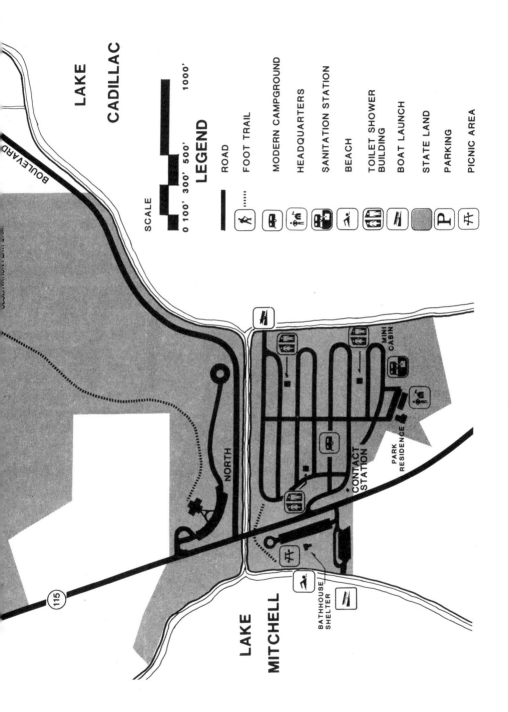

LAKE CADILLAC

LAKE MITCHELL

BOULEVARD

NORTH

CONTACT STATION

PARK RESIDENCE

MINI CABIN

BATHHOUSE/SHELTER

115

SCALE

0 100' 300' 500'   1000'

LEGEND

—— ROAD

...... FOOT TRAIL

MODERN CAMPGROUND

HEADQUARTERS

SANITATION STATION

BEACH

TOILET SHOWER BUILDING

BOAT LAUNCH

STATE LAND

P PARKING

PICNIC AREA

Canal between Lake Mitchell and Lake Cadillac

Area is a 2.5-mile hike whose trailhead is at the rear of the Carl T. Johnson Hunting and Fishing Center. The study area supports a variety of plants, and wildlife that includes whitetail deer, wild turkeys, beavers, great blue heron, and numerous species of waterfowl. The trail is a wood-chipped path with bridges and boardwalks for an easy hike around the wetlands. Near the area's southeast corner, an observation tower provides an even better view of wildlife. The Heritage Nature Study Area is also accessible by following North Boulevard east from M-15. Just after crossing Black River, turn left onto a dirt road opposite the city boat launch. A parking area and another posted trailhead are at the end of the road.

Interpretive Center: In 1992, the park opened up the Carl T. Johnson Hunting and Fishing Center, named after the founder of the Michigan Conservation Foundation and dedicated to the hunting and fishing heritage of Michigan. The center features a variety of exhibits and hands-on displays, including a marsh diorama, a wall-size aquarium stocked with native Michigan fish, and a full-size mounted elk, a species that was introduced to the state thanks to the effort of sportsmen's groups. Other exhibits outline the evolution of hunting equipment and practices from the first hunters in the state to the present ones, while a multimedia presentation in the auditorium shows the role hunters and anglers have played in restoring Michigan's wildlife.

The center is open year-round. Hours are from 10:00 A.M. to 6:00 P.M. daily except Monday from April through November, 1:00 P.M. to 5:00 P.M. on Friday, and 10:00 A.M. to 5:00 P.M. on Saturday and Sunday the rest of the year.

Fishing: Both lakes are noted as fine walleye fisheries and are heavily fished during the summer. The 1,150-acre Lake Cadillac is an extremely busy body of water, as it lies totally within the city limits of Cadillac and its shoreline is heavily developed. Most walleye anglers prefer drift fishing with live bait, either minnows or crawlers, early in the morning or at night. Lake Mitchell also attracts walleye fishermen, while both lakes provide good catches of perch, panfish, and bass. The quarter-mile canal that connects the two lakes is a popular place for children to shore fish in the park, and in the evening many can do well landing bullheads. The park maintains a boat launch in the Lake Mitchell day-use area.

Day-Use Facilities: The state park maintains a day-use area on Lake Mitchell with an entrance and parking lot that are separate from that of the campground. Along with the sandy beach and designated swimming area, facilities include a bathhouse (but no showers), picnic tables, grills, and a shelter.

Winter Activities: The campground is open year-round, and the heated bathroom facilities remain in operation throughout the winter. Visitors both ski and snowshoe in the Heritage Nature Study Area, and there are numerous Nordic trails and a downhill ski facility in the Cadillac area. Both lakes are very popular with ice fishermen, who can set up shanties on the frozen surface and jig for perch, panfish, and an occasional walleye.

Access and Information: The park is 2.5 miles west of Cadillac on M-115. For more information, contact Mitchell State Park, 6093 East M-115, Cadillac, Ml 49601; or call (231) 775-7911.

Newaygo State Park

Featuring 3 miles of frontage along Hardy Dam Pond, a lake that was created when Muskegon River was dammed in 1931, Newaygo State Park is in the center of Newaygo County. The 257-acre park is staffed during the summer but not the rest of the year, as almost 70 percent of its 35,000 annual visitors are campers. The terrain is a wooded area of oak and other hardwoods mixed with popple and softwoods.

The park has no foot trails other than a few that connect the campground to the lake. Its day-use area is a small sandy beach with no facilities, located east of the boat launch.

Camping: Newaygo has ninety-nine rustic sites along two loops on both sides of the boat launch. The area is heavily wooded, and the sites are well separated from each other. None are directly on the lake. In recent years the campground, despite being a rustic facility with vault toilets and no showers, has been filling up on weekends from mid-July to early August. Sites are easily obtained during the week and the rest of the year.

Fishing: The park maintains a boat launch on a small inlet off Hardy Dam Pond with parking for fifty cars and trailers. The 3,971-acre lake is almost 18 miles long and stocked with walleye annually. Many anglers target yellow perch, the most frequently caught fish in the lake, as well as black crappies and bluegill.

Access and Information: The park is 43 miles north of Grand Rapids and can be reached from US 131. Go west on Jefferson Road at the Morley exit for 7 miles and then go north on Beech Road to the park's entrance. During the summer the contact station is staffed and can provide information: (231) 856-4452. During the rest of the year, contact Silver Lake State Park, Route 1, P.O. Box 187, Mears, MI 49436; or call (231) 873-3083.

Lake Michigan

Warren Dunes State Park

▲ For many out-of-staters, Michigan's famous sand dunes begin at Warren Dunes State Park. The 1,952-acre unit is the first park reached along Lake Michigan when driving into the state, as it's located just 12 miles north of the state border in Berrien County. It's a Michigan park, but its dunes are well known throughout the Midwest. Warren Dunes draws close to 1.5 million visitors a year, the second highest total in the state park system, and more than 80 percent are from outside the state. Though the vast majority are from Illinois and Indiana, the park attracts people each summer from every corner of the country.

The attraction is 2.5 miles of sandy Lake Michigan shoreline and the dunes that border it. Near the water the dunes are wind-blown and high with several that rise 200 feet above the lake. They range from Mount Fuller and Pikes Peak at the south end of the park to Mount Edwards, a mostly wooded dune at the north end. Thousands climb these mountains of sand each summer for an excellent view of Michigan's southwest corner. The most noted dune, however, is Tower Hill, the highest at 240 feet. During the mid-1970s this hill became a haven for hang gliders, when on a windy weekend there would be almost 100 on the hill and twenty in the air at one time.

Although sandy beaches and wind-blown dunes are the main attractions, the majority of the park is hilly terrain heavily wooded in oak and hickory. From a naturalist's point of view, this is the most interesting aspect of the Warren Dunes: It is an excellent example of plant succession, from open sand and beach grasses to a climax beech-maple forest, as found in the Warren Woods Natural Area. Others simply like the brilliant autumn colors these forests provide, or their appearance from a ski trail in the winter, when every branch of a tree is laden with snow.

Camping: Warren Dunes has two campgrounds. A 182-site modern campground is in a wooded area of the park that offers shade and, surprisingly, for the

Lake Michigan shoreline in Saugatuck Dunes State Park

number of sites in it, a small degree of privacy between campers. On the southern loop are three mini-cabins and a foot trail that leads around Mount Randal to the day-use area on Lake Michigan. In 2000, Warren Dunes replaced its beach campground that overlooked Lake Michigan with a rustic campground. The rustic facilities include 20 sites and vault toilets; they are located in a wooded setting north of the modern campground.

The campgrounds are filled 90 percent of the time during the summer and every weekend from the beginning of May through October. The park also has an organization camp.

Hiking: There are more than 5 miles of maintained hiking trails in Warren Dunes, with most of it forming a 4-mile loop through the dunes in the park's interior, along Lake Michigan, and back to the modern campground. The trail passes through both wooded terrain and open dunes and can be picked up from the northern parking lot of the day-use beach area, the organization camp, and a small trailhead parking lot located just off the entrance to the modern campground. Plan on 2 to 3 hours for the entire hike.

Another trailhead is located at the end of Flora Lane, north of the park entrance on Red Arrow Highway, where there is a small parking area, trash cans, and a trail sign. From here there is a mile loop to the north that was originally built as part of the cross-country ski system. But after the park constructed a 400-foot boardwalk over the marsh, hikers began using the loop, especially in the spring when it is possible to sight a variety of birds.

Part of the trail system is posted as the Warren Dunes Nature Trail, a 1-mile loop featuring ten interpretive stops that correspond to a brochure. Pick up the nature trail at the small trailhead parking lot just south of the modern campground. Finally, a popular hike in early spring is to simply walk the beach from the park's

Trails across the Great Warren Dune

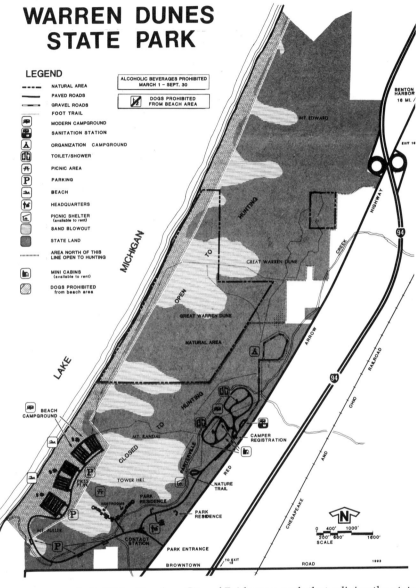

WARREN DUNES STATE PARK

LEGEND

- ---- NATURAL AREA
- —— PAVED ROADS
- --- GRAVEL ROADS
- .... FOOT TRAIL
- MODERN CAMPGROUND
- SANITATION STATION
- ORGANIZATION CAMPGROUND
- TOILET/SHOWER
- PICNIC AREA
- PARKING
- BEACH
- HEADQUARTERS
- PICNIC SHELTER (available to rent)
- SAND BLOWOUT
- STATE LAND
- .... AREA NORTH OF THIS LINE OPEN TO HUNTING
- MINI CABINS (available to rent)
- DOGS PROHIBITED from beach area

ALCOHOLIC BEVERAGES PROHIBITED
MARCH 1 – SEPT. 30

DOGS PROHIBITED FROM BEACH AREA

day-use area north to Weko Beach, a City of Bridgman park that adjoins the state park. At that time of year, the crowds are gone, the beach is hard for good footing, and you can still enjoy the beauty of the dunes and deep blowouts. Round trip to Weko Beach and back to the day-use area is a 5-mile hike.

Day-Use Facilities: Separated from the rest of the park by several towering dunes is the day-use beach area of Warren Dunes. The area has parking for more than 1,500 cars but still fills up on weekends during the summer. Occasionally the park staff sets up overflow parking for an additional 600 cars before they start turning vehicles away. There are three bathhouse/stores near the parking lots, much sand on the exceptionally wide beaches, and the towering dunes nearby to climb up. Warren Dunes also has a wooded picnic area with shelters bordered on one side by a wind-blown dune, located near the contact station.

Natural Area: The center of the state park, including almost a mile of Lake Michigan beach, is further protected as the Great Warren Dune Natural Area.

Winter Activities: Nordic skiing is a popular activity in both Warren Dunes. The state park has 3 miles of ski trails along a flat terrain east of the dunes. The trails cut through the modern campground and can also be picked up from the trailhead for the Warren Dunes Nature Trail just south of it or at the end of Floral Lane. The trails are not groomed, nor is there a ski rental concession in the park.

Hang Gliding: Warren Dunes is the only state park in Michigan that permits hang gliding, and is considered by most gliders to be the best place in the Midwest, if not the country, for soaring. What makes the park so attractive for these soaring adventurers, especially those just learning the sport, are the smooth winds that come off the lake and the soft and forgiving sand below. Back in the 1970s, when hang gliding hit its peak in Warren Dunes, the park staff was overwhelmed by the number of accidents occurring among unqualified flyers and instituted several regulations. All gliders must now be certified and must obtain a daily or annual gliding permit from the park headquarters.

For a list of instructors with permits to soar in Warren Dunes, check with the park office. Although not nearly as popular as it was in the late 1970s, it is still possible to witness the colorful gliders. Best time to come is on weekends from late September through October, when it is often possible to watch two or three gliders soar from Tower Hill.

Access and Information: Warren Dunes is reached from I-94 by taking exit 16 and following Red Arrow Highway south to the park entrance. For more information, contact Warren Dunes State Park, Red Arrow Highway, Sawyer, MI 49125; or call (616) 426-4013.

Warren Woods Natural Area

Administered by the staff at Warren Dunes State Park, Warren Woods Natural Area is a 311-acre state park unit located inland on the Galien River. The Woods were saved from loggers by Edward K. Warren in the nineteenth century, and today the tract is one of the last stands of virgin climax beech-maple forests in the state.

The Three Oaks merchant was a partner in a general store when, in 1879, he decided to purchase the land. He was ridiculed at the time for buying land with no intention other than preserving it. A conservationist far ahead of his time, Warren purchased the forest only seven years after Yellowstone National Park was acquired. He continued to purchase undeveloped tracts including the stretch of Lake Michigan dunes that eventually became Warren Dunes State Park in 1930.

Thanks in part to those 300-year-old trees, Warren Woods is designated a National Natural Landmark. The sluggish Galien River can make the tract something of a bug factory in June and July, but the woods are stunning in the fall when the hardwoods turn to shades of autumn. This far south, the leaves peak from late October to early November. The unit is also a frequent destination in the spring for birders, who walk the trails to view a variety of warblers, barred owls, flycatchers, and both redheaded and pileated woodpeckers.

Hiking: The park features an easy 3.5-mile trail that loops through the area between Elm Valley Road and Warren Woods Road and crosses the Galien River. The most impressive trees are in the northern half of the loop. The main trailhead is in the small day-use area reached from Elm Valley Road. There is also a posted trailhead off Warren Woods Road, 7 miles from Warren Dunes State Park.

Day-Use Facilities: There is no camping in Warren Woods. The only facilities are a small picnic area and parking lot off of Elm Valley Road.

Access and Information: Warren Woods is reached from I-94 by taking exit 6 and heading east on Elm Valley Road to the posted entrance of the natural area. For more information, contact Warren Dunes State Park, Red Arrow Highway, Sawyer, MI 49125; or call (616) 426-4013.

Grand Mere State Park

Grand Mere State Park is an undeveloped unit of 985 acres with such unique land formations and flora that it has been designated a National Natural Landmark. The glaciers that scooped out the Great Lakes 10,000 years ago also carved a number of small depressions along the western edge of Michigan that evolved into interdunal lakes, ponds, and wetlands. Grand Mere, a park in Berrien County, contains three such lakes that have been protected ecologically by a line of wind-blown sand dunes that stand between them and the Lake Michigan shoreline.

Although the park is day-use only with limited facilities, it attracts between 50,000 to 60,000 visitors a year, many of them educational groups that come to study an excellent example of plant succession from open sand to forested hills, or the many rare and endangered plants that can be seen, most notably around South Lake. The park also contains North and Middle Lakes and 2 miles of Lake Michigan shoreline that can only be reached on foot.

Day-Use Facilities: Three roads lead into the park, but the official entrance is off Thornton Drive between Grand Mere Road and Willow Road. The posted entrance is a paved road that leads a half mile to a picnic shelter and a sixty-vehicle parking lot. From here it is another half-mile walk to Lake Michigan through mostly wind-blown dunes.

The shortest route to the Great Lake is from the end of Grand Mere Road, where there is a trail sign and parking for a half dozen cars. From here the beach is a quarter-mile walk over a few steep sand dunes.

Hiking: Almost 4 miles of trails form a loop through open dunes and wooded areas of the park, but the only designated trail is a half-mile nature trail. The barrier-free trail extends from the picnic shelter around South Lake, passing ten numbered posts that correspond to interpretive notes on the back of the park map.

The rest of the trails, many of them old two-tracks, are neither posted nor maintained. The trails can be picked up at the end of Wishart Road and followed to the park road between South and Middle Lakes, while one loop swings west to Lake Michigan, skirting the south side of Baldtop, the tallest dune in the area.

Fishing: Anglers are attracted to both North and Middle Lakes for bass and a variety of panfish. Access to the lakes is off Grand Mere Road, where you pass a township park along North Lake, the larger of the two lakes. Further along the road there is a boat launch on Middle Lake. There is no access to South Lake.

Winter Activities: When there is sufficient snow, the park is popular with Nordic skiers, who enjoy an undeveloped, almost trailless, area to explore. Skiers can park at the end of Wishart, a half-mile drive from its junction with Willow Road. None of the trails are groomed, and there is no ski rental concession in the park. Snowmobiles and all other ORVs are prohibited from Grand Mere.

GRAND MERE STATE PARK

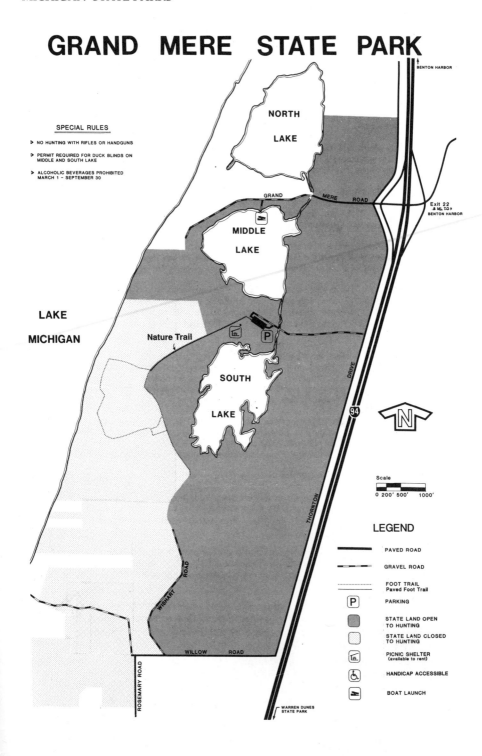

SPECIAL RULES

▷ NO HUNTING WITH RIFLES OR HANDGUNS

▷ PERMIT REQUIRED FOR DUCK BLINDS ON MIDDLE AND SOUTH LAKE

▷ ALCOHOLIC BEVERAGES PROHIBITED MARCH 1 – SEPTEMBER 30

NORTH LAKE

BENTON HARBOR

GRAND MERE ROAD

Exit 22
¼ MI TO ▶
BENTON HARBOR

MIDDLE LAKE

LAKE MICHIGAN

Nature Trail

SOUTH LAKE

THORNTON DRIVE

94

WISMART ROAD

WILLOW ROAD

ROSEMARY ROAD

WARREN DUNES STATE PARK

Scale
0 200' 500'   1000'

N

LEGEND

—————— PAVED ROAD

– – – – GRAVEL ROAD

.... FOOT TRAIL
Paved Foot Trail

P PARKING

STATE LAND OPEN TO HUNTING

STATE LAND CLOSED TO HUNTING

PICNIC SHELTER (available to rent)

HANDICAP ACCESSIBLE

BOAT LAUNCH

Access and Information: From I-94 take exit 22 and head east on John Beers Road, where you immediately come to an intersection with Thornton Road. Straight ahead, John Beers becomes Grand Mere Road. Turn south (left) on Thornton Road to reach the park entrance or Willow and Wishart Roads. For more information, contact Warren Dunes State Park, Red Arrow Highway, Sawyer, MI 49125; or call (616) 426-4013.

Van Buren State Park

Van Buren State Park, a 407-acre unit in Van Buren County, is located down the shoreline from South Haven. The park is composed of towering wooded dunes on its west side and a gently rolling terrain of oak, maple, and beech in its eastern half. But clearly its major attraction is its expanse of Lake Michigan shoreline, almost a mile of it. The sandy beach, bordered on one side by dunes and on the other by the sweeping blue views of the Great Lake, is the main reason the park draws 235,000 visitors a year.

Van Buren lacks both developed trails for biking or hiking and a boat launch for fishermen, but just 2 miles north of the state park is the western staging area of the 33.5-mile long Kal–Haven Trail.

Shoreline dunes in Van Buren State Park

Camping: Van Buren State Park's campground has 220 modern sites that are not on the water but are only a 5-minute walk from the beach. Some are well shaded in hardwoods or pines, but most are semi-open and a few are not shaded at all. The sites are well sodded but close together, and when the campground is full, they offer little privacy. Throughout the summer, from late May to early September, Van Buren is filled each weekend often by Thursday evening. The campground is open April to December but from mid-October to November, facilities include only vault toilets, electricity at sites, and spigots for water. The park also maintains an organizational campground.

Day-Use Facilities: The park has a day-use parking area for 520 vehicles that occasionally fills up during weekends at the height of summer. From there a walkway winds through a narrow cut between two steep dunes and you spill out onto some prime Lake Michigan real estate: a stroller's beach 30 to 40 yards wide, bordered on one side by towering bluffs of sand and on the other by the endless surf of a Great Lake. Near the parking area is an open picnic area, which includes a shelter that can be rented, while overlooking the beach is a bathhouse and concession store.

Winter Activities: The park is open year-round, but due to the lack of trails and facilities there is minimal use of the park in winter.

Access and Information: From I-196 take exit 13 and head west on 32nd Avenue and then north on Blue Star Memorial Highway. Turn west onto Ruggles Road and follow it to the park entrance. From South Haven head south on Blue Star Memorial Highway for 2 miles to Ruggles Road. For more information, contact Van Buren State Park, 23960 Ruggles Rd., South Haven, MI 49090; or call (616) 637-2788.

Kal–Haven Trail State Park

The second longest state park in Michigan, and one of the most narrow, is Kal–Haven Trail, a 33.5-mile rail-to-trail park that extends from Kalamazoo to South Haven on Lake Michigan. The project was approved in 1975, but the former railroad right-of-way wasn't acquired from Penn Central until twelve years later during the 150th anniversary of Michigan's statehood.

The former railroad right-of-way has a uniform width of 100 feet and contains a raised bed of crushed slag, making it ideal for hybrid and mountain bikes. Road bikes can be used on the trail but they require a little more effort on the part of the cyclist. The trail is also open to hikers, while from Bloomingdale to South Haven a 14-mile bridle path parallels the main trail.

The trail winds through a number of small towns and a variety of terrain, including wooded stretches, farmlands, and wetlands. There are also seven former railroad trestles that have been rebuilt into trail bridges. The most interesting one is at the west end where the trestle crossing the Black River has been converted into a covered bridge. In Bloomingdale, roughly the halfway point, a depot has been restored as a museum, while the caboose outside serves as an information center for trail users.

If you don't have time for the entire route, a particularly enjoyable stretch is the 10.5-mile segment from Gobles to Grand Junction, passing through Bloomington and crossing an unusual camelback bridge that spans the Barber Creek ravine. Bikes can be rented in Bloomington at the Kixx Stand Bike Shop (616-657-7625).

Winter Activities: There is no camping along the trail but it is open to cross-country skiers in the winter, and snowmobilers when there is a 4-inch snow base.

Staging Areas: The eastern trailhead is located just west of US 131 on 10th Street

An old railroad depot serves as an information center along the Kal-Haven Trail State Park

between G and H Avenues in Oshtemo Township, just north of Kalamazoo. The staging area includes parking for 150 vehicles, a picnic area, restrooms, and a restored caboose that serves as an information center.

The western trailhead is located west of I-196 on the Blue Star Highway just north of South Haven and two miles north of Van Buren State Park. Facilities here include a parking lot, restrooms, a picnic area, and trail display.

Access and Information: The trail is accessible from the staging areas or parking areas in the villages of Kibbie, Bloomingdale, Gobles, and Kendall. Trail use requires an individual or family pass, which can be purchased at the staging areas, Bloomingdale, or Van Buren State Park but does not require a state park vehicle permit. For more information on the Kal–Haven Trail, contact Van Buren State Park, 23960 Ruggles Road, South Haven, MI 49090; or call (616) 637-4984.

Saugatuck Dunes State Park

Probably the least-visited state park along the popular west Michigan shoreline is Saugatuck Dunes State Park, an undeveloped unit in Allegan County. The 1,008-acre park is a scenic area whose terrain ranges from rolling hills to steep slopes, with most of it forested in hardwoods and pines. It also includes a dedicated natural area and more than 2 miles of Lake Michigan shoreline. The sandy beach, bordered on one side by sand dunes from 20 feet to a towering 180 feet above the lake level, can only be reached after a walk of almost a mile.

Livingston Trail in Saugatuck Dunes State Park

The most unusual aspect of this park is that it used to surround a minimum secu-rity prison. Saugatuck was created in 1977 after the state purchased the St. August-ine Seminary and its 800 acres of Lake Michigan frontage. When word leaked out that the state planned to convert the facility into the Michigan Dunes Correctional Facility, residents of Holland and Saugatuck protested loudly and a compromise was reached. The prison was still built but occupied only 50 acres; later, in the early 1990s, it was removed. The rest of the tract became Michigan's newest state park.

Saugatuck Dunes is a day-use park only, and due to its walk-in beach and the lack of a campground, it draws only 50,000 visitors a year. To many, this is its most charming aspect. In this park you can stroll along a shoreline that isn't littered by blankets, coolers, and beach balls. Others like the 14 miles of trails that wind up and down the park's wooded dunes and spill out onto a beautiful stretch of Lake Michi-gan shoreline.

Day-Use Facilities: The only facility in the park is a day-use area, which in-cludes tables, grills, vault toilets, a picnic shelter, and parking for 50 cars. From here the various trails depart into the park. The shortest route to Lake Michigan is a mile walk along the Beach Trail.

Hiking: Winding throughout the park are 14 miles of trails; wide, sandy paths built for both hiking and skiing. The trails are divided into three sections. The

Lake Michigan

SAUGATUCK DUNES STATE PARK

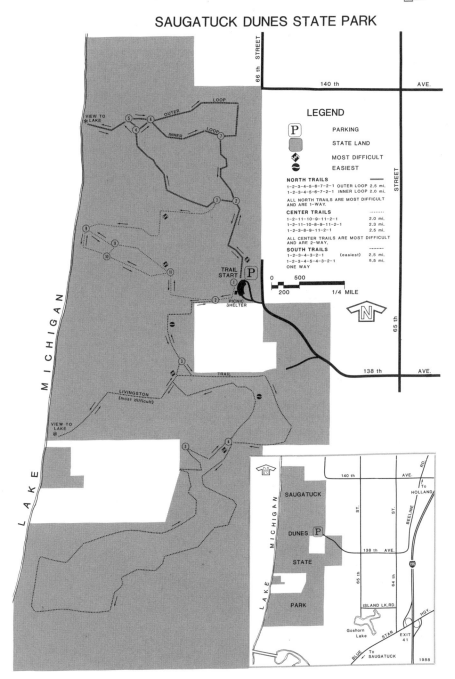

LEGEND

P — PARKING

STATE LAND

MOST DIFFICULT

EASIEST

NORTH TRAILS
1-2-3-4-5-6-7-2-1 OUTER LOOP 2.5 mi.
1-2-3-4-5-6-7-2-1 INNER LOOP 2.0 mi.

ALL NORTH TRAILS ARE MOST DIFFICULT AND ARE 1-WAY.

CENTER TRAILS
1-2-11-10-9-11-2-1   2.0 mi.
1-2-11-10-8-9-11-2-1   2.3 mi.
1-2-3-8-9-11-2-1   2.5 mi.

ALL CENTER TRAILS ARE MOST DIFFICULT AND ARE 2-WAY.

SOUTH TRAILS
1-2-3-4-3-2-1   (easiest)   2.5 mi.
1-2-3-4-5-4-3-2-1   5.5 mi.
ONE WAY

0   500
200   1/4 MILE

N

North Trail is two loops of 2 and 2.5 miles that include a scenic view of Lake Michigan at its west end. The Beach Trail is a 2-mile loop to Lake Michigan with connecting spurs to the North and South Trails. The South Trail is a 5.5-mile loop to the south end of the park, and along the way you pass the posted junction to the Livingston Trail. This rugged trail is a walk of a mile one way through a series of dunes to a view of Lake Michigan from the edge of a towering lakeside bluff. Within the day-use area, there are display maps showing the loops and distances.

Natural Area: The southern third of the park is protected as a dedicated natural area. The 300-acre tract is a prime example of a coastal dune system and contains three endangered plant species: Pitcher's thistle, spotted wintergreen, and American ginseng. The park is also well known among birders because it lies on a major migration route for hawks. Six species of hawks can be spotted in the spring and fall, including Cooper's hawk, broad-winged hawk, and rough-legged hawk.

Winter Activities: Saugatuck Dunes is a popular place to cross-country ski during the winter due to its hilly terrain and the abundance of snow that the Lake Michigan region usually receives. Traffic on the Livingston and Beach Trails is two-way during the winter; traffic on the other loops is one-way, and all pass views of Lake Michigan. The majority of the trails are rated "most difficult," for advanced skiers who can negotiate steep slopes. But the first half of the South Trail forms a 2.5-mile loop that is relatively flat and can be easily managed by novice skiers. The most challenging run for skiing is the Livingston Trail.

Access and Information: From I-196, just north of the town of Saugatuck, take exit 41 west onto Blue Star Memorial Highway and then immediately turn right onto 64th Street. Head north for a mile and then west onto 138th Avenue. Follow it to the park entrance and day-use area less than a mile away. For more information, contact Van Buren State Park, 23960 Ruggles Rd., South Haven MI 49090; or call (616) 637-2788.

Holland State Park

▲ Many argue Holland State Park has one of the best beaches in Michigan. The 150-foot-wide park beach, with its sugarlike sand, extends 1,800 feet along Lake Michigan and is crowned by "Big Red," the distinctively red Holland Harbor Lighthouse that was built in 1907 and is located across the channel. The beautiful beach and the scenic lighthouse have made Holland a very, very popular park.

Holland, an easy drive from several urban areas, including Grand Rapids, draws almost 1.5 million visitors a year, the most of any unit in the state park system. The vast majority arrive during the traditional summer season to camp or enjoy the beach, as the 142-acre park does not have any designated trails or natural areas. Located in the northwest corner of Allegan County, the park is two separate units with one area bordering Lake Macatawa and the other containing the beach on Lake Michigan.

Camping: Holland has two campgrounds for a total of 306 modern sites. Lake Macatawa Campground contains 208 sites that are located across Ottawa Beach Road from the inland lake. A few of the sites are on the edge of a wooded dune, but most of them are in an open area, close together with little shade. Lake Michigan Campground has ninety-eight sites laid out on blacktop adjacent to the day-use beach area of the park. This campground is completely open with little shade, and the sites are close together. Lake Macatawa Campground is connected to the beach area by a paved walkway/bicycle path.

The campgrounds are full practically every day from mid-May to September.

Day-Use Facilities: Along with the wide, sandy beach, the day-use area includes a bathhouse and store, playground equipment, and beach volleyball courts. To the south, the day-use area is bordered by the channel, which connects Lake Macatawa with the Great Lake. Along the waterway are picnic tables, grills, and benches, from which park visitors can watch the bustling boat traffic departing or entering Lake Michigan, with Big Red in the background. There is parking for 782 vehicles in the day-use area, but from mid-May to early September the lot fills every weekend, usually by noon, and additional cars are turned away.

Fishing: Lake Macatawa is the site of much fishing activity as anglers seek out bass, perch, and walleye, while on Lake Michigan a deepwater fishery is trolled during the summer for Chinook and coho salmon and lake trout. Holland maintains a boat launch on the inland lake across the road from Lake Macatawa Campground that is designated primarily for campers. The ramp is open to any park visitor, but there is no parking available for vehicles and trailers. Most shore fishing takes place along the pier reached from the southwest corner of the day-use beach. During the summer, anglers suspend minnows and nightcrawlers to entice perch, while in the fall and spring the spot is a popular place to cast spoons into Lake Michigan for steelhead, salmon, and brown trout.

Cycling: The bicycle path that connects the two units of Holland State Park is part of a 30-mile network in Park Township. Bike paths also extend north along Lake Shore Avenue, allowing cyclists to travel the 20 miles from Holland to Grand Haven.

Popular beach at Holland State Park

Access and Information: From US 31 exit onto Lakewood Boulevard and head west. Follow park signs to turn southwest onto Douglas Avenue, which becomes Ottawa Beach Road. The park is at the west end of Ottawa Beach Road, 7 miles from Holland. For more information, contact Holland State Park, Ottawa Beach Road, Holland, MI 49424; or call (616) 399-9390.

Grand Haven State Park

Grand Haven State Park contains only 48 acres but draws 1.5 million visitors a year, one of the highest totals in the state park system, and officials are quite candid about the reasons for its popularity. This is an urban park, and the city of Grand Haven, a popular summer destination, draws people to the state park as much as does its beautiful beach on Lake Michigan. The park is only a mile from the downtown area, and the two places are connected by a scenic boardwalk along the Grand River and a city-operated trolley that shuttles people between the stores and restaurants of Grand Haven and their campsites on the beach.

Located in the northwest corner of Ottawa County, less than 30 miles from Grand Rapids, the state park is open year-round but receives the vast majority of its

Pier and lighthouse near Grand Haven State Park

visitors during the traditional summer season. Besides its 2,500 feet of Lake Michigan beach, the park contains a campground and day-use area but no maintained trails or boat-launching facilities.

Camping: Grand Haven has 174 modern sites in a campground that is open with no shade and little space between sites. A few sites actually border the beach with an open view of Lake Michigan, and all of them are a short walk away from the surf. The facility is full daily from mid-June to the end of August, and on the weekends throughout June and most of September. Due to its overwhelming popularity, there is little chance during the summer of getting a site here without a reservation. The campground is open from April to November, with electricity and water available, but the restrooms are closed in mid-October.

Fishing: Adjacent to the park is the picturesque Grand Haven Lighthouse and the pier connecting it to the mainland. This is an extremely popular spot for fishermen, who jig for perch during the summer and cast spoons for salmon, steelhead, and brown trout during the fall and spring. The park maintains a fisherman's parking lot with a posted entrance off Harbor Drive. It opens at 5:00 A.M., as often the best fishing is early morning. There is also some surf fishing for salmon and trout off the park's beach in the fall and early spring. Lake Michigan is a noted deep-water fishery during the summer for salmon and trout, but there are no ramp facilities in the park. There are public boat launches in the city, however, along with a number of charter fishing boats at Chinook Pier along the Grand River.

Day-Use Facilities: Grand Haven's beach possesses some of the finest sand along Lake Michigan, and the day-use area is a colorful scene during the summer, filled with windsurfers, swimmers, and sunbathers. In the spring and fall, the beach is popular among kiters. There is parking for 800 cars in the day-use parking lot, and often on Saturday and Sunday from June through August the lot fills up and additional cars are turned away. People are then encouraged to park downtown and take the trolley to the beach for a small fee. Also located in the day-use area are picnic facilities, play equipment, a bathhouse, and a concession store.

Cycling: A bicycle path extends both north and south out of the state park. To the north it follows Lighthouse Connector Park, a preserved right-of-way along the Grand River that passes harbors, the displays devoted to the Coast Guard, Chinook Pier, and the many other attractions of Grand Haven. This riverside greenbelt is also popular with walkers and in-line skaters. To the south the path eventually goes to Holland State Park.

Access and Information: The park is a mile southwest of US 31 in Grand Haven along Harbor Drive. For more information, contact Grand Haven State Park, 1001 Harbor Avenue, Grand Haven, MI 49417; or call (231) 798-3711.

P. J. Hoffmaster State Park

The Dune Climb Stairway at P. J. Hoffmaster State Park is no easy climb. It's 165 steps to the top, a viewing platform on the crest of a dune 190 feet above the lake. So tiring is the climb for some people that the park staff has built benches along the stairway. No easy stroll but a magnificent view.

From the observation deck there is a panorama of Lake Michigan and its shoreline beach, but most of all there are dunes, almost every which way you look. Well forested or wind-blown, these steep hills of sand make up the majority of Hoffmaster's 1,043 acres. Most visitors know they are viewing a portion of the world's most extensive set of freshwater dunes, but don't realize these are among the youngest geological formations in Michigan, formed only 3,000 years ago and constantly changing in appearance, size, and their effect on the environment.

Michigan's sand dunes are perhaps its greatest natural treasure, and there may not be a better place to see them or understand their natural history than P. J. Hoffmaster State Park, just south of Muskegon on the southern edge of Muskegon County. A 10-mile network of trails loops through the park and allows visitors to view the entire plant succession of dunes, from the beach along Lake Michigan to pioneer dune grass, and foredune country to the barrier dunes with their white pines and black oak forests. There is also Gillette Nature Center, an interpretive center within the park, devoted to the state's sand dunes.

Hoffmaster draws about 500,000 visitors a year due to a wide range of activities, including camping and horseback riding. In the winter the park, with its heavy snowfall, becomes a popular area for Nordic skiers, and in the spring it's a favorite destination of wildflower enthusiasts.

Camping: Hoffmaster has a modern campground of several loops with 293 sites. The area is well forested with pine trees towering over every site and a sandy floor covered with needles. A quarter-mile trail leads from one loop west to a camper's beach on Lake Michigan. On a clear evening campers head down the trail to sit on the sandy bluffs above the beach and watch the sunset, applauding afterwards at Mother Nature's nightly performance.

The facility is a popular campground that fills up almost daily Wednesday through Sunday from late June through most of August. On Monday and Tuesday the campground is generally 75 percent full in the summer.

Hiking: A 10-mile network of foot trails loops through the park's dunes and along most of the 2.5 miles of Lake Michigan shoreline within Hoffmaster. The network basically forms a large loop, stretching from the campground on the northern end to almost its southern border, with several spurs cutting across it. There are several trailheads to the loop located at the campground, the day-use beach area, and the Gillette Nature Center. The interpretive center is a popular place for many hikers to start the day, as several trails begin here, including the Dune Climb Stairway, a half-mile trail to the park's designated quiet area, and a 2.5-mile loop that includes the Homestead Trail and a stretch along Lake Michigan.

It's important to note that mountain biking is not allowed on any of the park's trails.

Interpretive Center: The Gillette Nature Center was built in 1976 as a bicentennial project to serve as Michigan's sand dune interpretive center. The two-story center is, in fact, overshadowed by a huge, wind-blown dune that is best viewed from behind a glass wall on the west side of the lobby. The center also features an exhibit hall entitled "From a Grain of Sand," which guides you through the natural history of the dunes, and an eighty-two-seat theater that uses a nine-projector, multi-image slide show to further explain the dunes' delicate nature. On the ground floor there is a gallery that has hands-on exhibits to help children understand the environment of the park.

The nature center (231-798-3573) is open daily in the summer from 10:00 A.M. to 5:00 P.M. The rest of the year the hours are from 1:00 P.M. to 5:00 P.M. Tuesday through Friday, and from 10:00 A.M. to 5:00 P.M. Saturday and Sunday.

Day-Use Facilities: Hoffmaster maintains a day-use area on Lake Michigan with parking for 550 cars. The facility includes a bathhouse, a concession store, and a picnic area near a beautiful stretch of Lake Michigan beach. The facility is heavily used in the summer, and occasionally the lot is filled on the weekend. Further south, along the park road toward the nature center, there are other picnic areas situated in a wooded setting.

Dune overlook at P. J. Hoffmaster State Park

Natural Area: Almost a fourth of Hoffmaster, more than 200 acres, is a dedicated natural area. This tract is located in the southwest corner of the park and includes 1.5 miles of Lake Michigan shoreline. In the heart of this section is a half-hidden ravine, situated between a pair of forested dunes, called the Quiet Area. This special spot is a half-mile hike from the Gillette Nature Center but, seemingly, a million miles from anywhere. It is especially dazzling in the spring when the area explodes with trillium.

Trillium-lovers from around the state flock to Hoffmaster every Mother's Day weekend, when the park hosts its annual Trillium Festival, which includes guided walks into the woods to view the showy wildflowers.

Winter Activities: Nordic skiing is a popular activity in the winter, as Hoffmaster maintains 3 miles of ski trails with a trailhead and parking lot at the south end of the park road. The trail forms three loops through rolling to hilly terrain with runs rated for novice to advanced skiers. The trails are not groomed, nor is there a ski rental concession on site, but there is an open shelter with a fireplace near the trailhead.

It is equally as impressive in late winter to hike the shoreline on a windy day and watch the surf erupt through ice volcanoes along the frozen edge of Lake Michigan.

There is no snowmobiling in the park.

Access and Information: From I-96 take exit 4 and head south on 148th Avenue

P. J. HOFFMASTER STATE PARK

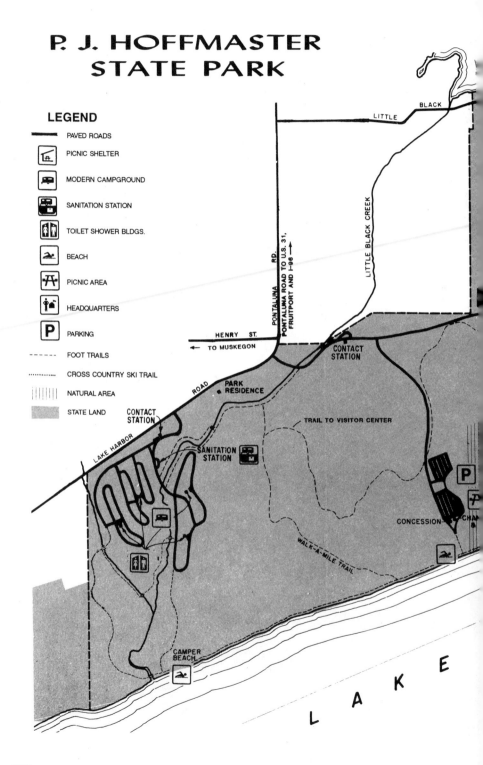

LEGEND

▬▬▬	PAVED ROADS
🏠	PICNIC SHELTER
🚐	MODERN CAMPGROUND
	SANITATION STATION
	TOILET SHOWER BLDGS.
	BEACH
🧺	PICNIC AREA
	HEADQUARTERS
P	PARKING
- - - - -	FOOT TRAILS
··········	CROSS COUNTRY SKI TRAIL
‖‖‖‖‖	NATURAL AREA
▒▒▒	STATE LAND

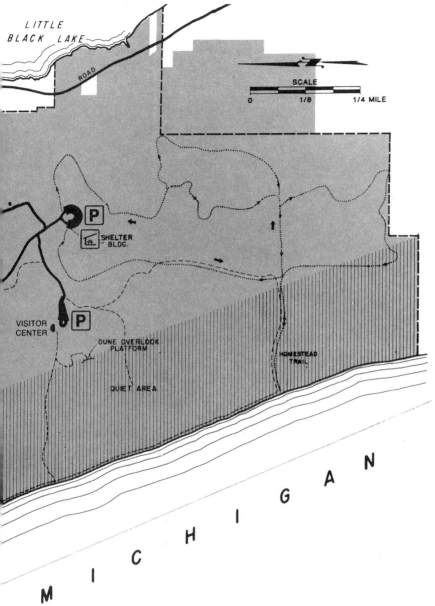

LITTLE
BLACK LAKE

ROAD

SCALE

0   1/8   1/4 MILE

P

SHELTER
BLDG.

VISITOR
CENTER

P

DUNE OVERLOOK
PLATFORM

HOMESTEAD
TRAIL

QUIET AREA

M I C H I G A N

and then immediately turn west (right) onto Pontaluna Road, which ends in 6 miles at the park entrance. From US 31 take Pontaluna Road, almost halfway between Muskegon and Grand Haven, and head west for 3 miles. For more information, contact P. J. Hoffmaster State Park, 6585 Lake Harbor Road, Muskegon, MI 49441; or call (231) 798-3711.

Muskegon State Park

▲ Not all of the features in Muskegon State Park are natural. Within the 1,165-acre park is the Muskegon Winter Sports Center, home of one of only four luge runs in the United States. The winter center is a popular and busy place, as it contains a biathalon range and almost 5 miles of lighted trails for night skiing.

The state park, located in Muskegon County, draws more than 500,000 visitors annually and is also a popular place in the summer. More than 2 miles of sandy beach along Lake Michigan is the most attractive feature for many people, while the rest of the park consists of large forested and wind-blown dunes, steep sandy bluffs overlooking the Great Lake, and a mile of Muskegon Lake shoreline. The park road is the southern end of Scenic Drive from Whitehall and winds 3 miles from the northern border of the state park through the dunes and along Lake Michigan before swinging east to end at the shore of Muskegon Lake.

Much of the park is a peninsula surrounded by the inland lake on the east side, Lake Michigan to the west, and a canal that connects the two bodies of water. Abundance of water and shoreline attracts more than 200 species of birds, which in turn attract birders from around the state. Among the waterfowl and shorebirds often spotted are cormorants, egrets, herons, and scooters, while warblers migrate through the area in May.

Camping: The park has 278 sites divided into three campgrounds. Lake Michigan Campground (also known as the North Campground) is one of the oldest camping areas on the west side of the state, built before motorhomes and car trailers appeared in the 1930s. Subsequently, many of its 110 modern sites are not level and can be used only by tent campers. The gently rolling area is well wooded in deciduous trees and bordered to the west by wind-blown sand dunes. Within the campground is a pair of mini-cabins. There are no sites on the water, but the sandy Lake Michigan shoreline is only a short walk away. Across the park road is the East Campground, a semi-modern facility of thirty sites with restrooms but no electricity. The former CCC camp is in an open area hemmed in by woods.

At the south end of the park is Channel Campground, a modern facility of 138 sites. The semi-open campground features black-topped camp pads that allow recreational vehicles to be parked on the sandy soil. A number of sites are located right on the channel and are extremely popular during the summer. The campground also has its own boat launch on Muskegon Lake. Both modern campgrounds are filled on the weekends from July through Labor Day and are usually near capacity during the week. There is also an organization campground in the park.

Hiking: The park maintains 12 miles of foot trails through a terrain of mostly well forested lowlands and dunes. Most of the network is a series of loops and side trails spread between Channel Campground and the East Campground, but you can also enter the system at the Blockhouse on Scenic Drive south of Lake Michigan Campground and from the Snug Harbor day-use area. Often the trails involve steep climbs to the crests of dunes where there are scenic views, particularly in the southern half of the park. The trails wind past such interesting spots as Devil's Kitchen,

Muskegon Lake, Muskegon State Park

the village site of Old Bay Mills, and Lost Lake, a small, isolated inland lake in the northern half of the park. There is no mountain biking on the trails.

Fishing: The park abounds with year-round fishing opportunities. The 4,150-acre Muskegon Lake is noted for its perch and bass as well as walleye, which the DNR Fishery Division has stocked annually since 1978. Anglers also use the channel during the summer to enter Lake Michigan to troll for Chinook and coho salmon and lake trout. Shore fishermen can park in the day-use area and follow the beach south to reach the rocky breakwall, where during the summer the catch is perch and an occasional bass. During the early spring and late fall fishermen cast spoons and spawn off the breakwall for steelhead trout and salmon or surf fish off the beach when the fish begin schooling just offshore prior to spawning runs.

Facilities for fishermen in the park include a boat ramp in the Snug Harbor day-use area and another near Channel Campground. There is also a fishing pier in Snug Harbor and two more along the walkway that borders the 4,000-foot channel, where occasionally anglers night-fish for walleye.

Winter Activities: The Muskegon Winter Sports Center is a unique facility located in the state park, and was founded by the Muskegon Sports Council in 1983. Today the council oversees a pair of Nordic ski loops, 1.5 and 3.1 miles in length, that are groomed and tracked daily and lit for night skiing. The sports complex (231-744-9629), located near the East Campground, also includes a warming lodge with food concession, lessons, and a ski rental service. Along with a vehicle fee to

135

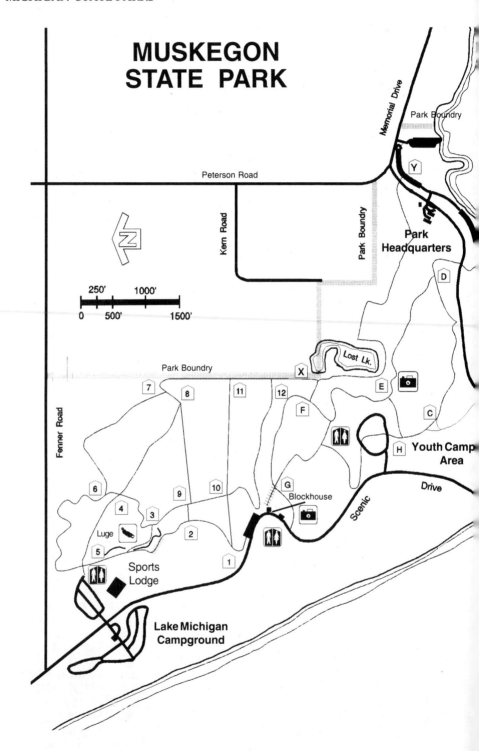

MUSKEGON STATE PARK

Lake Michigan

Muskegon Lake

Old Bay
Mills Village
Site

**Channel
Campground**

Devil's
Kitchen

IV

III

II

I

V

VI

VII

Navigation Channel

Bath
House

Beach

**Lake
Michigan**

nug
rbor

Hiking Trails

——————— Road

—/+++++ Trail / Steps

Interdunal Pond

Scenic View

Toilet

A	O	Devil's Kitchen - Green
Y	X	Lost Lake - Orange
1	12	Loop to Loop - Yellow
G	F	Scenic Ridge - Red
A	H	Hearty Hiker - Blue
A	VII	Dune Ridge - Brown

enter the park, there is a trail fee. The complex, which is open from 10:00 A.M. to 10:00 P.M. daily, operates a luge run that is open to the public as well as a lighted ice skating rink and a biathalon range, which combines skiing and marksmanship. For a fee, it's possible for children and adults to receive a helmet, a sled, and coaching, and be enjoying the luge within an afternoon.

There is no snowmobiling in Muskegon State Park.

Day-Use Facilities: One of two day-use areas is located on Lake Michigan at the south end of the park, where there is parking for 600 cars, a bathhouse/store, and a wide, sandy beach that is typical of this side of the Great Lake. A second day-use area borders Snug Harbor off Muskegon Lake near the south entrance of the park. The area has tables, grills, a shelter that can be rented, and a small sandy beach, though the water tends to be weedy here much of the summer. Snug Harbor, which also has a boat launch and fishing pier, is a favorite spot for wind surfers and those with small sail boats.

Scenic Viewpoint: In 1935, a CCC group built the original Blockhouse, a two-story log structure that provides a broad view of the park. The building burned down in 1962 but was rebuilt two years later. From the second floor, to the south you see the high point of the area, a wooded dune at 791 feet, while to the west is the water horizon of Lake Michigan. The Blockhouse is located on Scenic Drive between Lake Michigan Campground and the park's south entrance road.

Access and Information: From US 31 exit at M-120 and head southwest following park signs to Memorial Drive, which terminates at the park's south entrance. The park's north entrance can be reached by following Scenic Drive south from Whitehall. For more information, contact Muskegon State Park, 3560 Memorial Drive, North Muskegon, MI 49445; or call (231) 744-3480.

Duck Lake State Park

▲ Duck Lake State Park, which stretches from Lake Michigan along the northern shore of its namesake lake in Muskegon County, has only one sand dune, but it's almost impossible to miss the wind-blown hill of fine sand. It separates Lake Michigan from Whitehall Scenic Drive, and on its lake side is a steep bank into the Great Lake. On the other side it's a nuisance for road crews. The drifting dune is slowly spilling onto the pavement, which now must be plowed during the summer for sand like it is in the winter for snow.

The towering dune is atypical of the 729-acre park, whose terrain for the most part is level forests. Duck Lake State Park officially opened in 1988 as a day-use park. There are no camping facilities, nor are there any maintained trails. Still, the park registers more than 80,000 visitors a year, due in large part to the scenic Lake Michigan beach and Duck Lake.

Day-Use Facilities: There is a day-use area on Duck Lake that includes a wooded picnic area with tables and grills, and a shelter that can be rented, along with a small sandy beach and a bathhouse. Further west along the park drive is another parking area, from which a boardwalk leads around the end of Duck Lake to the Lake Michigan shoreline on the other side of Whitehall Scenic Drive. There are vault toilets but no bathhouse along the boardwalk.

Fishing: Off the boardwalk parking lot is a boat launch for Duck Lake, which attracts anglers interested in catching bass, crappie, and panfish. Fly fishermen often visit the lake in early summer to pop for nesting bluegill near the shore, while ice fishermen set up during the winter for northern pike. A small channel empties

Duck Lake into Lake Michigan, but due to a dam under the Whitehall Scenic Drive bridge, boats cannot enter the Great Lake from the boat launch.

Access and Information: The park is located 6 miles north of Muskegon. To enter the park head east onto Michillinda Road from Whitehall Scenic Drive north of the lake and look for the posted entrance. For more information, contact Muskegon State Park, 3560 Memorial Drive, North Muskegon, MI 49445; or call (231) 744-3480.

Silver Lake State Park

One of the most appealing features to visitors of Silver Lake State Park is its lack of trees. The 2,936-acre unit in Oceana County is another Lake Michigan park, with 1,800 acres of it forming a mile-wide strip between the Great Lake and Silver Lake. This area is unique dune country, as its ridges and valleys are mostly wind-blown sand, lacking trees, scrub, even dune grass, and often rangers compare its appearance to that of the Sahara Desert.

The strip of dunes is divided into three areas, with small sections at the north end designated for ORVs. The south end is occupied by a dune-ride concession. The majority in the middle is the pedestrian area, where visitors leave their cars and follow the ridges of open sand out to Lake Michigan. Silver Lake State Park contains almost 4 miles of Lake Michigan shoreline, and the wide sandy beach is the main drawing card for the park, as much of it is uncrowded and can only be reached by foot.

Silver Lake attracts more than a million visitors a year, many of them interested in its unusual ORV area. This is the only park in the state that has a designated ORV area, and riders come from throughout the Midwest to "ride the dunes." Almost as popular are the commercial dune rides that are offered by a concessionaire.

Camping: The park has 200 modern sites in a campground on the east side of Silver Lake. Divided in half by County Road B15, the campground is a lightly wooded area with shade but little space between campers, though in recent years the staff has removed forty-nine sites, making the area a bit more spacious. There are no sites on the water, but the day-use beach area is a short walk from any site. The entire east side of Silver Lake is now heavily developed for tourism, including seven private campgrounds nearby on Hazel Road, which has taken some pressure off the DNR facility. Still, during the months of July and August, the park campground fills up Wednesday through Saturday and is 90 percent full the rest of the week. Midweek sites are easy to obtain in June without a reservation and the campground is never full after Labor Day. The restrooms are closed in November and reopened on April 15.

Hiking: There are no maintained trails in the park, but there are the dunes. The pedestrian area is a series of wind-blown dunes that run east to west, and from the top of almost any ridge, there are good views of Silver Lake on one side and the endless horizon of Lake Michigan on the other. From the pedestrian parking lot, which holds ninety vehicles, it's a mile out to the Great Lake, or about a 20-minute walk for most people.

The most interesting trek is a 6-mile hike out to Lake Michigan and then south along the shoreline to Little Point Sable Lighthouse. This involves fording the mouth of Silver Creek to access Golden Township Park on the other side, and then following Lighthouse Drive briefly to reach the lighthouse, the halfway point of the walk and an ideal spot for an extended break or lunch.

The return begins by taking Lighthouse Drive for almost a mile to an old wooden bridge, where you can recross Silver Stream and climb to the top of the

139

dunes. You then follow the dunes to skirt Silver Lake and return to the Dune Pedestrian Parking Area. Almost half of this incredible hike is in the Sahara Desert-like terrain of open dunes, while most of the other half is spent strolling a stretch of Lake Michigan that is free of cottages and ice-cream stands.

The steep dunes tower over the inland lake's west shoreline, making it a popular area for running down the sandy slopes straight into the cooling waters of Silver Lake. The pedestrian area is reached at the end of Fox Road, which curves around the north end of the lake.

Day-Use Facilities: There is a day-use beach area next to the campground, a popular area for families because of its shallow swimming area. Facilities include a bathhouse, a picnic shelter that can be rented, and parking for 100 vehicles. The parking lot is also used for the boat launch and often is filled on weekends during the summer. Historic Little Point Sable Lighthouse, built in the 1880s, is the most picturesque feature of a second day-use area along Lake Michigan. The area is reached by continuing west where County Road B15 turns south at the Mac Woods Dune Rides and following the signs along the narrow dirt road. The lighthouse isn't open to the public but is a spectacular spot to view a sunset on a clear summer evening.

Dune Rides: Near the south end of the park, where County Road B15 curves

Hiker in a ghost forest, Silver Lake State Park

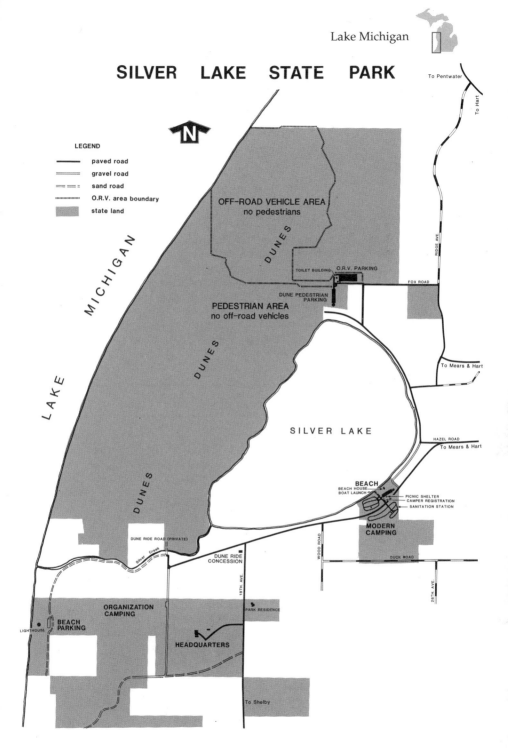

SILVER LAKE STATE PARK

Lake Michigan

To Pentwater

To Hart

LEGEND

— paved road
═ gravel road
═ ═ sand road
.... O.R.V. area boundary
▓ state land

N

OFF-ROAD VEHICLE AREA
no pedestrians

DUNES

TOILET BUILDING   O.R.V. PARKING

RIDGE AVE

FOX ROAD

DUNE PEDESTRIAN
PARKING

PEDESTRIAN AREA
no off-road vehicles

DUNES

To Mears & Hart

LAKE MICHIGAN

DUNES

SILVER LAKE

HAZEL ROAD
To Mears & Hart

DUNES

BEACH
BEACH HOUSE
BOAT LAUNCH
PICNIC SHELTER
CAMPER REGISTRATION
SANITATION STATION

MODERN
CAMPING

DUNE RIDE ROAD (PRIVATE)

Silver Creek

DUNE RIDE
CONCESSION

WOOD ROAD

DUCK ROAD

18TH AVE

28TH AVE

ORGANIZATION
CAMPING

PARK RESIDENCE

LIGHTHOUSE

BEACH
PARKING

HEADQUARTERS

To Shelby

141

south, is Mac Woods Dune Rides (616-873-2817), a park concession that has been offering trips through the dunes in open jeeplike vehicles for seventy years. The 40-minute rides wind 7 miles across the dunes between Lake Michigan and Silver Lake, stopping several times for passengers to view the terrain up close. Mac Wood's Dune Rides is open daily from mid-May through early October.

ORV Facilities: The unusual ORV area at the north end of the dunes is open to riders from April 1 to October 31. As well as a vehicle entry permit into the park, all ORVs (four-wheelers, dirt bikes, dune buggies) must have a current ORV registration that can be obtained from a Michigan Secretary of State office. There are a number of regulations for the area covering the use of helmets and harness straps, and riding in a one-way direction on the dunes, and all vehicles and riders are checked for proper safety equipment before they enter the area. The ORV parking lot holds 300 cars and trailers but often is filled on the weekends.

Fishing: There is some fishing on Silver Lake for bass and panfish. The lake is a busy place for motorboats and jet skis, however, so anglers tend to fish only in the early morning or after dusk. During the fall and spring, steelhead and salmon move into Silver Creek and offer opportunities for river anglers.

Access and Information: From US 31 exit at Shelby Road and head west for 6 miles to County Road B15 (16th Avenue). Head north (right) for 4.5 miles to reach the campground entrance. For more information, contact Silver Lake State Park, P.O. Box 254, Route 1, Mears, MI 49436; or call (231) 873-3083.

Hart–Montague Trail State Park

An abandoned track of the Chesapeake and Ohio Railroad was put to good use by the DNR after its days of ferrying freight were over. The 22.5-mile-long railroad right-of-way, which parallels US 31 from Muskegon County into Oceana County, was designated the Hart–Montague Trail State Park in 1987, with sections of it paved by 1989. The trail corridor is between 30 and 100 feet wide, while the paved trail itself is 8 feet wide, making it ideal for road bikes.

From the southern end in Montague, the trail heads north through a variety of terrain, ranging from flatlands to gently rolling hills, crosses several streams and creeks, and climbs to excellent overlooks of valleys and the East Golden Ponds. It passes through three small towns—Rothbury, New Era and Shelby—before reaching its northern trailhead in Hart, but the majority of the trip is through uninhabited and noncultivated areas of woodlots, wetlands, and fields that provide habitat for much wildlife.

The trail includes mileposts that begin at Hart and end at Montague. Near Mile 4 is an observation platform where you can view Golden Pond and the surrounding marshland, while a scenic overlook at the trail's high point is at Mile 6.

Trailside parks, which include picnic tables, shelters, restrooms, and parking areas, are in Shelby and New Era and at the Rothbury Community Park. There are also a handful of trailside rest areas with tables and bicycle parking, and information boards along the corridor. In Mears you can rent bicycles on the trail at The Wood Shed (231-873-4388).

Although its primary use is seen as a bicycle route, the Hart–Montague Trail is also used for Nordic skiing and snowmobiling in the winter. No other ORVs are allowed in the state park, and hunting is banned as well. There is no camping along the trail, but several communities offer private campgrounds.

Staging Areas: The southern terminus is Stanton Boulevard in the northeastern

HART–MONTAGUE STATE PARK

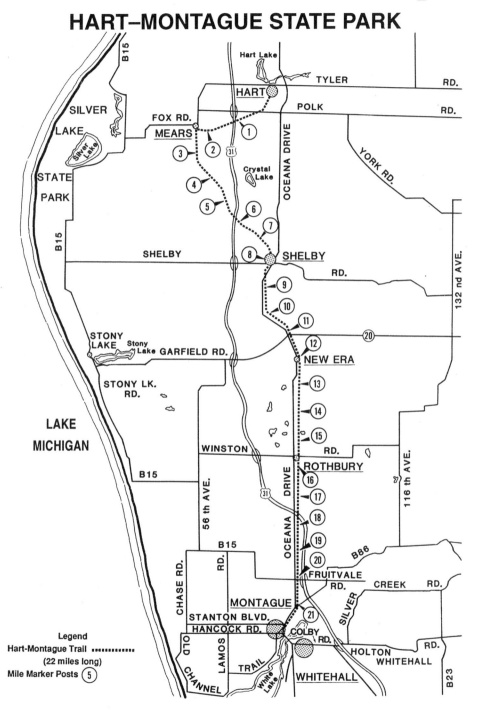

Lake Michigan

143

corner of Montague, near White Lake. The city of Montague plans to develop parking facilities here. The northern trailhead is in John Gurney Park in Hart, which features a large parking lot along with a campground, picnic facilities, and a swimming area.

Access and Information: The trail is accessible at the trailheads and in the villages it passes through. An individual or family trail permit is necessary to enter the park but a state park vehicle entry permit is not. Trail permits can be purchased at Silver Lake State Park or from various businesses along the trail. For more information, contact Silver Lake State Park, Route 1, P.O. Box 254, Mears, MI 49436; or call (231) 873-3083.

Charles Mears State Park

▲ A small unit of only 50 acres, Charles Mears State Park is one of the most popular camping areas along Lake Michigan. The park contains little more than a campground, 1,500 feet of Lake Michigan beach, and a dune named Old Baldy, but it is situated on the edge of Pentwater, a popular summer tourist town in western Michigan.

Pentwater was founded in 1853, but development really began when lumber baron Charles Mears arrived from Chicago three years later. Mears not only built mills, hotels, and docks, but straightened out the Pentwater River into its present location to assist ships in hauling away his timber. In 1920, Mears's daughter, Carrie Mears, deeded 13.7 acres along the North Channel for the establishment of a state park, but wouldn't sell any more land to the state as long as park officials allowed "nudes" on the beach (women not fully covered). The park wasn't enlarged until after Mears died in the 1940s.

Today Mears draws more than 300,000 visitors a year, with more than 90 percent of them arriving between Memorial Day and Labor Day.

Camping: Mears has a modern facility of 180 sites and is a destination campground, as the average stay at a site is 4 to 5 days. The campground features not only electricity and modern bathrooms but also paved pads for recreation vehicles. A small sand dune separates campers from Lake Michigan, while Old Baldy looms overhead to the east.

The campground is virtually filled every weekend from June to Labor Day, and everyday from mid-June to late August. Sites can be obtained without reservations on weekends in April and May and usually in September and October . . . just don't plan to do too much swimming in Lake Michigan at that time of year. Otherwise a reservation is necessary to camp here and should be made ten or eleven months in advance. The campground is open from April to December but the modern restrooms are closed before April 15 and after November 1.

Hiking: Located just off the campground loop is a posted trailhead and a set of stairs that lead up the wooded slope of the dune called Old Baldy. The entire trail is less than half a mile long, and within a few minutes of climbing you arrive at an observation platform and a view of the campground, the wide sandy beach, and the Pentwater Channel leading into Lake Michigan. From the viewing platform, it's a quick climb to Old Baldy's bald spot, a small blowout at the top of the sand dune where there is an excellent view of the town of Pentwater and its extensive boat harbor.

Day-Use Facilities: Mears has a beautiful beach on Lake Michigan along with parking for 200 cars, a bathhouse/store, outdoor volleyball courts, a picnic area, and a small shelter. Usually on weekends during the summer the parking lot will fill and other visitors must park in town and walk in.

Fishing: Bordering the park beach to the south is the Pentwater Pier, where anglers fish for perch and smallmouth bass during the summer. The busiest time on the pier, however, is late August to early September, when spoons or crankbaits are cast in search of steelhead trout and salmon. In late October and early November, anglers begin surf fishing from the beach for the same species. There is no boat launch in Mears, but there are several nearby in Pentwater.

Access and Information: From US 31 follow Business US 31 through Pentwater and look for a state park sign. Charles Mears State Park is four blocks from the downtown area. For more information, contact Charles Mears State Park, P.O. Box 370, Pentwater, MI 49449; or call (231) 869-2051.

Ludington State Park

Ludington is the largest state park along Lake Michigan, and one of the largest in the Lower Peninsula. The 5,300-acre state park, located in Mason County, includes 5.5 miles of Great Lake shoreline, 4 miles along popular Hamlin Lake, and a 1,699-acre Wilderness Natural Area. The terrain varies from wind-blown sand dunes to gently rolling pine forests. Many of the dunes, from Lake Michigan to a half mile inland, are treeless areas of dune grass and scrub. Others are covered in jack pine.

The state park's most picturesque fixture is Point Sable Lighthouse, an impressive tower amid the dunes that was built in 1867. From the lighthouse to the northern boundary is the park's Wilderness Natural Area, a trailless and undeveloped section of mostly forested dunes. This unique dune wilderness continues, as bordering Ludington to the north is Nordhouse Dunes, a declared federal wilderness that is managed by the Manistee National Forest.

In the mid-1800s, the park was the site of Hamlin, a lumbering town that was built after the Big Sable River was dammed and Hamlin Lake was created. The main purpose of the lake was to float logs to the mills in the village, where the timber was taken by tramway to Lake Michigan to be loaded onto ships. In 1888, the dam burst and the fury of the rushing water swept the town away, including forty homes, the mill, and more than a million board feet of white pine. Today there is a Michigan historical marker near the present dam noting the disaster, where it's still possible to the see the remains of the old mill and the village cemetery.

The miles of sandy Lake Michigan shoreline, the most of any unit in the state, the many coves and inlets of Hamlin Lake, and the appeal of dune country have made Ludington a popular park. Ludington draws 750,000 visitors a year as one of the most heavily used units in the state park system. Although there is year-round activity in the park, the majority of the visitors come during the summer to enjoy the beaches, campground, and scenic network of foot trails.

Camping: Ludington has 199 modern sites divided into three campgrounds. Pines Campground, which has 97 sites, is closest to Lake Michigan, separated from the shoreline only by a sand dune. Cedar Campground has 105 sites in the middle of the park, and Beechwood Campground features 97 sites near the Hamlin Lake day-use area and Lost Lake. All the campgrounds are well wooded, offering shady sites that now have a little space between them since the park staff removed 100 sites in the mid-1990s. Paved bike paths connect the campgrounds with the interpretive center.

Ludington's campgrounds are booked daily July through Labor Day, and are full on weekends beginning on Memorial Day. Late April is a particularly pleasant time to camp; reservations are unnecessary and the park is practically empty at that time of year. The campground is open year-round but the modern restrooms are available only from April 15 to November 1.

Hiking: There are eleven named and color-coded hiking trails in Ludington that form an 18-mile network. All the routes are located north of the Big Sable River, except for the mile-long Skyline Trail that circles the interpretive center and includes an extensive boardwalk along the crest of a dune. One of the more popular destinations for hikers is the Point Sable Lighthouse, a one-way walk of 2 miles along a work road open to park maintenance vehicles only. An excellent day hike is the 5-mile loop out to the historical structure, combined with a return along Lighthouse Trail and Logging Trail, passing two shelters and a well along the way. The trip begins and ends at the Pines Campground. Another scenic hike follows the Ridge Trail, which passes several high points with good views of Hamlin Lake, and then returns along Island Trail, which skirts the interesting shoreline between Hamlin and Lost Lakes. The trailhead for Ridge Trail is in Cedar Campground, while Island Trail begins at the day-use area of Hamlin Lake. The entire loop is a 4- to 6-hour hike. A park map, which can be picked up at the contact stations, lists all the routes, notes the color of their markers, and estimates hiking times.

Backpacking: An interesting overnight trek is to hike to Point Sable Lighthouse and then continue north along the beach to Lake Michigan Recreation Area. Within 2 miles of the lighthouse you pass a sign marking the border between the park and Nordhouse Dunes Wilderness, and once in the federal wilderness you can set up camp for the night. It is a one-way walk of 8 miles from the state park campgrounds to the Lake Michigan Recreation Area, a U.S. Forest Service campground on the north side of Nordhouse Dunes.

Canoeing: The most unusual trail in the park is the Ludington State Park Canoe Trail, a 6-mile, 3-hour paddle into a serene world of ponds, coves, and marshes along the southwest shore of Hamlin Lake. Built in 1992, the canoe trail was the first of its kind in a state park and is still the longest one in Michigan. It features directional signs to keep you on course and small landing docks, and interpretive brochures that explain the passing scenery are available. Six very short portages allow you to loop through protective bayous and ponds to totally escape the motorized traffic on Hamlin Lake.

Fishing: Hamlin Lake, with its many coves, inlets, and bayous, is a renowned warm-water fishery. There is heavy spawning of northern pike and tiger muskellunge in the shallow coves, and anglers frequently have landed muskies over fifteen pounds. The 4,490-acre lake, which is nearly 10 miles long, is also noted for bass and its excellent winter fishing for northern pike and bluegill. The lake has been stocked with tiger muskies since the early 1980s, and in 1987 a walleye-stocking program began. Ludington State Park maintains a boat launch on Hamlin Lake in the day-use area with parking for seventy-five vehicles and trailers.

Other fishing activity in the park includes surf fishing in the early spring and in October for salmon and trout off Lake Michigan.

Interpretive Center: On the south side of the Big Sable River is the Great Lakes Interpretive Center, open daily from Memorial Day to Labor Day from 10:00 A.M. to 5:00 P.M. and weekends in the spring and fall. The center looks at the creation and significance of the Great Lakes that surround Michigan through displays, exhibits,

Hiking in Ludington State Park

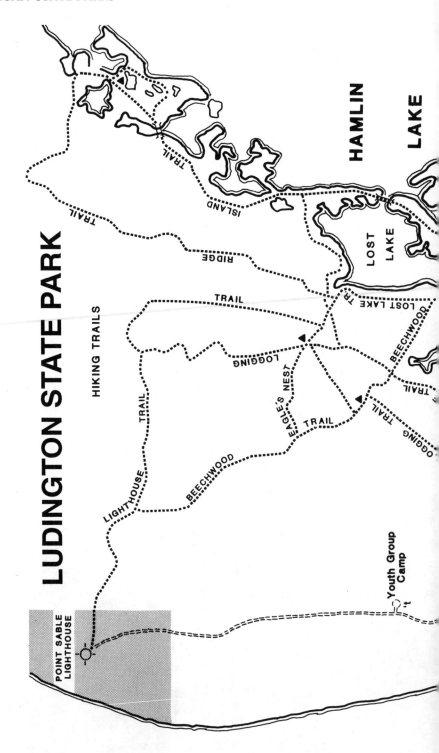

LUDINGTON STATE PARK

HAMLIN LAKE

HIKING TRAILS

ISLAND TRAIL

TRAIL

RIDGE

TRAIL

LOST LAKE

LOST LAKE TR

LOGGING

BEECHWOOD

EAGLE'S NEST

LOGGING TRAIL

TRAIL

TRAIL

BEECHWOOD

LIGHTHOUSE TRAIL

POINT SABLE LIGHTHOUSE

Youth Group Camp

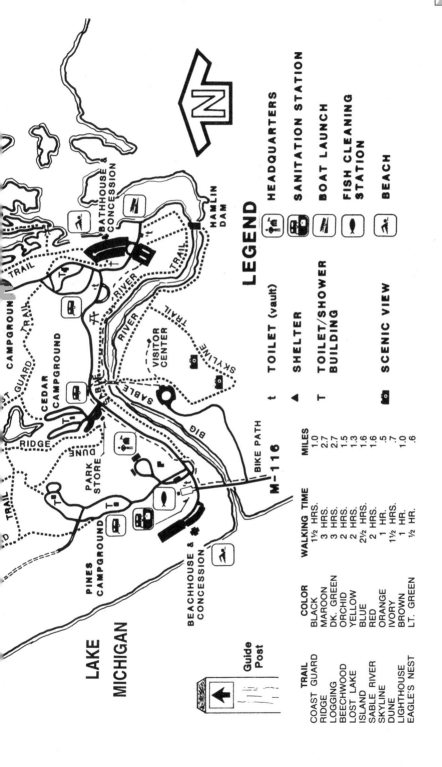

LAKE MICHIGAN

LEGEND

t TOILET (vault)

▲ SHELTER

T TOILET/SHOWER BUILDING

SCENIC VIEW

HEADQUARTERS

SANITATION STATION

BOAT LAUNCH

FISH CLEANING STATION

BEACH

Guide Post

TRAIL	COLOR	WALKING TIME	MILES
COAST GUARD	BLACK	1½ HRS.	1.0
RIDGE	MAROON	3 HRS.	2.7
LOGGING	DK. GREEN	3 HRS.	2.7
BEECHWOOD	ORCHID	2 HRS.	1.5
LOST LAKE	YELLOW	2 HRS.	1.3
ISLAND	BLUE	2½ HRS.	1.6
SABLE RIVER	RED	2 HRS.	1.6
SKYLINE	ORANGE	1 HR.	.5
DUNE	IVORY	1½ HRS.	.7
LIGHTHOUSE	BROWN	1 HR.	1.0
EAGLE'S NEST	LT. GREEN	½ HR.	.6

On the Canoe Trail in Ludington State Park

and a multimedia show. It also sponsors numerous naturalist-led walks and other activities throughout the summer.

Day-Use Facilities: The park maintains two day-use areas, one on Lake Michigan just north of where Big Sable River empties into the Great Lake and a second on Hamlin Lake. Both have parking, bathhouses, and concession stores, but the Hamlin beach is often the more popular of the two early in the year as its water warms up quicker. M-116 follows the Lake Michigan shoreline for almost 3 miles after entering the park, and it's common during the summer for visitors to pull over anywhere along the road to enjoy a section of the beach.

Winter Activities: Due to a very limited amount of trail open to motorized vehicles, there is almost no snowmobiling in the park during the winter. Nordic skiing, on the other hand or because of it, is a popular activity. Ludington has two designated ski trails, both relatively flat routes that follow fire access tracks. North of the Big

Lake Michigan

Sable River, there is a 6-mile loop that begins near the Hamlin Lake day-use area and follows the Loggers Trail most of the way. From the nature center, south of the Big Sable River, there is a loop with four cross-spurs for runs that range from 1.5 miles to over 4 miles in length. A local ski club grooms the trails when needed, but there is no equipment concession or warming shelter in the park. Skis can be rented in Ludington.

Access and Information: The state park is 8.5 miles north of Ludington at the end of M-116. For more information, contact Ludington State Park, P.O. Box 709, Ludington, MI 49431; or call (231) 843-8671.

Orchard Beach State Park

▲ Orchard Beach State Park's name is from an old apple orchard that occupied the area in the 1930s, and its beauty is from the steep bluffs that border Lake Michigan. Only a few of the apple trees remain in the campground, but the view from the bluffs is as scenic as ever. Visitors can stand in the grassy picnic area at the top to view the park's narrow beach below or miles of Great Lake shoreline stretching out to the north.

The 201-acre park is located just north of Manistee in Manistee County and attracts 100,000 visitors annually. It's split by M-110, and east of the road the park is a wooded area of hemlock and beech used predominantly by hikers in the summer and skiers in the winter. To the west of the road are the park facilities.

Camping: Orchard Lake has 174 modern sites and one mini-cabin in a scenic, semi-open campground that is sparsely wooded but well sodded compared to many other state park facilities on Lake Michigan. From June to Labor Day the campground is filled every weekend and often Thursdays as well. Sunday and Monday are the best days to obtain a site without a reservation.

Hiking: Across from the park entrance, off M-110, is a small parking area and the trailhead to Beech-Hemlock Nature Trail, a half-mile interpretive loop that takes about 30 minutes to cover. The contact station can provide an interpretive sheet to the trail. Another 2 miles of footpaths extend south of the Beech-Hemlock Nature Trail.

Fishing: Orchard Beach does not have a boat launch, pier, or even a pond to wet a line, but it does have a fish-cleaning station and is often considered a "fisherman's park." A large number of campers bring their boats with them and launch them at ramps in Manistee to spend the day trolling Lake Michigan for steelhead, lake trout, and salmon. The only actual fishing within the park is surf fishing from the beach, mostly in October, for predominantly steelhead and brown trout.

Day-Use Facilities: There is a picnic area at the northern edge of the park with tables, grills, a shelter that can be rented, and a good view of Lake Michigan. From here and at the southern end of the campground long wooden staircases lead down to the narrow sandy beach along the lake. The park has a day-use parking area for 500 vehicles that is rarely filled during the summer.

Winter Activities: In the winter, 2.1 miles of trails form three loops that are marked and called the "Little M Ski Trails" in a bit of a spoof on the Big M Ski Area, a well-known Nordic facility nearby in Manistee National Forest. The state park trail system makes for an easy ski but there is no ski rental concession or warming hut.

Access and Information: Orchard Beach is located 2 miles north of Manistee right on M-110. For more information, contact Orchard Beach State Park, 2064 Lakeshore Road, Manistee, MI 49660; or call (231) 723-7422.

151

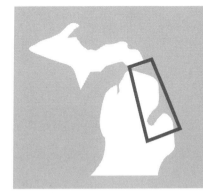

Lake Huron

Port Crescent State Park

⚓ In the mid-1800s, Port Crescent was a booming lumbering and fishing town of almost 700 residents, known for its salt wells, fine sand, and good docks. Today it's one of the most scenic and unusual state parks along Lake Huron, and all that remains of the village is a lone chimney from the Pack Woods Sawmill, and two salt mines. Although the last remnants and residents of the town vanished in the 1930s, there is an interpretive display next to the remains of the 120-foot chimney that recalls the industrial history of this Huron County state park located at "the tip of the Thumb."

Most of Port Crescent's 150,000 annual visitors, however, arrive to see the park's dunes rather than its artifacts. The 569-acre unit includes 3 miles of almost pure white beach along Saginaw Bay, a wooded interior of jack pine and oak, and the best set of sand dunes on the east side of Michigan. The wind-blown, open dunes occupy roughly 100 acres on the west side of Port Crescent's day-use area and drop down to the shoreline. They are nowhere near the size of those along Lake Michigan, but still they create a scenic area to wander through.

The state park, purchased in 1955 and formally dedicated eight years later, added its day-use area, which is separated from the campground by the Pinnebog River, in 1975. There are year-round activities at Port Crescent, including ice fishing and skiing in the winter.

Camping: Port Crescent State Park has 137 modern sites located in a partially wooded area in the east half of the park. Included in the hilly campground are 25 spots situated right off the beach and described by the DNR staff as "premium sites." The park has created a "lot-move" procedure that allows campers to sign up for a beachfront site after they have arrived at the campground. You cannot reserve them in advance. Port Crescent is filled on weekends and filled 95 percent in midweek from mid-June to mid-August. The park also has an organization camp

Fun at full throttle, Port Crescent State Park

reached from the intersection of Port Crescent Road and M-25 by an iron bridge over Old Pinnebog River Channel. The bridge is closed to vehicle traffic during the summer.

Hiking: The park has 7 miles of trails that offer the best hiking opportunities on Michigan's Thumb. The system is split into two segments with 3 miles on the east side of the park with a trailhead along the campground loop. Most of it is a 2.5-mile, figure-eight loop that winds through wooded dunes along the Pinnebog River and passes several scenic viewpoints of Saginaw Bay. The trail is also accessible from the trailhead reached after crossing the iron bridge over Old Pinnebog River Channel.

The other half of the system is west of the day-use area and is a main loop with four cross-spurs that total 4 miles. The trail crosses Pinnebog River Drain and passes through a variety of terrain, including hardwood forests, a stand of pines, marshes, and the open dunes that border Saginaw Bay. The trailhead and parking is near the contact station for the day-use area. Also in this side of the park is a 0.75-mile exercise trail with ten activity stations.

Due to the delicate nature of the dunes, mountain biking is banned from the park's trails.

Canoeing: The final mile of the Pinnebog River winds through Port Crescent and is a popular waterway for a leisurely and easy paddle. Tip-of-the-Thumb Canoe Rental (517-738-7656) is a canoe livery located just outside the park on M-25 along the banks of the Pinnebog. It is open daily during the summer.

Fishing: Saginaw Bay is renowned for its walleye fishery, which usually peaks in July and August. Anglers troll the bay, using crankbaits and planner boards, and walleyes in the 6- to 8-pound range are common throughout the summer. Closer to shore, anglers fish for perch and bass. Pinnebog River also attracts a number of fishermen during the summer searching for bass, panfish, and northern pike. During the spring, smelt dippers congregate at the river's mouth for the small silvery fish,

Time to try a different fly

Lake Huron

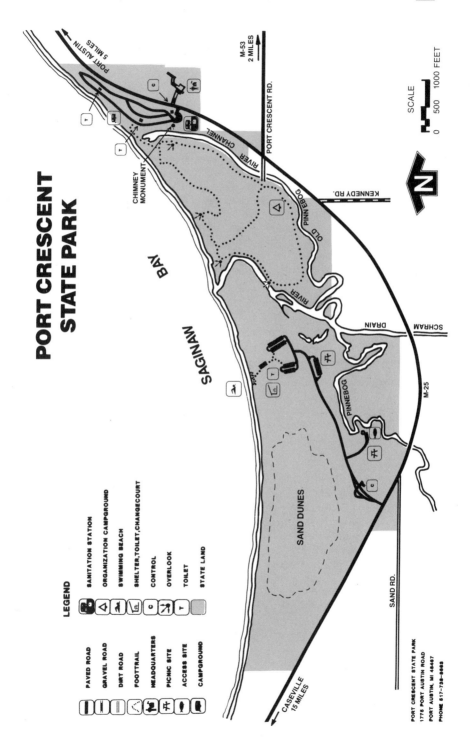

PORT CRESCENT STATE PARK

SAGINAW BAY

CHIMNEY MONUMENT

RIVER CHANNEL

PORT AUSTIN 5 MILES

M-53 2 MILES

PORT CRESCENT RD.

KENNEDY RD.

OLD PINNEBOG RIVER

SCHRAM DRAIN

PINNEBOG

M-25

SAND DUNES

SAND RD.

CASEVILLE 15 MILES

N

SCALE
0   500   1000 FEET

LEGEND

PAVED ROAD	SANITATION STATION
GRAVEL ROAD	ORGANIZATION CAMPGROUND
DIRT ROAD	SWIMMING BEACH
FOOTTRAIL	SHELTER, TOILET, CHANGECOURT
HEADQUARTERS	CONTROL
PICNIC SITE	OVERLOOK
ACCESS SITE	TOILET
CAMPGROUND	STATE LAND

PORT CRESCENT STATE PARK
1775 PORT AUSTIN ROAD
PORT AUSTIN, MI 48467
PHONE 517-738-8663

155

while in late September and October, river anglers fish for Chinook salmon using crankbaits, spoons, and spawn bags.

The park maintains an access site for hand-carried boats at Lot A of its day-use area, as well as a fishing pier on the Pinnebog River. The nearest boat ramp is located 5 miles northeast at Port Austin. Also at Port Austin are party boat charters for perch and charter boats that specialize in trolling Lake Huron for salmon and lake trout.

Day-Use Facilities: The west half of the park is a day-use area with its own entrance off M-25. The facility includes parking for 260 vehicles, two picnic areas along the Pinnebog River, and a beach shelter that can be rented. There is also a 1,000-foot-long boardwalk that provides barrier-free access across the dunes to observation decks and picnic tables above the beach.

Winter Activities: The east half of the park's trail system becomes ski runs during the winter that are groomed and tracked frequently. The ski trailhead is located near the organization camp, and vehicles are allowed to cross the old iron bridge to reach it. The trails make up a pair of loops, 1.1 and 1.2 miles in length, that wind through a gently rolling and wooded terrain. Ice fishing, predominantly for perch, is also popular during the winter.

Access and Information: The park is located 5 miles southwest of Port Austin along M-25. For more information, contact Port Crescent State Park, 1775 Port Austin Road, Port Austin, MI 48467; or call (517) 738-8663.

Sanilac Historic Site

After the residents of Holbrook put out a ground fire from the Great Fire of 1881 that swept across the Thumb, they made a startling discovery in the heart of the state's Thumb Region. The fire burned away the brush and grass along the Cass River and exposed petroglyphs, aboriginal rock carvings of animals, hunters, crosses, and mythological creatures. Holbrook is now a ghost town, but the carvings have been preserved within Sanilac Historic Site, a 238-acre park in Sanilac County that is administered by the state Bureau of History.

The main feature of the park is a large slab of sandstone with dozens of carvings on it that many archaeologists believe to be almost 1,000 years old, dating back to the Late Woodland Period. They are the only petroglyphs ever found in Michigan.

Interpretive Center: A large pavilion has been built over the slab of sandstone, which is a quarter-mile walk from a gravel parking lot. Most of the carvings—outlines of hands, animal tracks, birds, and spirals—are not visible at first glance. But a display near the entrance shows their locations, and this will help you identify most of the glyphs on the surface of the sandstone. The best viewing is on overcast days when you can use a flashlight to illuminate the petroglyphs from the sides. The most prominent carving is easy to see: a bowman with a single, long line depicting his arm and arrow.

From Memorial Day to Labor Day the state Bureau of History staffs the park with interpretive guides from 11:30 A.M. to 4:30 P.M. Wednesday through Sunday. Guides assist visitors in recognizing the carvings and lead walks along the park's trail system.

Hiking: From the pavilion, there is a 1.5-mile interpretive trail that winds toward the west side of the park and twice crosses bridges over a branch of the Cass River. The walk is interesting, as it's possible to see the remains of a timber cruiser's cabin, a Chippewa Indian village site, a huge white pine that survived the Great

Fire of 1881, and mortars, large holes that Native Americans carved in boulders to store and protect their food. Numbered posts along the trail correspond to an interpretive brochure available at the entrance of the park.

Access and Information: From M-53, 4 miles from its junction with M-81, turn east on Bay City–Forestville Road. In 3 miles turn south on Germania Road to the posted entrance. Petroglyph signs appear on both M-53 and Bay City–Forestville Road. For more information, contact Port Crescent State Park, 1775 Port Austin Road, Port Austin, MI 48467; or call the park at (517) 738-8663, or the state Bureau of History at (517) 373-1979.

Albert E. Sleeper State Park

▲ The only two state parks in Michigan's Thumb Region are practically next to each other. A short drive from Port Crescent is Albert E. Sleeper State Park, the 723-acre unit on the shores of Saginaw Bay in Huron County. Dedicated in 1927 as Huron State Park, Sleeper was renamed in 1944 to honor the Michigan governor from Bad Axe who signed the original bill that created the park system.

Although there are no Lake Huron sand dunes in Sleeper, the park is larger than Port Crescent State Park and features 4.5 miles of trails in a lightly used, wooded area of oak, popple, and other hardwoods. Most of Sleeper's 153,000 annual visitors arrive in the summer and are attracted to its half mile of wide, sandy beach on Saginaw Bay, or its large campground.

Camping: Sleeper maintains a campground of 280 modern sites situated on the south side of M-25. It's a wooded area with a pedestrian overpass connecting it to the day-use beach area on Saginaw Bay. The campground fills up on weekends during the summer, and often fills during the week from the July 4 weekend to early August.

Also located within the park is an outdoor center, featuring sixteen cabins that sleep up to 120 persons, a dining hall and kitchen, a council ring, and its own entrance off State Park Road. Groups interested in reserving the center should contact the National Wildlife Education Foundation at (248) 583-4863.

Hiking: Sleeper's 4.5-mile network of trails departs from the campground and winds through the undeveloped southern half of the park. The Mile Circle Trail is a half-mile walk that connects the two halves of the campground, while departing halfway along it is the Ridges Nature Trail.

This mile-long loop follows the low, wooded ridges that mark the former shoreline of Saginaw Bay and features fourteen interpretive markers along the way. A self-guiding brochure for the trail is available at the contact stations or park headquarters. Also departing from the Mile Circle Trail is the Deer Run Trail, a 2.5-mile round trip that passes the outdoor center before looping through the southwest corner of the park where deer are often spotted. There is also a trailhead and parking at the park headquarters off State Park Road just south of M-25.

Mountain Biking: The trail system at Sleeper is open to mountain biking and makes for an easy-to-moderate ride through a beech and maple forest. Keep in mind that during the summer camping season the trails are heavily used by hikers and campground visitors. Controlled speed, caution, and good biking etiquette are needed at this busy time of year.

Day-Use Facilities: On the north side of M-25, with a separate entrance from the campground, is Sleeper's popular day-use area. The park has a half mile of beach that, when the Great Lake is at normal water level, is up to 100 feet wide. A low, sandy ridge, with wooden steps down to the beach, lies between the parking lot and the shoreline. The parking area has room for 167 vehicles but often fills up on Sunday during the summer. Facilities include a bathhouse and a picnic area, and a shelter that can be rented.

Winter Activities: Nordic skiing is a popular activity during the winter when there is sufficient snowfall. The trailhead to three loops and parking for skiers is located adjacent to the park headquarters on State Park Road. Ski runs range from 0.5 mile to 2.5 miles for the Deer Run Trail through a terrain that is level and heavily forested. The trails are groomed and occasionally tracked, and skiers are allowed to use the park workshop, when it is open, as a warming shelter. The park also stages a number of candlelight skis during the winter when there is sufficient snow.

Access and Information: Sleeper State Park is located 4 miles northeast of Caseville on M-25. For more information, contact Sleeper State Park, 6573 State Park Road, Caseville, MI 48725; or call (517) 856-4411.

Bay City State Recreation Area

Created in 1923, this unit was originally called Bay City State Park and was ranked number one in attendance for state parks in the 1930s, when it attracted more than 1.5 million visitors a year. The park's attendance continued to run over a million well into the 1950s, and then the sludge came. Due to the shallowness of Saginaw Bay and an overload of nutrients from farmland runoff, a growth of algae and other organic material turned the park's pristine, white sandy beach into something of a shoreline wetland. Attendance plummeted.

But in the early 1990s, the park received a major facelift. The size was increased from 196 acres to more than 2,200 when adjoining Tobico Marsh was officially added to the park, and the name was changed to Bay City State Recreation Area. The Saginaw Bay Visitor Center was added, the campground was improved and, most important, a new beach and swimming area were built at the north end of the park.

Today the sand is as pure and fine as ever, and annual attendance at the state recreation area tops 400,000. The most unique aspect of the park, however, is Tobico Marsh, the largest remaining wetland along Saginaw Bay. In 1976, Tobico was designated a national natural landmark and in the early 1990s was connected to the rest of the park by a unique rail–trail. The 2,000-acre marsh is a popular destination for birders, especially during the spring and fall migrations when its lagoons and marsh attract thousands of waterfowl.

Camping: As part of the park's renovation, Bay City's campground was reduced to 190 sites, to provide more space and privacy in a lightly wooded area away from the bay. No sites have a view of the water, but the park's day-use area lies only a short walk away along a foot trail. The park offers both rent-a-tents and mini-cabins in the campground, as well as an organization camp for groups. The facility fills only on holidays and an occasional weekend during the summer.

Hiking: Two nature trails begin at the Saginaw Bay Visitor Center. To the east of the interpretive center is a short trail around Tobico Lagoon, the outlet of Tobico Marsh. Heading north to immediately cross M-247 is the Frank Andersen Rail–Trail, a 0.75-mile paved path that includes interpretive plaques and observation decks. Within a half mile, a spur departs from the rail–trail and heads west into Tobico Marsh. Tobico features a pair of loops, 4 and 1.5 miles in length, each with a

Blue heron

30-foot observation tower that provides an extensive view of the wetlands and the waterfowl that congregate there.

A second trailhead to the Tobico trails is a mile north of the intersection of Beaver Road and M-247 on Killarney Road, where there is a parking area and a pair of vault toilets. The Saginaw Visitor Center provides a birder's list of 127 species of birds that have been spotted in the marsh.

Mountain Biking: Both the Frank Andersen Rail–Trail and the Tobico trails are open to mountain bikes. From the visitor center, the trails can be combined for a 6-mile ride that is considered ideal for beginning mountain bikers.

Interpretive Center: The Saginaw Bay Visitor Center (517-667-0717) was dedicated in 1995 as the newest state park interpretive center. Formerly known as the Jennison Nature Center, the exhibit hall is the result of a million-dollar renovation.The exhibit explains how Saginaw Bay was formed and discusses the abundance of life found in a wetland. The facility features a 100-seat auditorium with a multi-image slide show, hands-on displays that help visitors to learn how to identify waterfowl, and a glass-walled observation room to observe wildlife. Perhaps the most intriguing exhibit is devoted to the long history of waterfowl hunting in Tobico Marsh, and tells how duck hunters saved the wetlands. The facility is open Tuesday through Sunday from noon to 5:00 P.M.

Day-Use Facilities: The park's reconstructed beach and designated swimming area are located north of the picnic area and reached by a boardwalk. A bathhouse/store is at the site of the old beach and is surrounded by a picnic area, shelters, and parking for 1,500 cars.

Fishing: The park does not have a boat ramp onto Saginaw Bay. The only fishing within the park is in Tobico Lagoon, where anglers, mostly children, try their luck off a fishing pier for panfish.

Access and Information: The park is 5 miles north of Bay City and is reached

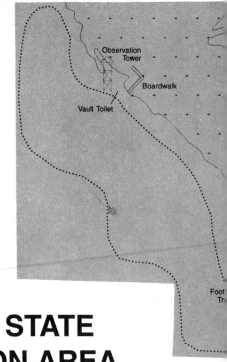

Observation Tower

Boardwalk

Vault Toilet

Foot Tr

BAY CITY STATE
RECREATION AREA

SCALE

0   1 MILE

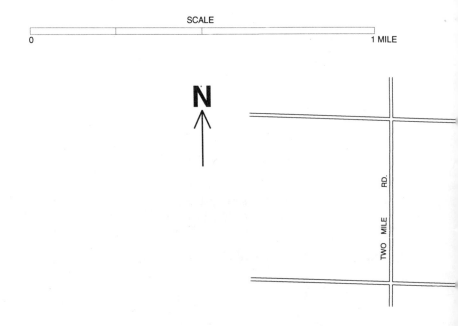

N

TWO MILE RD.

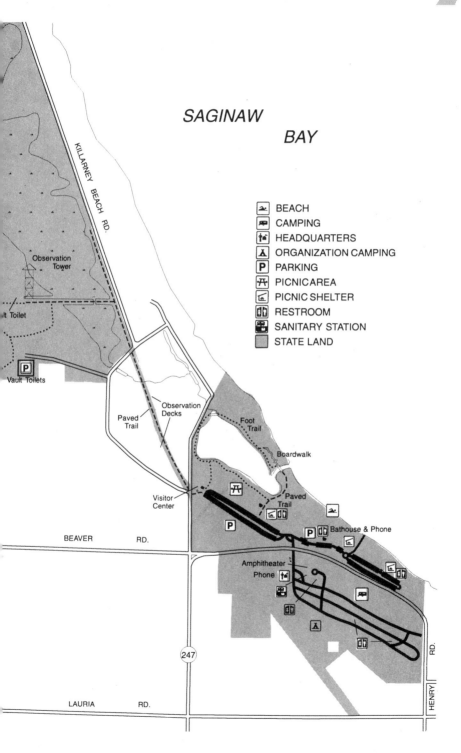

Lake Huron

SAGINAW
BAY

🏖	BEACH
🚐	CAMPING
🛉	HEADQUARTERS
🏕	ORGANIZATION CAMPING
P	PARKING
🏓	PICNIC AREA
🏠	PICNIC SHELTER
🚻	RESTROOM
🚰	SANITARY STATION
	STATE LAND

Observation
Tower

lt Toilet

P
Vault Toilets

Observation
Decks

Paved
Trail

Foot
Trail

Boardwalk

Visitor
Center

Paved
Trail

P

Bathouse & Phone

BEAVER   RD.

Amphitheater
Phone

247

LAURIA   RD.

KILLARNEY BEACH RD.

HENRY RD.

from I-75 by taking exit 168 and heading east on Beaver Road. It's almost 5 miles along Beaver Road to the park entrance, just past the intersection with M-247. For more information, contact Bay City State Recreation Area, 3582 State Park Drive, Bay City, MI 48706; or call (517) 684-3020.

Tawas Point State Park

▲ Occasionally referred to as the "Cape Cod of the Midwest," Tawas Point State Park is a 187-acre unit at the end of a sandy spit. The comparison to the East Coast is appropriate. Tawas Point features 2 miles of beautiful, white sandy beach that borders the blue water of Lake Huron, forms the east side of Tawas Bay, and is even crowned by a lighthouse. All this makes the state park a scenic spot in Iosco County that attracts almost 300,000 visitors a year.

Tawas Point was originally owned by the U.S. Coast Guard, which built the first lighthouse here in 1853 and the present one in 1876. The Coast Guard sold the point to the state, but retained the working lighthouse, which can be viewed but not entered except during special open houses. Tawas Point became a state park in 1960.

Swimmers and sunbathers flock to Tawas Point during the summer, but in the

A young visitor examines a roadside flower, Tawas Point State Park.

Lake Huron

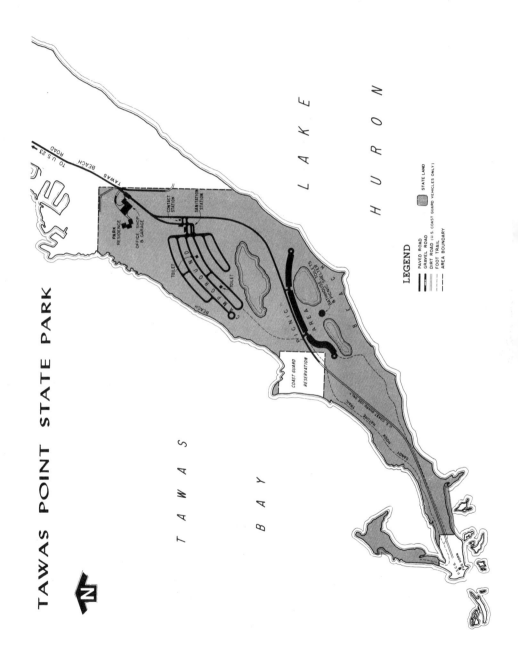

TAWAS POINT STATE PARK

N

T A W A S   B A Y

L A K E   H U R O N

TAWAS BEACH ROAD
TO U.S. 23

PARK RESIDENCE

OFFICE, SHOP & GARAGE

CONTACT STATION

SANITATION STATION

TOILET

TOILET

C A M P G R O U N D

BEACH

PICNIC AREA

TOILETS

BATHHOUSE-SHELTER

B E A C H

COAST GUARD RESERVATION

NATURE

U.S. COAST GUARD USE ONLY TRAIL

SANDY

U.S. COAST GUARD

LEGEND

PAVED ROAD
GRAVEL ROAD
DIRT ROAD (U.S. COAST GUARD VEHICLES ONLY)
FOOT TRAIL
AREA BOUNDARY

STATE LAND

spring and fall the park is a favorite spot for birders. The spit's location makes it a landfall for migrating birds crossing Saginaw Bay, and a birder's checklist put out by the park lists 205 species that have been spotted here. Listed are 17 species of waterfowl, including mallards and blue wing teals, which occasionally nest in one of the three ponds within the park. It also lists many unique shorebirds, such as red knots and piping plovers, an endangered species.

On the second weekend of June, the park is the site of Tawas Point Celebration Days, a popular festival that includes kids' fishing contests, lighthouse tours, demonstrations of traditional crafts, period encampments, and music.

Camping: Tawas Point has 210 modern sites and a pair of mini-cabins located in a loop on the bay side of the spit. An open area with little shade, the campground does have a few sites overlooking the sandy beach and shallow water of Tawas Bay. From the last weekend in June through mid-August the campground is filled daily, as well as Memorial Day weekend, Labor Day weekend, and most weekends in August. The modern restrooms are open from April 15 to November. Next to the campground there is an organization camp.

Hiking: Beginning at the day-use area parking lot, near the lighthouse, is Sandy Hook Nature Trail, a 1.5-mile loop that takes you to the end of the point. The trail follows the Tawas Bay shoreline out to the Coast Guard foghorn at the end of the spit and then returns along Lake Huron. The walk takes an hour or so, and the park has an interpretive brochure that points out the variety of plants seen along the spit, including wild grapes and strawberries, sand cherry, and red-osier dogwood.

Fishing: Tawas Bay is noted for its perch and walleye fishing and, to a lesser degree, bass. Coho and Chinook salmon also move into the bay during the spring and fall to make spawning runs up many nearby rivers. There is no boat launch in the park, but public ramps are located in Tawas City along with bait and tackle shops and charter fishing services.

Day-Use Facilities: The park's day-use area is located on Lake Huron, where the almost pure-white beach ranges from 100 to 300 feet in width, depending on the water level. There is a bathhouse and picnic shelter near the parking lot, which holds several hundred cars.

Access and Information: The park is located 3.5 miles from East Tawas. Follow US 23 just northeast of the town and then turn east onto Tawas Point Road and follow the signs to the park entrance. For more information, contact Tawas Point State Park, 686 Tawas Beach Road, East Tawas, MI 48730; or call (517) 362-5041.

Rifle River Recreation Area

▲ Rifle River, a state-designated Scenic Natural River, flows gently for more than ⊥ 50 miles before emptying into Saginaw Bay. Its beginnings can be found in Ogemaw County among the cluster of small lakes and streams that are protected in the 4,449-acre Rifle River Recreation Area, the tenth largest state park unit in the Lower Peninsula.

The recreation area was originally known as Grousehaven and was the private hunting retreat of H. M. Jewett, a pioneer auto manufacturer. In 1945 the tract was purchased by the then Department of Conservation and used as a field laboratory for fish and game research. The Parks Division acquired the area in 1963 and designated it Rifle River Recreation Area.

The river makes the park a haven for canoeists and fly fishers, while its size offers a variety of activities, including camping, hiking, mountain biking, and even scenic drives by car. The dirt roads wind through a terrain of high, rolling moraine hills broken up by ten lakes and numerous streams, all set in a dense forest, where it's easy to spot a variety of wildlife. The park draws 120,000 visitors annually, but due to its extensive facilities, especially campgrounds, it rarely seems overcrowded.

Camping: Grousehaven is the second largest lake in the park at 93 acres, and on its north shore is Grousehaven Campground, a modern facility of eighty sites. The campground is an open area with no sites directly on the water but with a scenic view of the lake. The facility has its own beach and swimming area separate from the day-use area at the east end of the lake. Devoe Lake is the largest in the park at 130 acres, and near its southwest corner is Devoe Campground. The rustic facility has fifty-eight sites that are well separated in a heavily forested area. None are on the lake.

Two other rustic facilities are located near the river off Rifle River Road. Ranch Campground is mostly an open, grassy flat with twenty-five sites, while Spruce Campground is located in a more wooded area and has eighteen sites with a handful right on the Rifle River, making them popular with fly fishers. Although Grousehaven Campground fills up on holidays and an occasional weekend in July, campers can generally count on an open site throughout most of the summer. The park also maintains an organization camp for large groups.

Canoeing: The headwaters of the Rifle River are located in the center of the park, which contains the first 2 miles of the waterway. At this point the river is a clear, gravel-bottomed trout stream. It picks up more volume and becomes 25 to 40 feet wide below Sage Lake Road. A common day trip within the park is to put in where Ranch Road crosses the river just west of DeVoe Lake. The paddle to the access site on Sage Road is a 2-hour trip, while a state forest campground is another 30 minutes to an hour beyond the bridge. The entire river is usually paddled in 2 or 3 days. There is no canoe rental concession inside the park, but several liveries are located near the entrance on Rose City Road.

Hiking: Rifle River Recreation Area has 14 miles of hiking trails that wind from the north end of the unit down to the southwest corner. Most of the trail network is an 11-mile loop that passes several scenic overviews of Rifle River's hilly interior. It also provides foot access to remote Lost Lake. The loop can be picked up at a variety of places, including Grousehaven, Devoe, and Ranch Campgrounds, and the day-use area. Across the park road from Grousehaven Campground is the trailhead for Pintail Nature Trail, a mile loop around a small pond with numbered posts. An interpretive brochure is available from the contact station or park headquarters.

Mountain Biking: The park's trail system is open to mountain bikers and in recent years has become a popular destination for off-road riding. The most challenging stretch of trail is the 2-mile loop north of Ridge Road that winds through the steep hills just west of Grebe Lake. Beginners, intimidated by single track, will simply enjoy riding the dirt roads within the park.

Fishing: The park is best known by fly fishers for its 7 miles of river and streams that harbor resident rainbow and brown trout. The cold-water fishery improved significantly after the Saginaw Chapter of Trout Unlimited completed a major bypass project at the outlet of Devoe Lake in the early 1990s that lowered the water temperature in the Rifle River by several degrees. The river, this far upstream, is easily waded by most anglers. Anglers also fish Gamble, Houghton, and Vaughn Creeks for trout.

The park also maintains access sites on Grousehaven, Grebe, Lodge, Devoe, and Jewett Lakes. Grebe, which is fished for northern pike, bass, and bluegill, has a pair of fishing piers on it with the second one featuring picnic tables and grills nearby. Jewett Lake is a catch-and-release fishery for walleye, bluegill, and perch, with a

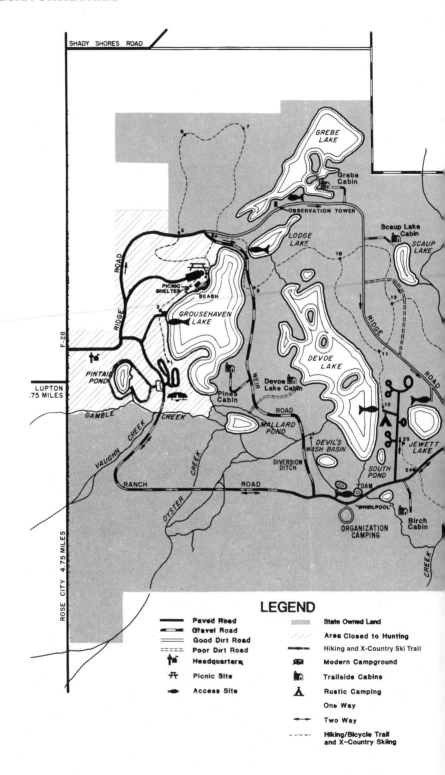

SHADY SHORES ROAD

GREBE LAKE

Grebe Cabin

OBSERVATION TOWER

Scaup Lake Cabin

SCAUP LAKE

LODGE LAKE

RIDGE ROAD

PICNIC SHELTER

BEACH

GROUSEHAVEN LAKE

F-28

DEVOE LAKE

RIDGE ROAD

PINTAIL POND

Devoe Lake Cabin

LUPTON .75 MILES

Pines Cabin

GAMBLE CREEK

CREEK

WEIR

ROAD

JEWETT LAKE

MALLARD POND

VAUGHN CREEK

CREEK

DEVIL'S WASH BASIN

DIVERSION DITCH

SOUTH POND

RANCH ROAD

ROAD

DAM

WHIRLPOOL

OYSTER CREEK

Birch Cabin

ORGANIZATION CAMPING

ROSE CITY 4.75 MILES

CREEK

LEGEND

Paved Road	State Owned Land
Gravel Road	Area Closed to Hunting
Good Dirt Road	Hiking and X-Country Ski Trail
Poor Dirt Road	Modern Campground
Headquarters	Trailside Cabins
Picnic Site	Rustic Camping
Access Site	One Way
	Two Way
	Hiking/Bicycle Trail and X-Country Skiing

RIFLE RIVER
RECREATION
AREA

LAKE	ACRES	DEPTH
Devoe	130	53
Grousehaven	95	54
Grebe	72.5	18
Lodge	16.8	16
Jewitt	12.9	17
Scaup	5.8	15
Pintail Pond	3.8	5
Mallard Pond	3.8	5
South Pond	1.3	19
Devils Wash Basin	1.3	15

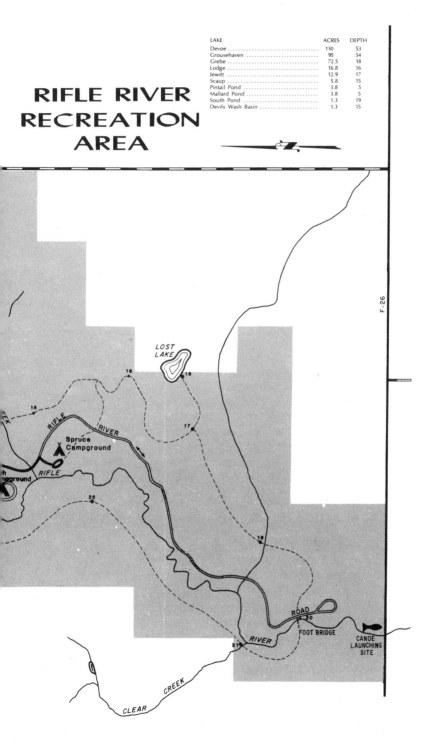

ban on live bait. Devoe is generally viewed as the most productive inland lake with anglers seeking bass, perch, and panfish.

Cabins: Rifle River has five frontier cabins that sleep eight persons each. All five can be reached by vehicle spring through fall, but in the winter the park roads are not plowed. When there is sufficient snow, the units can only be reached by cross-country ski, snowmobile, or dog sled for an unusual adventure.

Pines Cabin is nonrustic in appearance, near the southwest corner of Grousehaven Lake but not directly on the water. Grebe Cabin is perhaps the most scenic, tucked away on a small peninsula and within view of Grebe Lake, while Birch Cabin is located on the west side of the park 50 yards from Rifle River. The newest cabins are Scaup Lake and Devoe Lake Cabins. All five cabins are popular year-round and must be booked in advance through the park headquarters.

Scenic Viewpoints: Two one-way roads form scenic loops through the Rifle River's interior. Ridge Road departs east from the park entrance, passes some marshes and wetlands, and then climbs to a high point between Grebe and Lodge Lakes, which was the site of Jewett's massive hunting lodge in the 1920s. An observation tower has been constructed here, and from its platform there is a panorama of four lakes and the park's rugged terrain. Ridge Road then curves west and merges into Ranch Road for a 4.5-mile drive. Splitting off Ridge Road is Weir Road, which forms a shorter loop by winding west between Grousehaven and Devoe Lakes. The park has installed an auto tour along the roads featuring a series of habitat viewing signs.

Day-Use Facilities: Rifle River's day-use area is located near the east end of Grousehaven Lake and includes a beach and picnic area, and a shelter that can be rented.

Winter Activities: The trails are not groomed or tracked for cross-country skiing, and many sections, due to their rugged nature, are too challenging for most skiers. A lot of skiing during the winter is done on the park roads, which are not plowed beyond Grousehaven Campground.

Snowmobilers are also allowed on the roads, and ice fishing is popular, especially on Grebe Lake where anglers set up tip-ups for northern pike.

Access and Information: The park entrance is located 4.75 miles east of Rose City on County Road F28 (Rose City Road). For more information, contact Rifle River Recreation Area, P.O. Box 98, Lupton, MI 48635; or call (517) 473-2258.

Harrisville State Park

A half mile of wide, sandy Lake Huron beach, bordered by towering cedars and pines, is Harrisville State Park's most picturesque feature. The 107-acre unit in Alcona County draws 160,000 visitors a year, the vast majority of them campers who arrive during the summer hoping to obtain one of the park's beachfront campsites.

Established in 1921, Harrisville is one of the oldest state parks, and a unique one on the east side of the state in featuring a wooded campground within easy walking distance of a popular resort town. The park also has a day-use area, a boat launch, and a short trail that loops through its interior of cedar, pine, balsam fir, and maple trees.

Camping: Harrisville has a modern campground of 200 sites in a scenic area forested in pine and cedar. There are about 30 sites that lie near the beach, and these, naturally, are the first to go during the summer. Harrisville also maintains a Rent-a-Tent Program in its campground and two mini-cabins. The mini-cabin on

At the edge of Lake Huron, Harrisville State Park

site 186 is the typical saltbox design found in other state parks, but the other one is unique, an A-frame structure that used to be the contact station for the campground. This cabin is larger and heated by a wood-burning stove.

Expect the campground to be filled on weekends from the third week in June through Labor Day. Visitors have few problems obtaining a site in midweek throughout the summer.

Hiking: Departing from the campground is the Cedar Run Nature Trail, a 1-mile loop that takes about 45 minutes to enjoy. There are fifteen numbered posts on the trail, and an interpretive brochure, obtained from the contact station, points out the variety of trees at each stop.

Day-Use Facilities: At the south end of the park there is a day-use area with a bathhouse, picnic tables near the beach, and parking for seventy vehicles. There is also an access site here where hand-carried boats can be launched. Lake Huron is a noted deepwater fishery for salmon and lake trout, but the only actual activity within the park are anglers who surf fish off the beach during the fall.

Access and Information: The park entrance is a half mile south of the town of Harrisville on US 23. For more information, contact Harrisville State Park, P.O. Box 326, Harrisville, MI 48740; or call (517) 724-5126.

Negwegon State Park

Many believe the most beautiful and possibly the most isolated beaches on Lake Huron lie in Negwegon State Park. Words like "paradise" are often used by the DNR staff to describe the park's shoreline, a string of bays and coves stretching 6.5 miles from Alpena County into Alcona County. Lined by pine and cedar and featuring wide, sandy beaches, the bays are separated by rocky points of which South Point extends the furthest.

Day hikers in Negwegon State Park

The 2,400-acre park was acquired in 1962 and renamed from Alpena State Park to honor a Chippewa Indian chief. Negwegon is an undeveloped unit with a low, wooded interior of primarily cedar and white birch. Presently, there are few facilities and no campground, and the access road to the park can be a difficult drive for many vehicles. This will gradually change as the DNR develops the area.

Day-Use Facilities: The entrance of the park is a mile-long gravel road from Sand Hill Road to a forty-vehicle parking lot, where there is a water spigot, vault toilets, and an orientation sign for hikers. From the parking area it is a short walk to the park's largest bay—a crescent-shaped, sandy cove almost a half mile in length.

Hiking: Negwegon has a 10-mile network of hiking trails that form three loops through both the interior of the park and along the shoreline. There are trailheads at both the north and south end of the parking area. What is commonly referred to as the Beach Trail is a 3.3-mile loop that extends from the vehicle lot south along the shoreline before returning inland via an old two-track. The other two loops head north, and it's possible to follow portions of them along the shoreline to reach the tip of South Point, a very scenic spot. A one-way hike from the parking lot to South Point is a 2.1-mile walk.

Access and Information: To reach the park from Harrisville, head northwest on US 23 for almost 11 miles and then turn north (right) onto Fontaine Road. Follow the road for 1.6 miles until it dead-ends at Black River Road and then turn east (right). Sand Hill Road is the first road to the north, 0.2 mile from Fontaine, and appears as a very sandy, four-wheel-drive vehicle track. Caution must be used while following Sand Hill Road, as it is often covered with drifting sand and deeply rutted. Follow Sand Hill Road for 1 mile until the wide gravel park road, posted with a Negwegon State Park sign, heads east (right). For more information, contact Harrisville State Park, P.O. Box 326, Harrisville, MI 48740; or call (517) 724-5126.

Thompson's Harbor State Park

E. Genevieve Gillette, an ardent conservationist who was instrumental in the establishment of Porcupine Mountains Wilderness and Hartwick Pines State Park, died in 1986. But even after her death, the landscape architect was responsible for what DNR officials described as "one of the most important acquisitions of shoreline in more than twenty-five years." It was money Gillette willed to the people of Michigan that made Thompson's Harbor State Park a reality.

Gillette's bequest was used to purchase the heart of the 5,109-acre park located near Rogers City in Presque Isle County. Formally dedicated in 1988, Thompson's Harbor is a predominantly wooded area with a variety of terrain, including 7.5 miles of cobbled Lake Huron shoreline. Although the park lacks the sandy beaches so popular at Harrisville and Hoeft State Parks, it does feature unusual shallow marl beach pools, as well as marshes and conifer swamps that attract a variety of wildlife and birds.

The undeveloped park has no visitor facilities other than a pair of parking areas and a lightly posted trail system.

Hiking: The parking area closest to US 23 is the trailhead for the Thompson's Harbor 6-mile trail system of three loops. The loops depart north and skirt the shoreline before returning to the parking lot. Loop 3, which circles Bear Lake, is the longest at 2.6 miles, but keep in mind that the system is only lightly maintained and crisscrossed by old two-track roads. Following the trails can be challenging at times.

Mountain Biking: Mountain bikers are allowed on both designated roads open to vehicles and the trail system.

Natural Area: Within the park is the Thompson's Harbor Natural Area, which preserves the world's largest population of dwarf lake iris as well as the threatened Pitcher's thistle, Houghton's goldenrod, and many other plant species. Birding in the spring and fall is also very good within the park, with more than 100 species having been sighted and recorded.

Access and Information: From Rogers City, head southeast on US 23 for 12 miles and then east on a gravel road that is posted THOMPSON'S HARBOR DAY-USE AREA and leads to the two parking areas. Further south on US 23 is Old State Road, which is followed east to cross Grand Lake Outlet and skirt the natural area. For more information or a trail map, contact P. H. Hoeft State Park, US 23 North, Rogers City, MI 49779; or call (517) 734-2543.

P. H. Hoeft State Park

The 301-acre P. H. Hoeft State Park in Presque Isle County not only contains a mile of beautiful beach but also preserves a segment of the Huron Dunes. These low, gently rolling mounds of sand that separate the shoreline from the park's wooded interior are nowhere as grand as those along Lake Michigan or even the dunes found in Port Crescent. But they possess a charm of their own, and, when combined with the wide sandy beach, form one of the most interesting and scenic shorelines along Lake Huron.

The park land was deeded over to the state in 1922 by Paul H. Hoeft, one of the most successful lumber barons in northeast Michigan, and in 1938 a CCC unit built the distinctive stone and log bathhouse/shelter in the day-use area. But Hoeft receives light usage from day visitors, as it primarily attracts campers during the summer. Although the park draws only 63,000 visitors a year, the campground is busy throughout July and August.

Camping: It's easy to understand the popularity of Hoeft's campground. The modern facility has 144 sites that are well spaced in a forest of hemlock and pine. There are no sites near the water, but several border the low dunes and all are a short walk from the shoreline. Hoeft often fills up on weekends in July and August and occasionally during the week in mid-August, when the salmon and lake trout fishing out of Rogers City picks up. Hoeft also has a mini-cabin and an organization camp for large groups.

Hiking: Hoeft maintains a 4.5-mile network of trails centered around the Beach Trail. This 1.2-mile loop begins in the campground and passes through the Huron Dunes before returning through the park's wooded interior. At its east end, the Hardwood Trail departs south, crosses US 23, and then forms a 1.5-mile loop through a forest of oak, maple, and beech. Also extending from the east end of the Beach Trail is Nagel Creek Trail, which forms a 0.75-mile loop to the small creek.

Cycling: Mountain biking is not allowed on the park's hiking trails, but cyclists can enjoy a bike path that begins in the campground as a wood-chip path until it crosses US 23. On the other side, it extends a half mile to the south end of the park with a gravel surface. Once outside the park it continues another four miles to the downtown area of Rogers City as a paved path, allowing park visitors to reach the popular resort town without having to ride on US 23.

Fishing: Plantings of salmon, lake, and brown trout in Rogers City in recent years have resulted in an excellent deepwater fishery within a mile of the Lake Huron shoreline. There is no ramp in P. H. Hoeft State Park, but there are boat launching facilities in Rogers City and Hammond Bay. The only fishing in the state park is at Nagel Creek, which occasionally draws river anglers in the fall for spawning steelhead and salmon.

Day-Use Facilities: Hoeft's mile-long shoreline is a beautiful, wide beach that is ideal for beachcombing and setting up the lawn chair to watch lake freighters out

Campground, P. J. Hoeft State Park

Lake Huron

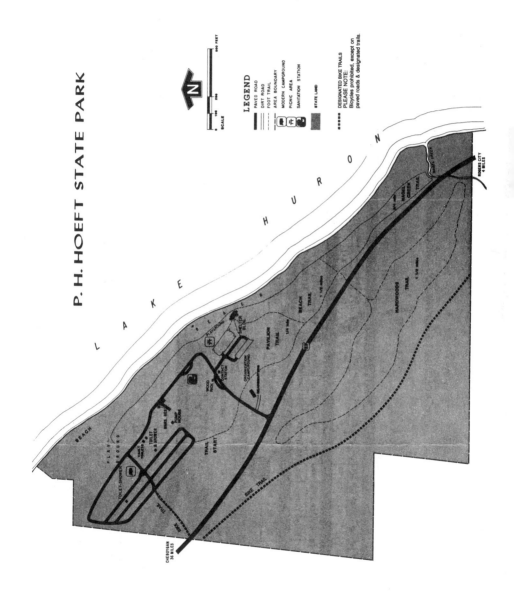

P. H. HOEFT STATE PARK

LEGEND

PAVED ROAD
DIRT ROAD
FOOT TRAIL
AREA BOUNDARY
MODERN CAMPGROUND
PICNIC AREA
SANITATION STATION
STATE LAND

DESIGNATED BIKE TRAILS
PLEASE NOTE:
Bicycles prohibited, except on
paved roads & designated trails.

SCALE

N

L A K E   H U R O N

BEACH

PLAY
GROUND

TOILET-SHOWER

TOILET
& SHOWER

PARK
WATER

BIKE RACK

DUMP
HOUSE

TRAIL
START

CONTACT
STATION

ROAD
RIGA

P.H. ROUND

SHELTER
BLDG.

PAVILION
TRAIL

BEACH
TRAIL 1 1/2 miles

1/4 mile

1/2 mile

ORGANIZATION CAMPGROUND

HARDWOODS
TRAIL 1 1/2 miles

MARSH
CREEK

NAGEL CREEK TRAIL

WAGE CREEK

ROGERS CITY
4 MILES

BIKE TRAIL

BIKE TRAIL

CHEBOYGAN
36 MILES

on the horizon. The day-use facility has a shelter on the edge of the beach and a picnic area with tables and grills well separated in the pine forest. Departing from the area is the Beach Trail, which crosses directly in front of the day-use pavilion.

Winter Activities: Hoeft's trails were widened for cross-country skiing, which draws a number of visitors to the park during the winter. The trails are occasionally groomed and tracked, and for the most part are quite level and ideal for novice skiers. There is almost no snowmobiling in the park due to the limited area open to ORVs.

Access and Information: The park is 4 miles northwest of Rogers City on US 23. For more information, contact P. H. Hoeft State Park, US 23 North, Rogers City, MI 49779; or call (517) 734-2543.

Cheboygan State Park

▲ A variety of terrain, including 4 miles of shoreline, extensive marshes and bogs, and even a stretch of wind-blown sand dunes, makes Cheboygan State Park an interesting place for hikers. A low number of visitors makes the 972-acre unit attractive to all other users, especially campers looking for an open site on a weekend.

Located in Cheboygan County, the park is a peninsula surrounded by three different bodies of water: To the north is South Channel of the Straits of Mackinac, to the west, protected Duncan Bay, and to the east, Lake Huron. It is along the Lake Huron and South Channel shorelines that a string of low sand dunes extends from the water to several hundred yards inland. Otherwise, the park is a lowland forest of cedar, poplar, maple, and oak broken by stretches of wetland and Little Bill Elliots Creek.

The park draws only 47,000 visitors annually, and they arrive throughout the year. Fishing, hunting, and viewing autumn colors are popular activities in the fall, while during the winter, the park offers the opportunity to ski to a rustic cabin for an overnight stay.

Camping: The park maintains a modern campground of seventy-five sites along Duncan Bay, 4 miles away from its day-use area. The campground is in a semi-open area with no sites directly on the bay but all a short walk away. Duncan Bay along the campground is a rocky shoreline with a heavy growth of aquatic plants, great for bass anglers but not too desirable for swimmers. The campground fills on holidays and a few weekends, especially Labor Day, when people arrive for the annual walk across the Mackinac Bridge, but there are usually available sites the rest of the summer.

Hiking: Cheboygan offers some of the finest hiking of any state park along Lake Huron. The park has more than 6 miles of trails, with the heart of the system a 4-mile loop that skirts the Great Lake and passes the three rustic cabins and a set of lighthouse ruins before reaching Cheboygan Point. It then loops back inland, first through an area of open dunes and then the shaded and cool forest of cedar. The loop is marked in yellow and red markers and can be picked up at a trailhead posted along Seffern Road, almost halfway to the campground.

You can also reach the loop via the Lighthouse Ruins Trail, a 1-mile trail that departs from near the campground contact station and is marked in orange footprints. Also beginning in the campground is the Swamp Trail, a 1-mile loop, marked in green, that includes an extensive boardwalk through a bog. Departing from the Swamp Trail is the Grass Marsh Trail, a half-mile side trip, and a spur that extends north to the shoreline loop. Keep in mind that all trails that cut across the

Lake Huron

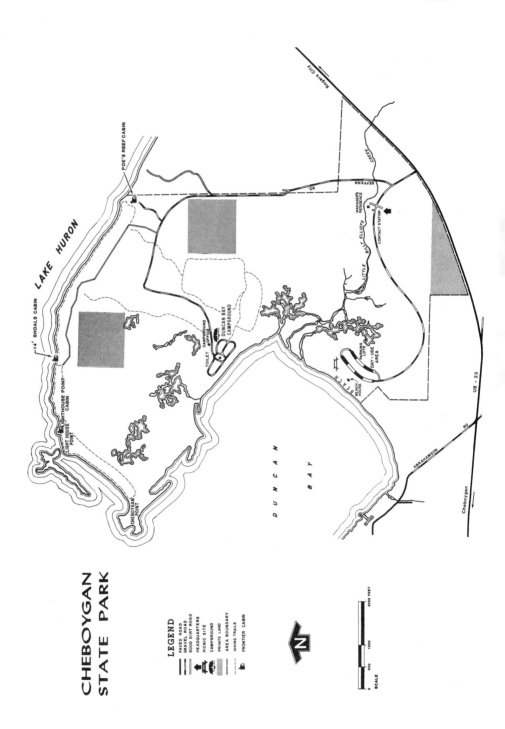

CHEBOYGAN STATE PARK

LAKE HURON

DUNCAN BAY

POE'S REEF CABIN

14' SHOALS CABIN

LIGHTHOUSE POINT CABIN

LIGHT HOUSE POINT

CHEBOYGAN POINT

TOILET

CAMPGROUND OFFICE

DUNCAN BAY CAMPGROUND

BEACH HOUSE

BEACH

PARKING LOT

DAY-USE AREA

SEFFERN RD

LITTLE BILLY ELLIOT'S CREEK

CONTACT STATION

MANAGER'S RESIDENCE

Rogers City

US - 23

ABRAHAMSON RD

Cheboygan

LEGEND
PAVED ROAD
GRAVEL ROAD
GOOD DIRT ROAD
HEADQUARTERS
PICNIC SITE
CAMPGROUND
PRIVATE LAND
AREA BOUNDARY
HIKING TRAILS
FRONTIER CABIN

N

SCALE
0   500   1000   2000 FEET

175

interior of the park and even parts of the shoreline loop pass through cedar swamps that make for some wet hiking at times.

Fishing: Cheboygan abounds in opportunities for anglers. Perhaps the biggest attraction to fishermen are the brook trout in Little Bill Elliots Creek. Using primarily worms, anglers wade in or work the banks of the stream in early summer in order to land the trout. Duncan Bay is best known for smallmouth bass, and fishermen do especially well in the shoreline weed beds that extend from the campground to Cheboygan Point. Duncan Bay is also fished for perch and northern pike. The park does not have a boat ramp in its day-use area, but there is an access site in the campground where hand-carried boats can be launched.

Cabins: Cheboygan has three frontier cabins that are all rustic in appearance, each set up for eight people, and all overlooking the water. Poe's Reef Cabin is on the east side of the park on Lake Huron, while farther to the west is Fourteen-Foot Shoal Cabin, on a sandy beach. Lighthouse Point Cabin is the newest structure and one of the few two-room cabins in the state park system. The structure is the farthest drive in and is situated on a dune overlooking the beach and its namesake point on the North Channel. During the winter the cabin road is not plowed, and the cabins are reached by ski, snowshoe, or snowmobile. The cabins are extremely popular and should be reserved well in advance of any anticipated trip.

Lighthouses: Within the park are the ruins of the Cheboygan Point Lighthouse, reached by hiking 1.5 miles of the shoreline loop from the park road trailhead. First built in 1851 on a pier in Lake Huron and then rebuilt in 1859 on the mainland, the lighthouse was operated until the U.S. Lighthouse Service put it out of service in 1932. Today all that remains are the foundation and partial rock walls of the lightkeeper's house. While hiking along the beach, you can also view the offshore lighthouses that replaced it: first the Poe Reef Light, and then the Fourteen-Foot Shoals Light.

Day-Use Facilities: On the south side of Little Bill Elliots Creek, the park maintains a day-use area with a bathhouse/store, picnic area, and parking for 200 vehicles. The beach here is wide and sandy, the designated swimming area shallow, and the view of the bay excellent.

Winter Activities: The park grooms and tracks almost 6 miles of cross-country ski runs when there is sufficient snow. The ski trailhead is located on Seffern Road, almost halfway to the campground. Skiers park along the road. A ski trail departs north and then, near Poe's Reef Cabin, joins the cabin access road, which is not plowed during the winter but is tracked for skiers. It is about a 1-mile ski to Fourteen-Foot Shoals Cabin and a 1.75-mile trip to Lighthouse Point Cabin. There is no ski rental concession within the park, but several sport shops in the city of Cheboygan rent equipment.

Access and Information: The park entrance is 3 miles east of the city of Cheboygan on US 23. For more information or reservations, contact Cheboygan State Park, 4490 Beach Road, Cheboygan, MI 49721; or call (231) 627-2811.

Onaway State Park

▲ Onaway State Park is a small unit that borders one of Michigan's largest inland lakes. The 10,150-acre Black Lake is more than 6 miles in length and almost 4 miles at its widest point, making it the eighth largest in the state. The beautiful lake is known for its walleye, and in the past it has been rated by DNR biologists as one of Michigan's best walleye fisheries.

The popular game fish has made Onaway what its staff describes as a "fishermen's park." The 158-acre unit is well forested in a variety of trees, including white and red pine, maple, oak, and birch, which draws mushroom hunters in the spring. Although the park contains almost a mile of lakefront, there is very limited beach and only a mile of foot trails that wind around the campground and to an overlook shelter in the northwest corner. The annual attendance at the park is 40,000 visitors with the vast majority of them arriving during the summer.

Camping: Onaway has ninety-nine modern sites well scattered in a campground that is shaded by towering white and red pine. A few sites lie near the shoreline of Black Lake, while the rest are uphill with a fine view of the water. The campground fills on the Fourth of July weekend and on a few other weekends during the summer, but generally, campers can expect to find an open site.

Fishing: The popularity of fishing on Black Lake prompted the park staff to rebuild its boat launch in the late 1980s. The improved ramp is located west of the campground and has parking for twenty-five vehicles and trailers. The large lake not only has good populations of walleye and perch, but also has a self-sustaining population of Great Lakes muskie, northern pike, and sturgeon. Sturgeon often range in age from nineteen to thirty-six years, in which time they can easily exceed 100 pounds in weight. They are primarily bottom feeders and can only be caught during a February season by spearing.

Day-Use Facilities: On the shore of Black Lake are tables, a shelter that can be rented, and parking for seventy-five vehicles. There is little sand here or elsewhere in the park, as most of the shoreline is rocky.

Access and Information: The park is located 6 miles north of the town of Onaway on M-211. For more information, contact Onaway State Park, 3622 North M-211, Onaway, MI 49765; or call (517) 733-8279.

Fishing in Black Lake, Onaway State Park

177

Clear Lake State Park

▲ Many geologists believe Clear Lake is a product of glaciation 10,000 years ago, when a huge chunk of ice broke off the mile-thick glacier and rammed into the earth's surface. After the glacier retreated and the block of ice melted, what remained was a body of water more than 100 feet deep. Today the lake is indeed "clear," and is the outstanding feature of Clear Lake State Park, a 300-acre unit in Montmorency County.

Although glacial evidence in the form of moraine hills surrounds the area, the park itself is relatively flat, forested primarily in jack pine and oak. It has two separate entrances off M-33, one for its day-use area and the other for its campground. Between the two facilities Clear Lake draws 87,000 visitors annually.

Camping: The park has a modern campground with 200 sites well spaced along several loops. The campground is located in a semi-open area, lightly forested in pines, and has its own beach and designated swimming area as well as a mini-cabin. Also nearby is a boat launch for campers (no parking near the ramp) and an organization camp. The campground fills most weekends from late June to mid-August, but sites are generally available for those without reservations the rest of the summer and during the week. The campground is open from mid-April to December but the modern facilities only from May to November.

Backpacking: Although there is less than 2 miles of footpaths within the state park, Clear Lake provides access to more than 70 miles of trails. Within the campground is the northern trailhead of the Clear Lake–Jackson Lake Pathway, a one-way hike of 3.5 miles south to Jackson Lake. The pathway is marked by yellow posts and ends at a state forest campground on Jackson Lake, allowing hikers to turn it into an overnight adventure.

Trails in the campground also merge into the High Country Pathway that skirts the state park to the south and east. The High Country Pathway is a 50-mile loop through the Lower Peninsula's elk country, linking Clear Lake with Pigeon River County State Forest to the west and more than a half dozen state forest campgrounds. One possible overnight trek on the pathway is to hike the 12 miles between Clear Lake and Shoepac Lake State Forest Campground to the north. An extra day can then be spent exploring the famed sinkholes in the area before returning to Clear Lake State Park.

Fishing: The 133-acre Clear Lake is a popular recreation lake with much boating activity during the day. Anglers do best fishing early in the morning or at dusk for smallmouth bass. Due to its depth, 100 feet at its maximum, the lake has been stocked in the past with rainbow trout and more recently, splake. Along with a camper's boat ramp, the state park maintains a boat ramp in the day-use area with a parking lot for fifty vehicles and trailers.

Day-Use Facilities: South of the campground is the entrance to the park's day-use area, which features a sandy beach and shallow swimming area, bathhouse, picnic area, and parking for 150 vehicles.

Winter Activities: The park grooms the Clear Lake-To-Canada Creek Cross Country Ski Trail throughout the winter and maintains a trailhead and vault toilets for skiers in the campground. The 4.5-mile ski trail is a level ski with two loops that stay entirely in the state park, and a third that heads west into Mackinaw State Forest where it skirts a bluff overlooking Canada Creek before returning to Clear Lake.

Access and Information: The park is off M-33, 8 miles north of Atlanta. For more information, contact Clear Lake State Park, 20500 M-33, Atlanta, MI 49709; or call (517) 785-4388.

Lake Huron

CLEAR LAKE STATE PARK

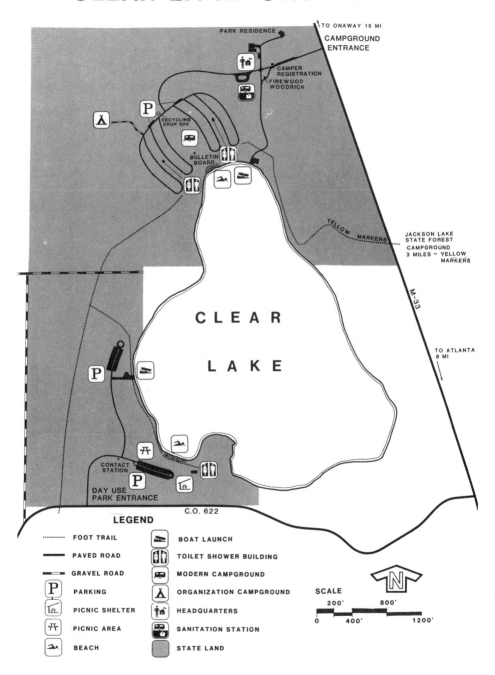

Northwest Michigan

South Higgins Lake State Park

▲ South Higgins Lake State Park features two lakes of opposite character. The 962-acre unit is split in half by County Road 100, and to the north is the huge campground and day-use area on busy Higgins Lake. South of County Road 100 is Marl Lake and 700 acres forested in maple, oak, and pine—the park's quiet half, best seen on foot or by paddle.

The state park contains almost a mile of shoreline along Higgins Lake, a large spring-fed body of water known for its clarity and its popularity. The 9,600-acre lake is a busy place, with anglers and recreational boaters during the summer, and snowmobilers and ice fishermen in the winter, and is the main reason the park draws 300,000 visitors annually. But across County Road 100, lying totally within the state park, is Marl Lake, considerably smaller, shallower, and with a shoreline free of cottages and other development. Marl Lake's deepest section is only 3 feet, limiting visitors to canoes and small motorboats.

Camping: South Higgins features the largest campground in a state park. The facility has 470 modern sites and one mini-cabin, situated close together in an area well shaded by hardwoods. There are no sites on the lake, but all are only a short walk from the lakeshore. Despite its size, the campground fills up daily from the Fourth of July holiday to early August and on weekends after that to the Labor Day holiday.

Hiking: South Higgins has almost 6 miles of trails, all of it, with the exception of a short nature trail, south of County Road 100. The network is a huge loop that skirts the south side of Marl Lake to The Cut, a channel that was dredged to float logs to Houghton Lake during the lumbering era. The loop then swings away from the lake and returns inland to the trailhead and parking area. Trail C is the entire loop, a 5.5-mile walk that is marked in blue and takes most people more

The Fox Island viewing platform in Leelanau State Park

Hiking around Marl Lake, South Higgins Lake State Park

than 2 hours to hike. But there are also two spurs that form shorter trips. Trail B, marked in red, is a 3.5-mile trip, or a 1.5-hour hike, while Trail A, coded in green, is a 2-mile loop. The Marl Lake area of the park has a separate entrance and parking area just north of the campground entrance on County Road 100.

Mountain Biking: The Marl Lake trail system is open to mountain bikers and is considered an easy and nontechnical ride. Cyclists need to remember that during the summer, the trail is heavily used by hikers.

Fishing: Higgins Lake stretches 7 miles between two state parks and reaches depths of up to 135 feet. It is best known by many anglers for its perch and lake trout. The lake has been stocked with lake trout, brown trout, and splake since 1971, and during the winter it is one of the best places in Michigan to take a laker or smelt through the ice. There is also fishing activity for smallmouth bass, northern pike, and whitefish. The park maintains an improved boat launch in a small basin next to the day-use area. There is parking for sixty-nine vehicles and rigs, but usually more than 100 boats are launched daily during the summer.

Other fishing opportunities can be found in Marl Lake, which holds perch, smallmouth bass, and northern pike. Because of its shallow depth, shore fishing is usually unproductive. Most anglers use a canoe or small motorboat and fish the center of the lake. Fishermen also dip into The Cut, where they seek out bass and pike. There is an unimproved access site for hand-carried boats in the Marl Lake parking area.

Day-Use Facilities: South Higgins' day-use area is on Higgins Lake and consists primarily of a grassy bank with many picnic tables only an arm's length away from

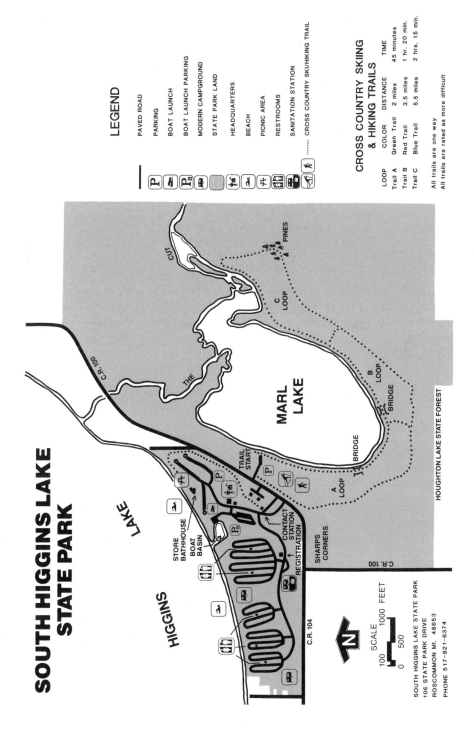

Northwest Michigan

LEGEND

PAVED ROAD
PARKING
BOAT LAUNCH
BOAT LAUNCH PARKING
MODERN CAMPGROUND
STATE PARK LAND
HEADQUARTERS
BEACH
PICNIC AREA
RESTROOMS
SANITATION STATION
.... CROSS COUNTRY SKI/HIKING TRAIL

CROSS COUNTRY SKIING & HIKING TRAILS

LOOP	COLOR	DISTANCE	TIME
Trail A	Green Trail	2 miles	45 minutes
Trail B	Red Trail	3.5 miles	1 hr. 20 min.
Trail C	Blue Trail	5.5 miles	2 hrs. 15 min.

All trails are one way
All trails are rated as more difficult

SOUTH HIGGINS LAKE STATE PARK

PINES
CUT
C LOOP
THE
MARL LAKE
B LOOP
BRIDGE
BRIDGE
A LOOP
C.R. 100
HOUGHTON LAKE STATE FOREST

HIGGINS LAKE

STORE
BATHHOUSE
BOAT BASIN
TRAIL START
CONTACT STATION
REGISTRATION
SHARPS CORNERS
C.R. 100
C.R. 104

N

SCALE   FEET
100   500   1000

0

SOUTH HIGGINS LAKE STATE PARK
106 STATE PARK DRIVE
ROSCOMMON MI. 48653
PHONE 517-821-6374

183

the water. There is little in the way of a sandy beach, but the designated swimming area has a sandy and shallow bottom ideal for young children. There are two picnic shelters, a bathhouse/store, and parking for almost 500 vehicles, although the lot fills up most weekends in July and additional visitors are forced to leave their cars outside the park and walk in. A boat rental concession rents out canoes, rowboats, small motorboats, sailboats, and even pontoons, and is open daily from Memorial Day to Labor Day.

Winter Activities: The Marl Lake trails are groomed and tracked during the winter for level loops of 2, 3.5, and 5.5 miles in length. There is no ski rental concession in the park, but 3.5 miles north of County Road 100 is Cross-Country Ski Headquarters (517-821-6661), which has equipment available from late November through March. There is no snowmobiling in the park.

Access and Information: From I-75 take exit 239 and head west on M-18, but immediately turn north (right) onto Robinson Lake Road. Robinson will curve west into County Road 100, which is followed south to the park entrance. From US 27 go east at the Higgins Lake exit and follow County Road 104 to County Road 100 at Sharps Corner. The park entrance is less than a half mile away. For more information, contact South Higgins Lake State Park, 106 State Park Drive, Roscommon, MI 48653; or call (517) 821-6374.

North Higgins Lake State Park

▲ At Hartwick Pines State Park, the interpretive center recounts the amazing story
⊥ of Michigan's lumbering era. After the trees had been cut and the loggers departed in the early 1900s, much of Michigan was a stump-ridden wasteland. The next chapter in the saga, the recovery of the land, began at what is now North Higgins Lake State Park. It was here in 1903 that the state built its first forest nursery in an effort to replace what had been taken by the lumbermen.

Interpretive buildings and a nature trail on the north side of County Road 200 take visitors back to the time when much of the state was a scene of fire-scarred stumps, and the CCC was planting pine seedlings and fighting forest fires. The area presents a fascinating account of the return of Michigan's "northwoods," but for many people the outstanding feature of the park lies on the other side of County Road 200. Within the 429-acre unit is 1,500 feet of shoreline along Higgins Lake, one of the most popular recreation lakes in the state. The water is so clear in the spring-fed lake that it attracts scuba diving clubs from around Michigan and the Midwest.

North Higgins also serves as the trailhead of 10 miles of trail that extend onto state forest land and, combined with the campground and fishing opportunities on Higgins Lake, draws 168,000 visitors a year.

Camping: The park features 210 modern sites and two mini-cabins located along two separate loops. The campground is a mix of open sites and partly wooded areas and is surrounded by hardwoods and pine. There are no sites on the water, but a foot trail that connects the two loops passes the day-use beach. From late June to early August, the facility is usually filled daily and on weekends through Labor Day.

Hiking: On the north side of County Road 200, there are three trail loops that begin at the park's interpretive center. All three loops overlap and are connected down the middle by a shortcut spur. The shortest hike is the Uplands Nature Trail, a 1.5-mile loop with twenty interpretive posts that winds through a pine plantation and a field of fire-scarred stumps. An accompanying brochure is available at the

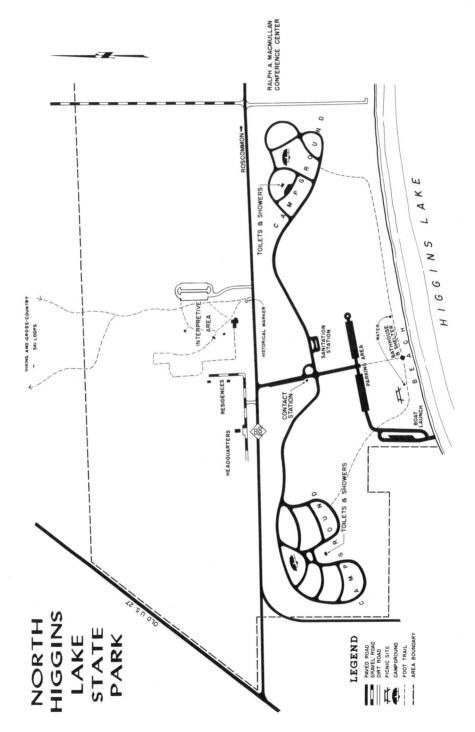

NORTH HIGGINS LAKE STATE PARK

RALPH A MACMULLAN CONFERENCE CENTER

ROSCOMMON →

HIKING AND-CROSS-COUNTRY SKI LOOPS

INTERPRETIVE AREA

HISTORICAL MARKER

RESIDENCES

HEADQUARTERS

CONTACT STATION

SANITATION STATION

TOILETS & SHOWERS

CAMPGROUND

PARKING AREA

WATER

BATHHOUSE & SHELTER

BEACH

BOAT LAUNCH

TOILETS & SHOWERS

CAMPGROUND

HIGGINS LAKE

OLD U.S. 27

LEGEND

PAVED ROAD
GRAVEL ROAD
DIRT ROAD
PICNIC SITE
CAMPGROUND
FOOT TRAIL
AREA BOUNDARY

185

trailhead that covers Michigan's past reforestation practices and efforts. Extending further into the state forest is the Bosom Pines Trail, a 3.8-mile loop, while the Beaver Creek Trail is a 6.5-mile trip that takes the hiker to the edge of the creek before returning.

Mountain Biking: Beaver Creek Trail is open to mountain biking and makes for an easy to moderately difficult ride for most bikers. The 6.5-mile loop is wide in most places but does include a few descents and climbs.

Interpretive Center: Within the park's interpretive area is the CCC Museum, dedicated to the federal program that was created by President Franklin Roosevelt to help the vast numbers of unemployed men during the Great Depression. It was signed into law on March 31,1933, and by July of that year Michigan had forty-two CCC camps that were employing 18,400 men. The CCC did many things, including constructing numerous log shelters seen in state parks today. But they are best known for planting trees, and the Michigan CCC led the nation by planting 485 million seedlings. The museum is a replica of a CCC barracks with displays of the spartan lifestyle, while nearby is the original cone barn, ice house, and the state's first iron fire tower. The museum is located on the north side of County Road 200 and is open from 10:00 A.M. to 6:00 P.M. daily from the second weekend of June through the weekend after Labor Day.

Fishing: Higgins Lake is a popular fishery (see Fishing, South Higgins Lake State Park). The park has an improved boat launch with parking for thirty-eight vehicles and rigs, and sets up temporary parking along the park roads when the lot is filled, as is often the case on summer weekends.

Day-Use Facilities: North Higgins features a narrow, sandy beach that is lined with pines and has a designated swimming area that drops off gradually. Facilities include two shelters that can be rented, a park store, a picnic area, and parking.

Winter Activities: The trail system from the interpretive center is groomed and tracked during the winter for cross-country skiing. Most of the tracks are flat, although there are hilly stretches along the Beaver Creek Trail rated "more difficult" and "most difficult." The track distances are the same for the hiking loop, and a trail map is available at the trailhead near the parking lot. On the first Sunday of February the AuSable Valley Nordic Ski Club stages its Beaver Creek Challenge at North Higgins Lake State Park. The event includes a 7.4-mile (12K) and 3.7-mile (6K) freestyle race, a children's 1.2-mile (2K) race, and unique beaver stump trophies for the winners. There is no warming shelter or equipment concession at the park, but skis can be rented nearby at Cross-Country Ski Headquarters (517-821-6661) on County Road 100.

Access and Information: From I-75 take exit 244 and head west for 4.5 miles to the park entrance. From US 27 take the Military Road exit and head east 1 mile. For more information, contact North Higgins Lake State Park, 11252 North Higgins Lake Drive, Roscommon, MI 48653; or call (517) 821-6125.

Interlochen State Park

One of the first things most visitors notice in Interlochen State Park is the well-preserved "Big Wheel," the device loggers used to haul timber out of the woods at the turn of the century. It's a bit ironic, of course. Interlochen was one of the first state parks preserved because loggers and their big wheels had passed it over.

The 200 acres of virgin white pine that somehow escaped the lumbermen's axes were preserved as Michigan's second unit in 1917 by the state legislature, which

Early morning angler on Duck Lake, Interlochen State Park

paid $60,000 for the land, the price of the timber on it. Although its trees were spared, there was a large sawmill located near Interlochen's northern campground that produced barrels from logs that were floated across Duck Lake.

Today the 200-acre park is probably best known not as one of the few remaining stands of virgin pine but as the park next to renowned Interlochen National Music Camp. The state park might be the only place in Michigan where you can bed down to Bach or Beethoven. Interlochen is actually the thin strip of land between Duck and Green Lakes and features almost a mile of lakeshore along with its towering pines. The park draws 320,000 visitors annually with the vast majority arriving in the summer.

Camping: With a total of 490 sites split between two lakeside campgrounds, Interlochen offers more sites than any other unit in the state park system. A campground along Duck Lake features 430 modern sites along two loops on each side of the day-use area. The area is well shaded by white pine, and many sites are located along a steep bank overlooking the lake. Along Green Lake is a rustic campground with 60 sites. Many of them have a good view of the lake from the heavily forested shoreline. The modern campground is filled weekends from the Fourth of July holiday through Labor Day, and often the Green Lake facility is as well. Sites in one or the other can usually be obtained Sunday through Wednesday when the campgrounds are usually 70 percent full. The park also has a Rent-a-Tent Program with four wall tents and a tipi in its modern campground, along with two mini-cabins. All of them are extremely popular during the summer and should be reserved three to four weeks in advance.

Hiking: Interlochen has only one trail, the Pines Nature Trail, a mile-long loop that winds through the towering stand of white pine. It begins at the south loop of Duck Lake Campground and has sixteen interpretive stops. An accompanying brochure can be picked up at the contact station.

Fishing: There is a considerable amount of fishing activity in both Duck and Green Lakes for a variety of species. The 1,930-acre Duck Lake reaches depths of 98 feet and has been stocked with both brown trout and lake trout. The lake is best known for smallmouth and largemouth bass, as well as northern pike that can exceed 30 inches at times. Anglers also do well with perch and bluegill and northern pike. The park maintains two boat launches on Duck Lake, one off each loop of the modern campground.

Green Lake, slightly larger and deeper than Duck Lake, is better known for its trout fishery. The lake is stocked annually with brown trout and lake trout by the DNR and has produced lake trout in excess of 24 inches. The lake also has a good smallmouth bass fishery. The park has a paved boat launch at the rustic campground on Green Lake.

Day-Use Facilities: Interlochen maintains a day-use area on Duck Lake that features a wide, sandy beach, designated swimming area, and picnic shelter that can be rented. Surrounding the beach is a wooded picnic area and parking for 200 vehicles. A boat rental concession has rowboats on both Duck Lake and Green Lake and is open daily from Memorial Day to Labor Day.

Access and Information: Interlochen is located 15 miles southwest of Traverse City. The park's entrance is on M-137, 3 miles south of US 31. For more information, contact Interlochen State Park, South M-137, Interlochen, MI 49643; or call (231) 276-9511.

Traverse City State Park

The only state park on Grand Traverse Bay is Traverse City State Park, appropriately named as it lies only 2 miles from downtown in the heart of a popular resort area. This 45-acre urban unit in Grand Traverse County features little more than a large campground on one side of US 31 and a day-use area on the other.

The park's outstanding feature is a quarter mile of beautiful beach on Grand Traverse Bay, one of the few segments near Traverse City that is not developed. The beach and a campground draw 220,000 visitors annually.

Camping: The park has a campground of 343 modern sites on the east side of US 31. The sites lack privacy, but the area is well shaded and there is a pedestrian overpass that crosses the busy highway to the beach on Grand Traverse Bay. The facility is full weekends from the end of June through Labor Day, particularly during the Traverse City Cherry Festival in mid-July. Generally there are openings in the middle of the week. The campground is also maintained throughout the winter with heated restrooms, showers, electricity, and water.

Cycling: From a gate at the back of the campground, an access spur connects the state park to the Traverse Area Recreational Trail, the paved rail–trail that locals call TART for short. TART begins at M-72 in Acme and presently extends west 11 miles to the intersection of US 31 and M-72 on the west side of the city. In between, the urban trail allows cyclists, in-line skaters, and walkers to reach the downtown area, three beautiful beaches, and the city zoo while bypassing the rush-hour-like traffic of US 31. Future plans call for extending TART to Suttons Bay on the Leelanau Peninsula.

Fishing: Mitchell Creek empties into Grand Traverse Bay at the west end of the day-use area, and its mouth is a popular spot to fish for steelhead in spring and fall. Anglers do best with spawn or spoons, fishing from April to March or late September through November.

Day-Use Facilities: The park's day-use area is on the north side of US 31 and has a separate entrance from the campground. Along with a quarter mile of wide, sandy beach, the facility features a grassy picnic area overlooking the bay, bathhouse, and parking for 125 vehicles. Frequently on summer weekends, the parking lot will be full. Additional visitors must park outside the area and walk in.

Access and Information: The park entrance is 2 miles east of downtown Traverse City on US 31 and is well posted. For more information, contact Traverse City State Park, 1132 US 31, Traverse City, MI 49686; or call (231) 922-5270.

Leelanau State Park

Preserving the tip of Michigan's "little finger" is Leelanau State Park, a 1,350-acre unit of spectacular views that are seen along 1.5 miles of lakeshore, from platforms on top of dunes, even from the tower of a lighthouse. The park, located in Leelanau County and guarding the entrance of the Grand Traverse Bay, is separated into two main regions. The smaller section preserves the tip of the Leelanau Peninsula and includes the campground, day-use area, and historic Grand Traverse Lighthouse.

Located to the south along Cathead Bay is the bulk of the park. This undeveloped area, a rolling terrain of low dunes forested in hardwoods of maple, beech, white ash, and birch, contains most of the park's shoreline and all of its trails. It also features the park's best beach, a wide, sandy shoreline that can only be reached after a mile hike from a parking lot.

Together the two sections draw 180,000 visitors throughout the year. The park is not only popular during the traditional summer season but also in autumn for fall colors, while the undeveloped area receives its greatest use during the winter from Nordic skiers.

Camping: The state park has a campground of fifty-two rustic sites located at the tip of the Leelanau Peninsula. Although the shoreline here is composed of pebbles and stones, ten sites are right along the water and another twenty-five have a fine view of Lake Michigan. These, naturally, are the first to go and are often claimed by campers transferring from another site. The area, which also includes two mini-cabins, is well wooded and, despite primitive facilities, is still a very popular campground, filling daily from July through Labor Day and often more than 50 percent full during June.

Hiking: Leelanau has an excellent trail network that forms 6 miles of loops through the undeveloped region of the park. The trailhead and parking lot is at the end of Densmore Road, located 5 miles south of the campground via County Road 629. The longest hike is Mud Lake Tour, a 2- mile loop through the hilly interior and along the shoreline of the inland lake. Those intent on reaching the sandy beach along Cathead Bay follow Lake Michigan Trail, a 1.5-mile loop that passes a short

Lighthouse, Leelanau State Park

spur down to the water. Also along this trail is Manitou Overlook Spur. The short spur follows a long stairway to the top of a dune, where there is an observation deck. The view from here is spectacular, and on a clear day you are able to see the Fox Islands out in Lake Michigan. It's also a superb place to catch the sunset as the orange orb melts over the Fox Islands. Two other spurs shorten the Mud Lake Tour. Maple Ridge Cutoff makes it a 0.75-mile, 45-minute walk, while the Tamarack Cutoff turns it into a 1.5-mile loop.

Interpretive Center: The Grand Traverse Lighthouse, built in 1916, is the most recent lighthouse in a series that have been guiding ships around the peninsula since 1852. A private historical society has since renovated the light and turned it into a maritime museum. You can climb the tower for a grand view of Lake Michigan. The museum is open throughout the summer, while the remains of an earlier light are posted along the campground loop.

Day-Use Facilities: The Grand Traverse Lighthouse towers over the park's picnic facility making the grassy area an especially scenic place to enjoy an outdoor meal. There is parking for fifty cars and a picnic shelter but no bathhouse facilities or swimming area, as the shoreline is composed of pebbles and stones. Petoskey stone hunters can often be seen searching the beach here for the state stone.

Winter Activities: The most popular use of the park's undeveloped area is for cross-country skiing. Trails are groomed and tracked, and skiers have a choice of a number of loops. Much of the north end of the Mud Lake Tour, however, is not suited for novice skiers. Densmore Road and the trailhead parking lot are plowed, but there is no ski rental concession in the park. There are several shops that rent equipment in Northport, 4 miles to the south.

Northwest Michigan

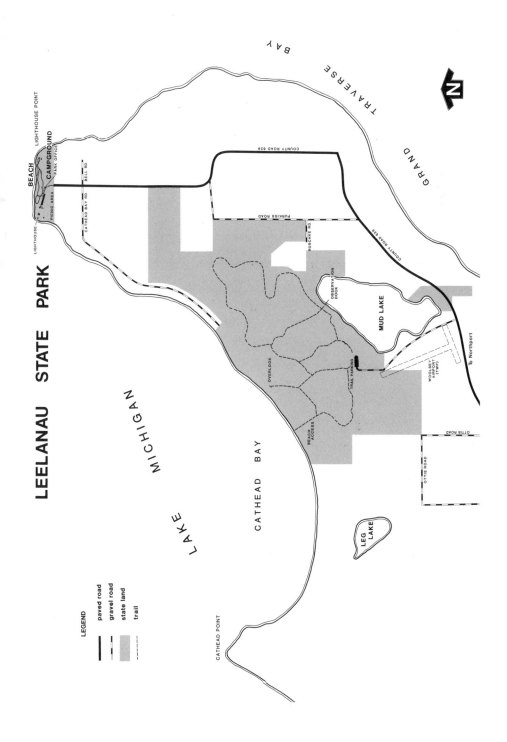

LEELANAU STATE PARK

GRAND TRAVERSE BAY

COUNTY ROAD 629

PURKISS ROAD

RUSCHKE RD.

COUNTY ROAD 629

OBSERVATION DOCK

MUD LAKE

To Northport

WOOLSEY AIRPORT (TWP)

OTTIS ROAD

OTTIS ROAD

OVERLOOK

TRAIL PARKING

BEACH ACCESS

BEACH

LIGHTHOUSE POINT

CAMPGROUND

PICNIC AREA

PARK OFFICE

BELL RD.

CATHEAD BAY RD.

LIGHTHOUSE

LAKE MICHIGAN

CATHEAD BAY

CATHEAD POINT

LEG LAKE

LEGEND

paved road
gravel road
state land
trail

191

Access and Information: The park's campground is located 8 miles north of Northport on County Road 629. Access to the trailhead in the undeveloped section is 4 miles north of Northport on Densmore Road. For more information, contact Leelanau State Park, 15310 North Lighthouse Point Road, Northport, MI 49670; or call (231) 386- 5422, summer only.

Young State Park

▲ Young State Park is located at the east end of beautiful Lake Charlevoix, also ⊥ known at one time as both Pine Lake and Long Lake, and a place frequently fished by a youthful Ernest Hemingway. The author's family owned a summer cottage on nearby Walloon Lake, but Hemingway occasionally spent his days on Lake Charlevoix, where he liked to fish for trout in Horton Creek. He even once evaded a conservation officer by boating across the lake from Horton Bay to his uncle's place on a spot known today as Hemingway Point.

Young State Park, a 563-acre unit in Charlevoix County, is a mix of gently rolling terrain, lowlands, and cedar swamp covered in hardwoods, aspen, and balsam fir. The wooded area, traversed by a good trail system, attracts morel mushroom hunters and wildflower enthusiasts every spring. But, unquestionably, the main features of the park that draw 150,000 visitors annually are the same as when Hemingway frequented the area—a beautiful lake, an undeveloped shoreline, and good fishing.

Camping: Young State Park has 297 modern sites spread out in three campgrounds. Oak Campground has 70 sites, including a row of them right on the shoreline of Lake Charlevoix, while next to it is Terrace Campground with an additional 56 sites. Both are wooded areas with well-shaded sites to make camp. Spruce Campground, north of the day-use facility, is the largest, with 169 sites situated in an open, grassy area. The three campgrounds fill up almost daily from the Fourth of July weekend to mid-August.

Hiking: Young has 3 miles of hiking trails that loop through the southeast half of the park. Deer Flats Nature Trail is the longest walk, a 2-mile trip from near the contact station to Terrace Campground. Looping off Deer Flats is White Birch Nature Trail, a 0.75-mile spur that skirts the lakeshore and three dry pond beds. A popular walk is to combine this trail with a portion of Deer Flats for a 1.5-mile loop out of Terrace Campground.

Fishing: Lake Charlevoix, a 17,260-acre body of water with depths up to 122 feet, has an exceptionally diverse fishery. It's stocked annually with rainbow, brown, and lake trout, with the latter two often caught during the summer by trolling the open water areas. Rainbow are often found in or near the mouths of most streams emptying into the lake, while Boyne River, near the park at the east end, supports a strong salmon run in the fall. The 13-mile-long lake, particularly the East Arm near Ironton, also has good spawning areas for bass, perch, and panfish. The only launching facility the park maintains is an unimproved ramp in Terrace Campground for boats under 16 feet in length. There is a modern ramp, however, 2 miles away at Boyne City.

Day-Use Facilities: There are 1.5-miles of lakeshore within the park, including a wide, sandy beach in its day-use area. Overlooking the beach and grassy picnic area is a classic log building, built in the 1930s by the CCC, which today houses a concession store but no bathhouse.

Winter Activities: Nordic skiing is an increasingly popular winter activity in

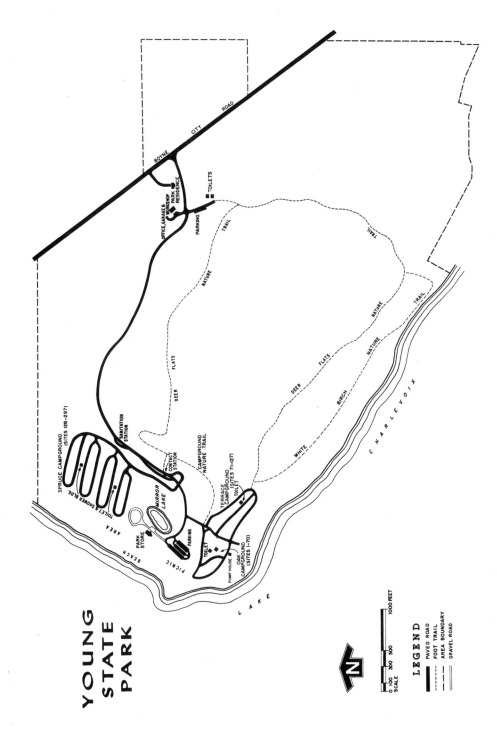

YOUNG STATE PARK

LAKE CHARLEVOIX

SPRUCE CAMPGROUND (SITES 128–297)

SANITATION STATION

CONTACT STATION

CAMPGROUND NATURE TRAIL

TERRACE CAMPGROUND (SITES 71–127)

OAK CAMPGROUND (SITES 1–70)

TOILET & SHOWER BLDG.

MIRROR LAKE

PARK STORE

PICNIC AREA

BEACH

PUMP HOUSE

TOILET

PARKING

NATURE TRAIL

DEER FLATS

BIRCH FLATS

WHITE

NATURE TRAIL

DEER FLATS

NATURE TRAIL

OFFICE, GARAGE

WORKSHOP

PARK RESIDENCE

TOILETS

PARKING

BOYNE CITY ROAD

LEGEND

PAVED ROAD
FOOT TRAIL
AREA BOUNDARY
GRAVEL ROAD

0 100 300 500 1000 FEET
SCALE

N

Young State Park, which offers three runs for novice skiers. The ski trailhead and parking area is located across the road from the park headquarters, and from here skiers have a choice of runs 1.9, 2.5, and 2.8 miles long. All begin on a hiking trail but return along the park road, which is not plowed. The trails are groomed, but there is no ski rental concession in the park.

Access and Information: From Boyne City head northwest on Boyne City Road (County Road 56) 1.5 miles to the park entrance. For more information, contact Young State Park, 02280 Boyne City Road, Boyne City, MI 49712; or call (231) 582-7523.

Fisherman's Island State Park

Michigan's state stone is not really a stone at all. Petoskey stones are actually petrified coral, leftover fragments of the many coral reefs that existed in the warm-water seas from Charlevoix to Alpena some 300 million years ago. Today the stone is collected by rock hounds, and many of them end up polished and used in jewelry, paperweights, and other decorative items. Dry Petoskey stones are silvery with no apparent markings to the untrained eye, but when the fossils are wet, it's easy to see the ringlike pattern that covers them.

You can search for the stones in several state parks, including Leelanau and Petoskey, but the best place is the 5 miles of undeveloped Lake Michigan shoreline in Fisherman's Island State Park. The 2,678-acre unit in Charlevoix County features a park road that extends 2.5 miles along the shoreline from the main entrance to a day-use area, passing along the way stretches of pebbled beaches that are havens for gemstone enthusiasts.

Away from the shoreline, the park's terrain is made up of rolling "old dunes" covered with secondary growth maple, birch, and aspen forests and broken up by bogs of cedar and black spruce. The park is almost divided into two regions by a large parcel of private land, with the northern half containing the campground, gravel park road, day-use area, and contact station. The southern half is completely undeveloped and the least visited portion of the park, reached only by a rough two-track trail off of Norwood Road that ends at a parking area on Whiskey Creek.

Fisherman's Island draws only 56,000 visitors annually, the vast majority during the summer and fall, as the access roads into the park are not plowed regularly during the winter. For visitors interested in searching for Petoskey stones, the contact station has some handout material on finding Michigan's most famous fossils.

Camping: Fisherman's Island State Park has ninety rustic sites located on two loops that are a mile apart. The sites are heavily wooded, well shaded, and very secluded. A row of sites, ten to fifteen of them, are located right on a sandy stretch of Lake Michigan shoreline, tucked away in the trees with a table and a spot to pitch a tent only a few feet from the lapping waters of the Great Lake. These are some of the most beautiful campsites in the state park system and are always the first to be picked. Be prepared to camp inland the first night or two and then hope to transfer to a lakeshore spot when available sites are handed out at 8:00 A.M. Despite being a rustic facility, the campground is full on weekends from the Fourth of July holiday to mid-August, and often daily if the weather is nice during that period.

Hiking: The park has almost 5 miles of maintained trail in its northern half. The trail begins across from the contact station and heads south past the first camping loop, across McGeach Creek and then past the second camping loop. It follows a dune ridge before ending near the day-use area at Inwood Creek. Almost halfway along the trail, a short spur leads back to the park road. The trail passes through

FISHERMAN'S ISLAND STATE PARK

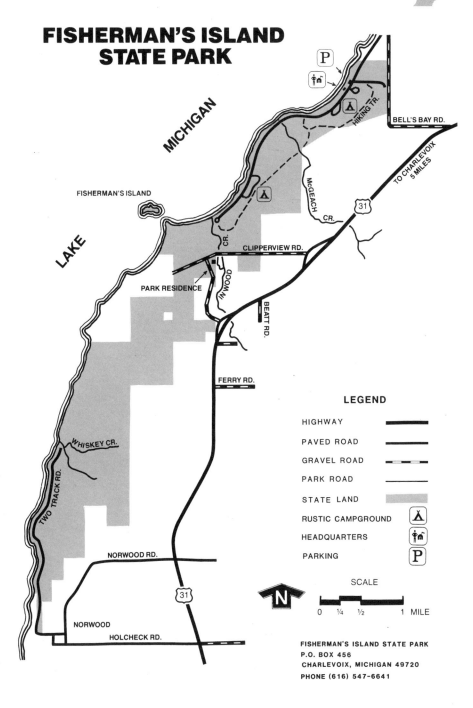

MICHIGAN

FISHERMAN'S ISLAND

LAKE

BELL'S BAY RD.

TO CHARLEVOIX 5 MILES

McGEACH CR.

31

CLIPPERVIEW RD.

PARK RESIDENCE

INWOOD CR.

BEATT RD.

FERRY RD.

WHISKEY CR.

TWO TRACK RD.

NORWOOD RD.

31

NORWOOD

HOLCHECK RD.

LEGEND

HIGHWAY	
PAVED ROAD	
GRAVEL ROAD	
PARK ROAD	
STATE LAND	
RUSTIC CAMPGROUND	Ⓐ
HEADQUARTERS	👤🏠
PARKING	Ⓟ

SCALE

N

0   ¼   ½   1 MILE

FISHERMAN'S ISLAND STATE PARK
P.O. BOX 456
CHARLEVOIX, MICHIGAN 49720
PHONE (616) 547-6641

195

both forest and open fields that are thick with wildberries, including blackberries, in August.

Also found throughout the southern half of the park are unposted, unmapped two-track trails that wind through the area.

Fishing: Fishing in the state park is limited to river angling for steelhead and Chinook salmon near the mouths of McGeach and Whiskey Creeks, with the best runs taking place during March and April. Fisherman's Island does not have any ramps along Lake Michigan, but there are numerous places along the park road where small hand-carried boats can be launched.

Day-Use Facilities: The park has a small day-use area almost 3 miles from the contact station that features a wide, sandy beach and shallow swimming area. The facility includes limited parking, tables, and vault toilets.

Winter Activities: Since the Bells Bay Road from US 31 to the park's entrance is not plowed regularly, there is little winter activity. A small number of Nordic skiers, however, will ski in and camp overnight at the rustic campgrounds for an unusual winter experience.

Access and Information: To reach the park's main entrance, head 5 miles south on US 31 from Charlevoix and turn west (right) on Bells Bay Road. The posted entrance is 2.5 miles from US 31. To reach Whiskey Creek in the southern half of the park, head 11 miles south on US 31 and turn west (right) onto Norwood Road to Norwood Township Park. A two-track road begins at the back of the park and ends at the creek. For more information, contact Fisherman's Island State Park, P.O. Box 456, Charlevoix, MI 49720; or call (231) 547-6641.

Petoskey State Park

Petoskey State Park is not misleading in its name. The 304-acre unit, located next door to the town of Petoskey in Emmet County, has a beautiful beach along Little Traverse Bay and a unique campground. In the winter it is a haven for cross-country skiers. But a good number of the 430,000 annual visitors come to the park for only one reason—to search for Petoskey stones.

The northern Michigan ritual of beachcombing and washing pebbles off in the Great Lake is a common activity in the state park. Visitors stroll along the park's 1.25 miles of shoreline but pay close attention to the patches of pebbles and small rocks at the south end of the park. It takes a trained eye to spot the distinct coral pattern when the stone is dry, but they stand out in a handful of pebbles when held just under the clear surface of Lake Michigan. Some of the Petoskey hunters are "lapidaries," persons who enjoy the art of cutting and polishing stones. But most are just visitors hoping to find a little piece of Michigan to take home.

Away from the shoreline, the state park is a gently rolling to hilly area of old dunes covered mostly in deciduous forests along with small stands of conifers. There is one small pond but little fishing activity within the park and no boat launching facilities.

Camping: Petoskey has 170 modern sites divided between two campgrounds. To the south is Tannery Creek Campground, a semi-open area with 100 sites and paved pads, making it ideal for large recreational vehicles. There are no sites directly on Little Traverse Bay but all of them are only a staircase and a short walk away.

The Dunes Campground is located in a well forested area with seventy sites that

Shifting dunes invade a campsite at Petoskey State Park

PETOSKEY STATE PARK

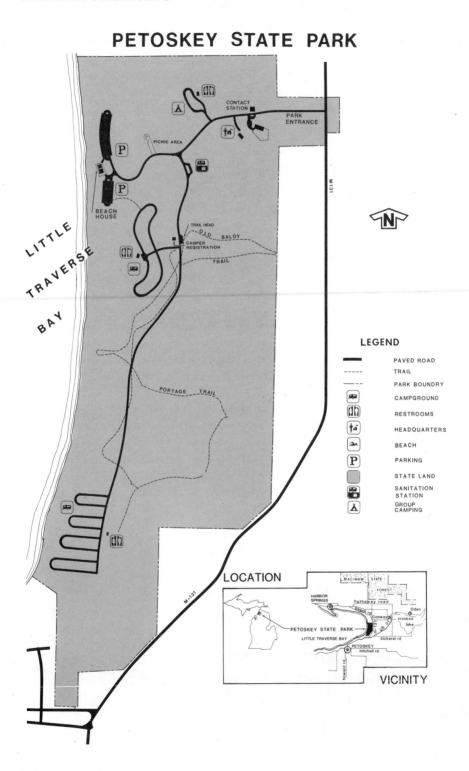

Hunting for Petoskey stones in Petoskey State Park

are shaded and, most unusual for popular state parks, offer considerable privacy between campers. Many sites are surrounded by migrating dunes, and in several places retaining walls have been constructed to keep sand out of a site. The camp-grounds fill up daily from July 4 weekend to mid-August and are up to 85 percent filled through Labor Day. Petoskey also has an organization camp.

Hiking: The park has 3.5 miles of trails along two loops that begin at a trailhead near the Dunes Campground. Old Baldy Trail is a 0.7-mile trek to the top of an old dune where hikers are greeted with a good view of Little Traverse Bay. The 30-minute walk involves some climbing, but stairways assist hikers. The other loop is Portage Trail, an easy hike of 2.8 miles that swings by Lake Michigan, a small in-land lake, and Tannery Creek Campground before returning to the trailhead. The loop takes about 1.5 hours to complete and can be picked up from either campground.

Cycling: Crossing the entrance of the park is a portion of Harbor Trailway, a paved path that someday might connect Charlevoix to Harbor Springs. Presently the trail extends only a mile south of the park and then resumes after Bay View to the waterfront of Petoskey.

Day-Use Facilities: Petoskey has a wide, sandy beach along Little Traverse Bay, bordered in many places by partly wooded dunes. The scenic shoreline, its close proximity to major resort towns, and the possibility of finding the state stone make it a popular place. The day-use parking area holds 300 cars. Other facilities include a bathhouse and a small picnic area separated from the beach by a line of low dunes.

Winter Activities: Nordic skiing along the Portage Trail is the park's main attraction in the winter. Although the trail is not machine groomed, it is a popular area for locals and thus usually tracked. Skiers can park at the trailhead near Dunes Campground. The 2.5-mile ski trail has some gently rolling sections but is ideal for novice skiers. There is no ski rental concession in the park, but shops in Petoskey rent equipment.

Access and Information: The park is 4.5 miles north of downtown Petoskey. Follow US 31 to M-119 and then go north (left) for 1.5 miles to the park's entrance. For more information, contact Petoskey State Park, 2475 M-119, Petoskey, MI 49770; or call (231) 347-2311.

Hartwick Pines State Park

▲ The Monarch has died. The star attraction of the Hartwick Pines State Park, and easily the most recognized and beloved tree in Michigan, was a 350-year white pine that somehow escaped the swinging axes of the lumberjacks who marched through Crawford County in the late nineteenth century. In 1996, however, park naturalists noticed that what little green the tree had produced the year before had not returned.

Basically, the 155-foot-tall white pine, the largest tree most people ever saw in Michigan, died of old age, but not until it had overwhelmed millions with its size and grandeur.Children especially would stand and gaze at that massive trunk and unknowingly gain a sense, and maybe even an appreciation, for old-growth forests. Plans are underway to crown a new Monarch, a 130-foot-tall white pine with a diameter of almost 44 inches, reroute the Virgin Pines Trail toward the tree, and erect a fence around it.

For most park visitors, such white pines are their only glimpse, other than faded photographs, of the towering trees that blanketed Michigan a century ago. The loggers, lumber barons, and pines made Michigan the greatest lumber-producing state in the country between 1869 and 1900. There were an estimated 700 logging camps, and more wealth was made off of Michigan white pine than by miners in the Klondike gold rush. By 1910 only a few parcels of virgin pine had escaped the cutting, and by far the most popular one is this 49-acre tract north of Grayling, the heart of Hartwick Pines State Park. Laid among the pines is a reconstructed logging camp, big wheels, and a logging museum that recounts Michigan's White Pine Era from 1840 to 1910.

The interpretive area is fascinating, but there is more to this Crawford County state park than virgin white pine. At 9,672 acres, Hartwick is the largest unit in the Lower Peninsula and has a diverse terrain that includes four small lakes, stands

Old logging equipment, Hartwick Pines State Park

of virgin jack pine and hemlock, and rolling high hills that overlook the broad valley of the AuSable River's East Branch. The park offers activities year-round, everything from morel mushroom hunting and trout fishing in the spring to mountain biking in the summer and Nordic skiing in the winter. It draws 225,000 visitors annually.

Camping: Hartwick Pines State Park's campground was rebuilt in 1994 and is now located in a much more isolated corner of the park. The modern campground is almost twice as large as its former size, with 116 sites. Most of them are situated in an open grassy area, but along the edge are wooded sites that offer a surprising amount of privacy for a modern campground.

Along with sanitation for RVers and modern restroom/shower buildings, the campground also has paved sites, many of them drive-through for larger recreational vehicles. Hartwick Pines is the only state park facility that offers full hookups, with both water and electricity at thirty-six sites. The campground is filled every weekend from late June through early October when the fall colors are peaking, and is 70 to 80 percent filled midweek throughout most of the summer.

Cabin: Hartwick Pines has a rustic cabin near Glory and Bright Lakes with a foot trail that connects it to the rest of the park. The stone and log cabin sleeps six and is just off M-93.

Hiking: Hartwick has 6 miles of designated foot trails with the longest walk being the AuSable River Trail. The 3-mile loop has a trailhead at the day-use parking area and begins by immediately crossing M-93 and then Scenic Trail Drive. The trail passes through a hardwood and conifer forest, twice crosses the East Branch of the AuSable River, a noted trout stream, and at one point reaches the height of 1,240 feet for a good view of the river valley before looping back. The Mertz Grade Trail shares the same trailhead with the AuSable River Trail but swings south after crossing M-93. This 2-mile trail loops around Hartwick Lake before recrossing M-93. The other designated foot trail is the popular Virgin Pines Trail, a mile loop through the tract of old-growth white pines. All three paths are marked with numbered stops and corresponding trail brochures.

Mountain Biking: The ski trails at Hartwick Pines are open to mountain bikers spring through fall and make for a 10-mile system that basically forms a 7.5-mile loop with two crossover spurs. The route is a wide path through a rolling forested terrain and is rated for beginning and intermediate bikers. The bike trailhead is in the day-use area parking lot at the end of the park road.

Interpretive Center: The park's stand of virgin pine is best enjoyed by first visiting the Michigan Forest Visitors Center. The history and growth of the Michigan forest is traced through a number of hands-on, computer generated exhibits, displays, and photos of the men who cut the trees and the camps they lived in. An especially popular exhibit is the talking "Living Tree." There is also a 105-seat auditorium that features a multi-image slide show on the history of logging. During the summer the center is open 8:00 A.M. to 7:00 P.M. daily except Monday. After Labor Day, the center switches to winter hours: 9:00 A.M. to 4:00 P.M. Tuesday through Sunday. From the interpretive center you then follow Virgin Pines Trail, a paved path that winds through this rare stand of white pine. Along the way you pass a "big wheel," the device used to haul the massive logs out of the forest, the Monarch, and a reconstructed logging camp of several buildings that was built by the CCC. Within the camp there is a bunkhouse and mess hall you can walk through, the camp boss' quarters, a blacksmith's shop, and a steam-powered sawmill. The park sponsors three major events during the summer in the interpretive area. Guides in period costumes give demonstrations in logging techniques and camp life. The events are Old Time Days in June, Milltown Festival in July, and Black Iron Days in August.

Day-Use Facilities: Hartwick Pines has no swimming area but there is a picnic area with shelters at the end of the park road. Departing from the parking lot are the trailheads for the Mertz Grade Trail, AuSable River Trail, and mountain biking system.

Fishing: The East Branch of the AuSable River, which flows 16 miles from its source southwest into the main stream, is especially scenic in Hartwick Pines. Here the river is a crystal-clear stream that gurgles over gravel beds and undercuts the banks around deadheads and trees. Too narrow to be a good canoeing waterway, the East Branch is an excellent brook trout stream, overlooked by many anglers. Fly fishers turn to short rods in the 6- to 7-foot length and use roll casts to work the East Branch, which is 15 to 20 feet wide in most places. Most anglers, however, are spin or bait fishermen using worms to entice the brookies or the brown trout that have been known to exceed 20 inches at times. Access to the river is along the Scenic Trail, which crosses it twice, or the AuSable River Trail.

The state park also has four inland lakes of which three are stocked annually. Bright and Glory Lakes lie side by side off M-93, south of the park entrance, and possess a good population of smallmouth bass and are stocked with trout. There is an unimproved boat launch at each lake and a fishing pier on Bright Lake. Hartwick Lake is a short walk from either M-93 or the campground and is stocked with a hybrid strain of sunfish.

Scenic Drive: The Scenic Trail is an 8-mile drive through a variety of vegetation,

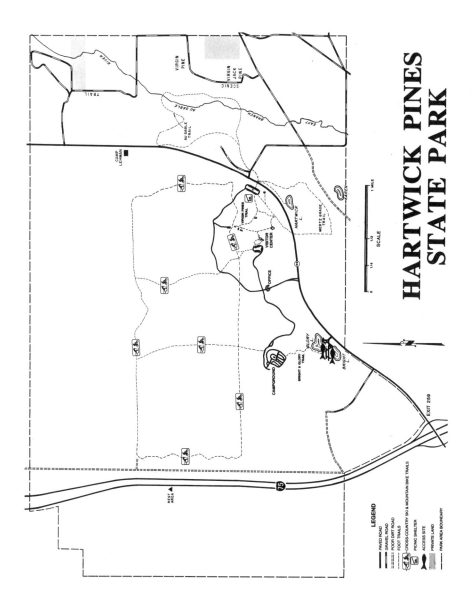

HARTWICK PINES STATE PARK

LEGEND

PAVED ROAD
GRAVEL ROAD
POOR DIRT ROAD
FOOT TRAILS
CROSS-COUNTRY SKI & MOUNTAIN BIKE TRAILS
PICNIC SHELTER
ACCESS SITE
PRIVATE LAND
PARK AREA BOUNDARY

SCALE

0   1/4   1/2   1 MILE

topography, and history. Twice the gravel road crosses the East Branch, providing access for trout fishermen, and it also passes through virgin stands of jack pine, where whitetail deer are often spotted. The drive begins across M-93 at the day-use picnic area and ends 3 miles north of the park entrance.

Winter Activities: Hartwick Pines has 10 miles of groomed ski trails that form three loops. The longest and most challenging is the 7.5-mile Weary Legs Trail, while the 5-mile Deer Run Trail and the 3-mile Aspen Trail are rated for novice to intermediate skiers. The ski trailhead is in the parking lot of the interpretive center, which doubles as a warming shelter in the winter. There is no ski rental concession in the park, but the trail system is connected to Forbush Corner (517-348-5989), one of the state's top touring centers. Forbush Corner rents out equipment and has its own network of trails that are groomed for both skating and striding. There is also snowmobiling in the state park on a separate trail system.

Access and Information: From I-75 north of Grayling, take exit 259 and head north on M-93 for 3 miles to the park entrance. For more information, contact Hartwick Pines State Park, Route 3, P.O. Box 3840, Grayling, MI 49738; or call (517) 348-7068.

Otsego Lake State Park

The name Otsego is Iroquois for "beautiful water," and came to Michigan from New York, where there is another Otsego Lake. But at one end of Michigan's Otsego Lake is a large rock where Native Americans once gathered to trade goods, and eventually the meaning of the name evolved to "place where meetings are held." Today both seem appropriate when describing Otsego Lake State Park.

The 62-acre unit in Otsego County includes 0.75 mile of shoreline along the scenic lake that features a distinct point forested in conifers and hardwoods, a wide, sandy beach, and a line of low bluffs overlooking the water. The park, which is entirely developed, is also a meeting place, as it is ideally located for travelers heading north on I-75. Otsego draws more than 100,000 visitors a year, most of them campers who arrive during the traditional summer season.

Camping: The park maintains a campground of 203 modern sites situated along two loops. The area is well shaded, but the sites are close together. None of them are directly on the lake, but a row of sites in the southern loop overlooks the water, including one with a mini-cabin in it. Part of the northern loop is situated on a line of low bluffs where stairways lead to the shoreline below. Due to its proximity to I-75, the campground is filled almost daily from July to mid-August. Otsego also has two organization camps for groups.

Fishing: The 1,972-acre Otsego Lake is often regarded as one of the best smallmouth bass lakes in the county and is stocked with tiger muskies as well. Anglers also pursue perch during the summer and through the ice in the winter, and do well with crappies in the spring as well as bluegill and northern pike. The park maintains a fish-cleaning station along the northern loop of the campground and an improved boat launch with parking for nineteen trailer rigs.

Day-Use Facilities: Within Otsego there is a wide, sandy beach that extends around the point. The point itself is a beautiful picnic area with tables near the shoreline and a view of the water on three sides. The day-use area also has a playground and a bathhouse, and a concession that rents boats with motors, canoes, paddleboats, and a pontoon boat.

Otesgo Lake

Access and Information: The park is 7 miles south of Gaylord. From I-75 go west at exit 270 where you immediately enter the town of Waters. Turn north (right) onto Old US 27 and follow signs to the park entrance. For more information, contact Otsego State Park, 7136 Old US 27 South, Gaylord, MI 49735; or call (517) 732-5485.

Burt Lake State Park

The heart of Michigan's Inland Waterway is Burt Lake, and located at its southern end in Cheboygan County, almost in the middle of this historic water route, is Burt Lake State Park. The Inland Waterway is a 40-mile chain of four lakes and three rivers that was first used by Native Americans as a safer and shorter alternative than paddling along the coast from Lake Michigan to Lake Huron. The route actually begins at Conway on Crooked Lake, 6 miles from Petoskey on Little Traverse Bay, and ends with the Cheboygan River flowing into the Straits of Mackinac.

Today the popular route is paddled, sailed, and motored in recreational vessels and houseboats, many of which stop at Burt Lake State Park, one of two state parks along the route. The 406-acre unit is bordered on one side by Burt Lake and to the north by the Sturgeon River. It draws 250,000 visitors a year, primarily during the summer, when people are attracted to the park's campground or the beach in its day-use area.

Camping: Burt Lake has 300 modern sites in a campground that is lightly forested in hardwoods. There are no sites on the lake, but all are a short walk from the beach in the day-use area. Campers have their own boat launch at the west end of the campground. Burt Lake also features a rent-a-tipi and a mini-cabin and maintains an organization camp for youth groups. The campground is filled most weekends July through mid-August and often in the middle of the week as well. Families interested in the rent-a-tipi or mini-cabin should book it 3 to 4 weeks in advance.

Hiking: Burt Lake only has one trail, a half mile long, that departs from the boat launch parking area and runs along the Sturgeon River.

Fishing: The 17,260-acre Burt Lake is the fourth-largest lake in the state and one of the most heavily fished. It's regarded as an excellent walleye fishery, and anglers are most productive with the gamefish from late May to mid-July and again in the fall. The lake, which is almost 10 miles long and 73 feet at its deepest point, also supports a healthy population of perch as well as largemouth and smallmouth bass, rock bass and other panfish, and northern pike to a lesser degree. There are also steelhead and brown trout in the lake, but many anglers wait until spring or fall to fish for them in the Sturgeon River, using nightcrawlers, floating Rapalas baits, or spawn bags. Along with a ramp in the campground, the park maintains a boat launch, where there is parking for fifty vehicles.

Day-Use Facilities: There is a beautiful, sandy beach along the entire length of the park between the two boat launches that is bordered by a picnic area in a stand of towering hardwoods and pine trees. The day-use area has parking for 200 vehicles, while other facilities include a bathhouse, a shelter that can be rented, and a

Wake-robin

park store that rents rowboats, motors, and paddleboats daily from Memorial Day to Labor Day.

Scenic Viewpoint: Along M-68, south of the park entrance, there is a scenic viewpoint with an 18-foot observation tower that provides a good view of the park and Burt Lake. Originally, some thirty years ago, this was just a scenic pullover until the growth of the trees obscured the fine view and necessitated the construction of the elevated platform.

Access and Information: From I-75 take exit 310 at Indian River and head west on M-68 (also called Old US 27) as it curves around the southern end of Burt Lake. The park entrance is reached in 1.5 miles. For information, contact Burt Lake State Park, 6635 State Park Drive, Indian River, MI 49749; or call (231) 238-9392.

Aloha State Park

Also located on the northern portion of the Inland Waterway is Aloha State Park, a 122-acre unit that has a scattering of a few large ash and many smaller ones that were planted in the 1960s—but no palm trees. The park picked up its unusual name in the 1800s, when the president of the Detroit and Mackinac Railroad, having just returned from a trip to Hawaii, named his newly built train station near Mullett Lake Aloha Depot. A small town developed there, and eventually the park, which was established in 1923, picked up the out-of-place name.

Aloha is a totally developed area featuring almost a mile of shoreline along Mullett Lake. It draws 183,000 visitors a year but few during the winter.

Camping: Most of Aloha State Park is a campground, as the park has 287 modern sites located on several loops. The area is well sodded but open with little shade or privacy. On the northern loop there is a row of sites directly on Mullett Lake, while more sites in the lower half of the park overlook a large boat basin that flows into the inland lake. The campground is generally filled daily for three weeks in July, during weekends through mid-August, and always on Labor Day weekend due to the Mackinac Bridge Walk.

Fishing: Mullett Lake, a 16,630-acre body of water, is probably best known for a 193-pound lake sturgeon that was speared in 1974, the largest fish ever taken from Michigan waters. But sturgeon can only be caught during a one-month season in February. In the summer anglers seek out northern pike, yellow perch, smallmouth bass, and especially walleye. DNR fisheries biologists have in the past rated Mullett Lake as one of the top walleye fisheries in the state. The lake, which is 148 feet deep at one point, has also been stocked with walleyes as well as brown and rainbow trout. Aloha has an improved launch at the east end of its boat basin and a fish-cleaning station nearby. Although piers are not nearly as productive, anglers fish off the park's three piers: two on each side of where the basin enters the lake and the third an old wooden jetty near the day-use beach.

Day-Use Facilities: Aloha's day-use area includes a wide, grassy picnic area with tables, grills, and a shelter that can be rented. But the park has only a small swimming area on the lake, with a narrow strip of beach.

Access and Information: The park is located 9 miles south of Cheboygan. Head south on M-27 for 4 miles and then veer south on M-33 for another 5 miles to M-212. Turn west (right) on M-212 and follow it 0.75 mile to the park entrance. For more information, contact Aloha State Park, 4347 Third Street, Cheboygan, MI 49721; or call (231) 625-2522.

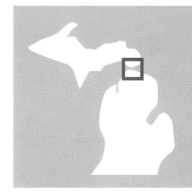

Straits of Mackinac

Wilderness State Park

⚑ Wilderness State Park in Emmet County may have cabins for rent, a boat launch, two campgrounds, and a day-use area on Lake Michigan, but for most visitors the outstanding feature is its undeveloped nature. The 8,286-acre unit, the second-largest state park in the Lower Peninsula, contains more than 30 miles of shoreline, a dedicated natural area, and a vast network of trails that attracts those who want to photograph wildflowers, identify birds, or spend a day hiking through its forested terrain of pines and hardwoods.

Michigan began acquiring the land for the park in the early 1900s and in 1922 named it Emmet State Game Area before dedicating it as Wilderness State Park in the mid-1930s. Although its outdoor center was used at one time by the U.S. Navy and later as a prison camp in the 1950s, the park itself has always remained undeveloped. Today the park is one of the largest undeveloped tracts in the Lower Peninsula, featuring 5 miles of sandy beach along Sturgeon Bay, as well as the islands and Waugoshance Point, which separate the bay from the Straits of Mackinac.

The point, a designated natural area, is an especially popular place for birders, as over 100 species either migrate through the area or nest here, including the rare piping plover. The park is also a haven for whitetail deer, black bear, and beaver, and someday possibly wolves. In 1997, a Coast Guard pilot sighted a pair of wolves along the shoreline of the park after they had apparently made the 5-mile trek across the frozen Straits of Mackinac. As packs increase in the Upper Peninsula, many biologists believe it is only a matter of time before they move permanently into this corner of the state. Wilderness State Park draws 94,000 campers and 77,000 day visitors annually with a variety of year-round activities that range from kayaking and hiking to mountain biking and winter camping.

Camping: The park has 250 modern sites divided between two campgrounds. The Lakeshore Campground is situated along Big Stone Bay in a semi-open area,

Cross-country skiers on Mackinac Island

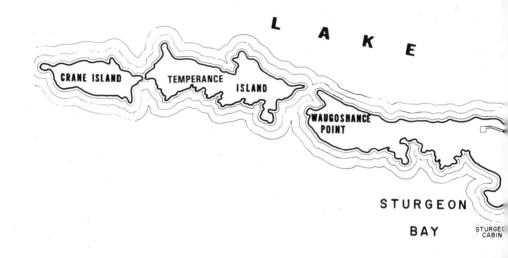

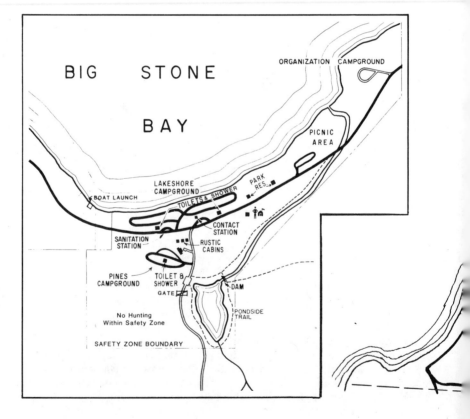

WILDERNESS STATE PARK

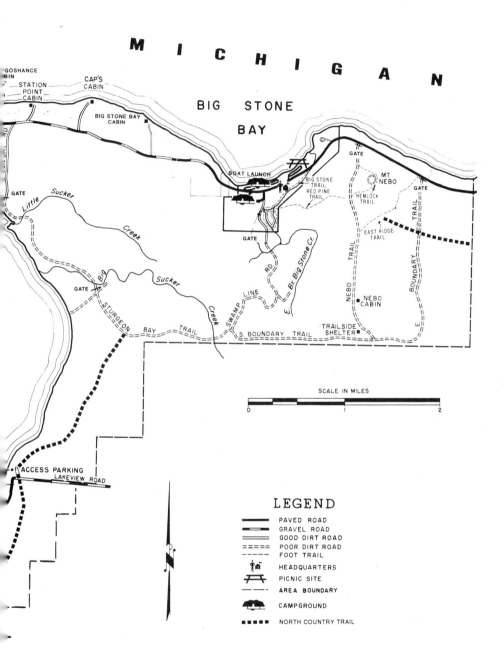

M I C H I G A N

GOSHANCE
BIN
STATION
POINT
CABIN
CAP'S
CABIN

BIG STONE BAY
CABIN

BIG STONE BAY

BOAT LAUNCH

GATE

BIG STONE TRAIL
RED PINE TRAIL

MT. NEBO

HEMLOCK TRAIL

GATE

GATE

Sucker

Little

Creek

EAST RIDGE TRAIL

GATE

Big

Sucker

Creek

SWAMP LINE

RD.

E. Br Big Stone Cr.

NEBO

TRAIL

NEBO CABIN

BOUNDARY

GATE

STURGEON BAY TRAIL

S. BOUNDARY TRAIL

TRAILSIDE SHELTER

E.

SCALE IN MILES

0   1   2

ACCESS PARKING
LAKEVIEW ROAD

LEGEND

▬▬▬▬	PAVED ROAD
══════	GRAVEL ROAD
═══════	GOOD DIRT ROAD
≡≡≡≡≡	POOR DIRT ROAD
- - - -	FOOT TRAIL
🚻	HEADQUARTERS
⛱	PICNIC SITE
— - —	AREA BOUNDARY
⛺	CAMPGROUND
▪▪▪▪▪	NORTH COUNTRY TRAIL

Father and son fish for smallmouth bass at Wilderness State Park

and within the 150 sites is a row right off the beach. Pines Campground, across Wilderness Park Drive, was rebuilt in the early 1990s and now has 100 sites, most of them with paved pads and situated in a grove of mature pines. Both campgrounds tend to be filled weekends from early July to mid-August but usually have sites available midweek throughout the summer. The exception is the last week of August through Labor Day, when the park is filled daily due to the Mackinac Bridge Walk. The park also maintains an organization camp on the shores of Big Stone Bay.

Hiking: Wilderness State Park has more than 20 miles of designated foot trails throughout the park. Many of them are old forest roads that are closed to vehicles by locked gates. The longest, Sturgeon Bay Trail, can be combined with Swamp Line to form a 5-mile hike from Sturgeon Cabin to a parking area at Goose Pond. Other tracks that begin off Wilderness Park Drive are the Boundary Trail, a 3.5-mile walk to its junction with Swamp Line, and Nebo Trail, a 2-mile route to the halfway point of Boundary Trail. Near the junction of Nebo and Boundary Trails, there is a trailside shelter for day-use only. Another popular hike is from the parking lot at the west end of Wilderness Park Drive to Waugoshance Point, a one-way, 2-mile trek along a pebbled and rocky shoreline. Check with DNR staff first, as parts of the shoreline are closed in spring and early summer when the endangered piping plover is nesting.

Goose Pond is the trailhead for a number of short nature trails. Pondside Trail is a quarter-mile walk around the pond, while heading east is Red Pine Trail, a 1.25-mile walk to Nebo Trail. Here hikers can continue along Hemlock Trail, a half-mile walk that climbs to the top of Mount Nebo, before returning to Nebo Trail. Hikers can combine Red Pine, Hemlock, a portion of the road, and Big Stone Trail to form a 3.5-mile loop from the parking area near Goose Pond. Also passing through the park is a 5.5-mile segment of the North Country Trail, the national scenic trail that some-day will extend from North Dakota to New York. The NCT enters the park from the east and merges into the East Ridge Trail. It then follows a portion of Nebo Trail, Boundary Trail, and Sturgeon Trail before splitting off and continuing south along Sturgeon Bay. The NCT leaves Wilderness State Park at its southernmost border.

Mountain Biking: The two-lane tracks are open to mountain bikers for almost 11 miles of nontechnical riding in a wildernesslike setting. The longest loop is an 8-mile ride that combines Boundary Trail, Sturgeon Trail, and Wilderness Park Drive, but keep in mind that you'll encounter several wet areas. The driest loop is the 6-mile ride of Nebo Trail, a portion of Boundary Trail, and Swamp Line Road. Mountain bikers are not allowed on the nature trails or North Country Trail.

Cabins: The park has six rustic cabins scattered throughout the park and three 24-bed bunkhouses located in an outdoor center near the campgrounds. Four of the trailside cabins are situated on the Straits of Mackinac and a short walk from Wilderness Park Drive. Cap's Cabin and Waugoshance Cabin sleep eight each, while Station Point Cabin, an old log structure with wooden floors, has four bunks. Sturgeon Cabin, a short walk from the end of Sturgeon Bay Road, sleeps five and is a favorite among anglers during the spring for the nearby bass fishing in the bay. Nebo Cabin, another log structure that sleeps five, is reached only after a 2-mile hike along Nebo Trail. All cabins are well used and should be reserved far in advance.

Nebo Cabin in the winter, Wilderness State Park

Fishing: The park's most noted fishing opportunity is for smallmouth bass in the spring and early summer in the north end of Sturgeon Bay. This stretch, especially along the south side of Waugoshance Point, is a spawning area for bass, and fishermen use waders and rig nightcrawlers to work the beds near the shoreline. Bass season in Michigan opens the Saturday before Memorial Day. The park also has an improved boat launch located just west of Lakeshore Campground.

Day-Use Facilities: The day-use area is located just east of the campgrounds on Big Stone Bay and includes tables (some right on the shoreline), vault toilets, and a wide stretch of sandy beach.

Winter Activities: Skiers can enjoy 12 miles of groomed trails during the winter. The most popular run is a 6-mile loop that follows Nebo Trail, a portion of the Boundary Trail and Swamp Line for an easy ski with only a moderate hilly terrain to contend with. The cabins are also well used during the winter. Getting to Nebo is a 2-mile trip and Waugoshance Cabin a 2.5-mile run, as Park Drive is not plowed beyond the end of the pavement. The other structures lie along a 12-mile snowmobile trail and can be reached by either skis or snowmobile. Sturgeon Cabin is the longest trip into the park, a 3.5-mile trek; Station Point, 2 miles; and Cap's Cabin, 1.5 miles.

Access and Information: The park's east entrance is 8 miles west of Mackinaw City and is reached by following County Road 81 and continuing west on Wilderness Park Drive after crossing Carp Lake River. There is also an entrance and parking lot at the south end of Sturgeon Bay off Lakeview Road, reached from US 31 by turning west on Gill Road 4 miles south of I-75. For more information, contact Wilderness State Park, P.O. Box 380, Carp Lake, MI 49718; or call (231) 436-5381.

Colonial Michilimackinac State Park

▲ The northern tip of the Lower Peninsula, a point between two Great Lakes, has been a strategic spot throughout history. It was a place where Native Americans naturally congregated and fur traders passed through. French and British troops occupied the spot, and eventually it would become one end of Michigan's most impressive bridge. Today the tip is part of Colonial Michilimackinac State Park, a 25-acre unit in Emmet County that features a reconstructed fort and an incredible view of the straits and the Mackinac Bridge.

Native Americans gathered along the Straits of Mackinac for centuries, and a small trading post appeared in 1715. It became a more substantial fur-trading town, and finally the French built Fort Michilimackinac as a military base from which to attack rebellious Native American tribes, most notably the Fox Indians in Wisconsin. The British took over the fort in 1761 after winning the French and Indian War and, despite its superb military design, were uncomfortable defending it from the approaching Americans during the Revolutionary War. In 1780 Lieutenant Governor Patrick Sinclair decided to move the British post to Mackinac Island and troops began dismantling the fort. What they couldn't ship across the channel, they burned.

Using information collected from archaeological digs and historical records, Colonial Michilimackinac was reconstructed in 1959. Combined with the maritime area and museum, the park presents a vivid lesson in the long history of the Straits of Mackinac, using guides in period dress, live demonstrations, shops and homes with eighteenth-century furnishings, even a military latrine. The park has a picnic area but no camping facilities.

Guides in period costume at Colonial Michilimackinac State Park

Interpretive Centers: Visitors enter the park through its Orientation Center, located beneath the Mackinac Bridge. The center houses a gift shop, displays, exhibits, and a small auditorium where a multi-image slide presentation is given throughout the day.

On the west side of the bridge is the reconstructed Fort Michilimackinac. The fort features eighteen buildings and structures inside or just outside the stockade walls. They include the Northwest Rowhouse, which contains an archaeology exhibit, the Soldier's Barracks with a museum of the fort's history, and the Chevalier House with a display of eighteenth-century weapons and the preserved remains of an original powder magazine. Outside you can explore a Native American encampment, a barnyard and corrals, or a display of birch-bark canoes. Regularly throughout each day, a light and sound show is given at the Church of St. Anne, as well as live demonstrations, musket firings, and cannon salutes within the fort. Also throughout the summer are interpreter-led tours of the fort and a special children's program in which a British soldier, French fur trader, and missionary priest visit with groups of children.

Day-Use Facilities: To the east of the bridge is picturesque Old Mackinac Point Lighthouse, an 1890 tower on "the busiest crossroads of the Great Lakes," and surrounding it is a picnic area with restrooms, tables, and panoramic views of Mackinac Bridge and Mackinac Island.

Access and Information: To reach the park depart I-75 at exit 339 and follow signs to the parking lot and Orientation Center under the Mackinac Bridge. The park is open from mid-May to mid-October. There is a per-person entry fee into the park, and there are also family tickets and package tickets available that allow you entry into Mill Creek and Fort Mackinac on Mackinac Island as well. For more information, contact Mackinac Island State Historic Parks, P.O. Box 370, Mackinac Island, MI 497957-0370; or call (231) 436-5563 or (906) 847-3328.

Historic Mill Creek State Park

▲ When the British moved their military post from Fort Michilimackinac on the mainland to Mackinac Island, they created a huge demand for lumber—more lumber than could possibly be supplied by pitmen and top sawyers, two-man teams sawing logs into planks by hand. Robert Campbell, a Scottish trader, saw a golden opportunity with the construction of the new fort on Mackinac Island and seized it.

In the 1780s he purchased a 640-acre tract of land with the only stream in the area

A top sawyer and pitman demonstrating the two-saw technique at Historic Mill Creek State Park

that had enough power for a mill. He built a 10-foot cedar dam and then constructed an ingenious sawmill, powered by Mill Creek, in which one man and a pair of oxen could cut fifteen to twenty times more planks than the best pitman-top sawyer in Northern Michigan. Later Campbell added a grist mill, blacksmith shop, and orchards, and the area became one of the earliest industrial centers in the Midwest. The Campbell heirs sold the mill in 1819, and twenty years later the site was abandoned as being unprofitable. But in 1972 Mill Creek was "rediscovered," and since then archaeologists have located the dam, two homes, and a barn. Archaeological digs continue, but Mill Creek State Park, a 625-acre unit, was opened in 1984 after a working duplicate of the 1790 water-powered sawmill was built. Like Colonial Michilimackinac, there are no camping facilities, but Mill Creek does have an extensive nature trail system.

Interpretive Centers: Visitors enter the park through its Orientation Center, which houses a museum dedicated to the eighteenth-century industrial center, a book store, and an auditorium. A slide and sound presentation is given throughout the day that further explains the role Mill Creek played in the construction on Mackinac Island. The main attraction in the park is the Water-Powered Sawmill, located below the mill dam. Demonstrations are given hourly that show how a system of wheels and gears used water power to cut the huge logs into planks. Boards that are cut during the demonstrations will be used in the future to reconstruct other homes and workshops uncovered in the area.

Hiking: Although many visitors overlook it, Mill Creek has 600 acres of undeveloped wooded terrain that is laced by almost 4 miles of nature trails. The system is composed of five loops that skirt the bluffs on both sides of Mill Creek, allowing families to enjoy easy treks of a half mile to 2.5 miles in length. The longest and the most intriguing loop is the 2.5-mile Beaver Pond Trail, which provides access to an active beaver colony in the upper reaches of this historic stream as well as a series of interpretive displays about the animal. The shortest loop is the half-mile Mill Pond Trail that includes two overlooks where, on a clear day, you can view Mackinac Island.

Access and Information: The park is located 3.5 miles south of Mackinaw City on US 23. It is open daily from mid-May to mid-October with extended hours during the summer of 9:00 A.M. to 6:00 P.M. Entry is a per-person or per-family ticket, not a motor vehicle permit. There are also combination tickets that provide entry to Mill Creek, Colonial Michilimackinac, and Fort Mackinac. For more information, contact Mackinac Island State Historic Parks, P.O. Box 370, Mackinac Island, MI 497957-0370; or call (231) 436-7301 or (906) 847-3328.

Mackinac Island State Park

It's called "magical Mackinac." It's the feeling that sweeps over visitors when they step off the ferry onto this 2,000-acre island that has seemingly defied time ever since it was first settled by British troops in 1780. Automobiles were banned from Mackinac Island in 1896 and were replaced by horse-drawn carriages and bicycles. These traditional, and slow, means of transportation, combined with the stunning Victorian architecture of the city of Mackinac Island and the restored British fort, makes it easy for visitors to take a step back in history. Mackinac was first viewed as a military post by Lieutenant Governor Patrick Sinclair, who moved his British troops from Fort Michilimackinac on the Lower Peninsula across the straits in 1780. Sinclair was sure the Americans were on their way and did not want to

MACKINAC ISLAND STATE PARK

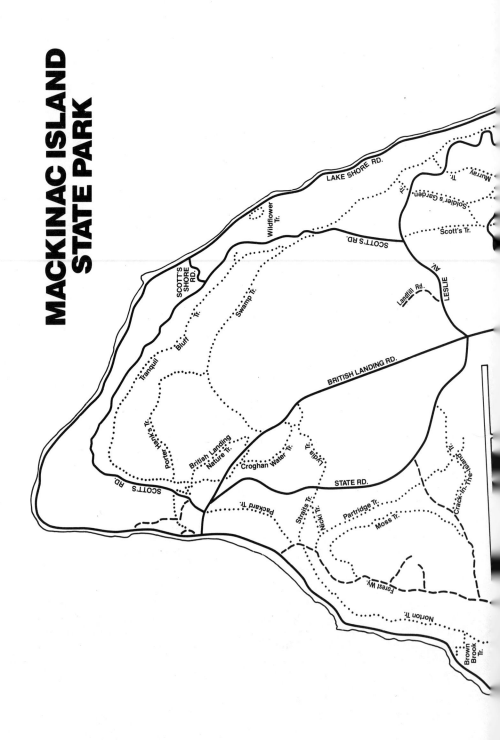

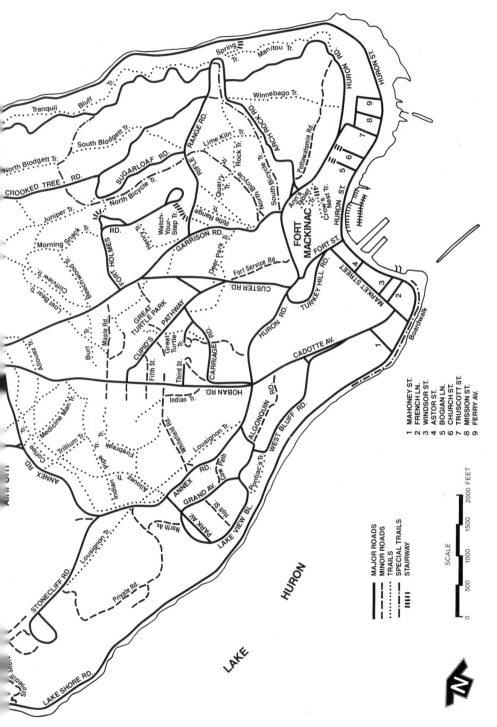

1 MAHONEY ST.
2 FRENCH LN.
3 WINDSOR ST.
4 ASTOR ST.
5 BOGIAN LN.
6 CHURCH ST.
7 TRUSCOTT ST.
8 MISSION ST.
9 FERRY AV.

MAJOR ROADS
MINOR ROADS
TRAILS
SPECIAL TRAILS
STAIRWAY

SCALE

0   500   1000   1500   2000 FEET

Cannon demonstration at Fort Mackinac

defend the mainland fort. The island, with its high limestone bluffs, was better suited for repelling the impending attack. The American troops never came but rather took over the island diplomatically after the Revolutionary War ended.

Then, in one of the most celebrated moments in Mackinac's history, the British recaptured the island during the War of 1812. They totally surprised the American garrison by secretly landing on the northwest shore, a spot now called British Landing, and dragging a cannon across the island to the bluffs above the fort. When the Americans woke up to the sight of a gun aimed at them from above, they gave up without firing a shot. Another treaty passed the island back to the United States, and in 1875 the federal government preserved Mackinac as the country's second national park, only three years after Yellowstone was dedicated. The island was returned to Michigan in 1895, and the legislature preserved it as their first state park.

Almost 83 percent of the island, some 1,800 acres, lies in Mackinac Island State Park, a unit that draws more than a million visitors a year. You cannot drive on Mackinac Island, nor can you drive to it. The DNR Waterways Division maintains a public marina on the island for boaters, but the vast majority of visitors arrive on one of several ferries that connect it to the mainland. There are no camping facilities on Mackinac, but there are numerous hotels, historic inns, and bed and breakfast establishments for overnight lodging.

Cycling: Bicycles can be carried over on the ferries to the island or rented at a number of liveries downtown. There are also two bike shops on the island in case your bike suffers an unexpected breakdown. The most popular ride, one of the most popular in Michigan in fact, is on M-185, also known as Lake Shore Road. The "round-the-shore" trip is an easy 8.4-mile ride that takes visitors along the entire perimeter of the island, passing many of the park's natural features and outstanding shoreline scenery. Another popular trip is to ride "across the Turtle's back" by following Garrison Road and British Landing Road 3 miles north to British Landing, the site of the park's nature center.

Bicyclists share the roads with horses and carriages but have one route set aside just for them. The 2.5-mile paved route begins at the south end of Garrison Road near the fort and is posted as South Bicycle Trail. This leads to Arch Rock, where cyclists then follow a half-mile stretch of Leslie Avenue before looping back to Garrison Road along North Bicycle Trail.

Hiking: In the center of the island is a vast network of trails that are used by hikers, mountain bikers, and equestrians. The longest and most scenic trek on the island is enjoyed by combining Manitou Trail with Tranquil Bluff Trail. The 4-mile walk begins off Huron Road (not to be confused with Huron Street in the downtown area) southeast of the fort where Manitou Trail extends north a half mile to Arch Rock. You then pick up Tranquil Bluff Trail at Arch Rock and continue north for another 3.5 miles to end just up the road from British Landing. Both trails skirt the limestone bluffs on the east side of the island and provide excellent views of Lake Huron. There are also two nature trails with interpretive displays on the island. Along the east shore with a trailhead on M-185 is the Wildflower Nature Trail, a quarter-mile walk around a pond and cedar swamp. This trail is best enjoyed in early summer when many of the rare orchids and endangered flowers are in bloom, including yellow lady's slipper. Departing from the British Landing Nature Center is the British Landing Nature Trail, a half-mile path that features twenty interpretive stops.

Mountain Biking: In recent years, more and more mountain bikers have discovered the interior trails of Mackinac Island State Park. There is little rhyme or reason in how the trails are laid out and most of them are short segments, forcing you to stop often at intersections and ponder which direction to head. Some trails, like Manitou and Tranquil Bluff Trails, are technical and challenging rides, but most of them are only moderately difficult. The trails with the greatest elevation change are those surrounding Fort Holmes, including Henry Trail, Beechwood Trail, and Morning Snack Trail. Most of the bike liveries on the island are now renting mountain bikes as well as road bikes.

Equestrian Facilities: The oldest horse livery in the country, predating the Civil War, is Mackinac Island Horse Carriages (906-847-3323). The livery offers both taxi services and 2-hour tours of the island. Other liveries offer drive-yourself carriages, hourly carriage rental, and saddle horses. Official tours and horse taxis are based downtown, while private liveries are available at the foot of Marquette Park at the corner of Front and Huron Streets. The state park provides a current list of horse and bicycle liveries.

Interpretive Center: Fort Mackinac is the most noted historic landmark on the island. Open from May to mid-October from 9:00 A.M. until 6:00 P.M., the fort features almost twenty historic buildings and structures within its walls. Among them is the Officers' Stone Quarters, built in 1781, the oldest building on Mackinac Island and the site of the Fort Tea Room, where visitors enjoy lunch and spectacular views on the terrace. Each building has interpretive displays that focus on a particular aspect of life in the military fort, while guides in period dress lead tours of them and perform live demonstrations including musket firings and cannon salutes.

Outside the fort, the state park maintains six other museums: Mission Church, the oldest surviving church in Michigan, Indian Dormitory with displays and craft demonstrations on Native American cooking and weaving, Biddle House, McGulpin House, Beaumont Memorial, and Benjamin Blacksmith Shop. All of them are in the downtown area and within easy walking distance of the fort.

At British Landing is the British Landing Nature Center, which features displays and a naturalist who conducts programs and leads hikes daily from June 15 to Labor Day.

Arch Rock, Mackinac Island (Photo courtesy Mackinac Island State Park Commission)

Natural Attractions: The limestone that enticed the British to move their fort across the Straits of Mackinac has also graced Mackinac Island with several unusual prehistoric geological formations. The most impressive by far, and the reason most people venture beyond the fudge shops on main street, is Arch Rock. The natural bridge stands 150 feet above Lake Huron and is almost a perfect 50-foot-wide arch. It was created 4,000 years ago when the higher levels of the Great Lake dissolved the softer materials of what was then a bluff. As the lake eroded away the base, the soft rock in the middle crumbled into the water, leaving the firm Breccia limestone arch standing.

Most people follow South Bicycle Trail or Arch Rock Road through the interior of the park to see the arch. But you can also reach it from Lake Shore Road via a long stairway of 192 steps. At the top are restrooms and observation platforms from which you can peer through the arch itself and see cyclists far below on Lake Shore Road.

Also located on the trails and roads of Mackinac Island State Park are Sugar Loaf, a 75-foot-high limestone stack, Skull Cave, and Devil's Kitchen. There's even a Lover's Leap, a limestone pillar that rises 145 feet above Lake Huron, where, yes, a Native American maiden jumped to her death over a boyfriend.

Scenic Viewpoints: Even if you don't venture into the fort, walk the long ramp to the South Sally Port entrance. The view of the downtown area and busy harbor are worth the climb up. An even better view is obtained at Fort Holmes, the highest point of the island and the spot where the British set up a six-pound cannon and re-took the fort from the Americans in 1812 without firing a shot. The fort is reached either by Fort Holmes Road or a 137-step staircase off Rifle Range Road.

Winter Activities: Mackinac Island is Michigan's most unusual Nordic skiing destination. After the first of the year, skiers fly to the state park on small planes out of St. Ignace and then ride horse-drawn sleighs from the island airstrip to the down-town area where a handful of inns and bed-and-breakfasts remain open. The island is divided into two sections with snowmobilers restricted to the western half and M-185. Cross-country skiers enjoy the trails on the east side, which include such noted attractions as Arch Rock, Sugar Loaf, and the view point from Fort Holmes. A small network of trails are groomed and tracked, with the heart of the system being the 2.5-mile loop formed by South and North Bicycle Trails. Many other trails are skier-set by locals. Between the 400 year-round residents who use snowmobiles for transportation and the safaris of sleds visiting from the mainland, Mackinac Island is also a haven of snowmobilers. Most recreational snowmobilers arrive via the ice trail from State Street in St. Ignace and then follow M-185 around the island. For transportation in the winter, call Great Lakes Air Service at (906) 643-7327. For a list of year-round accommodations, call the Mackinac Island Chamber of Commerce at (906) 847-3783.

Access and Information: Three companies provide ferry transportation from both the Upper and Lower Peninsulas. From Mackinaw City, Arnold Transit (906-847-3351), Shepler's Mackinac Island Ferry (616-436-5023), and Star Line (906-643-7635) run the 8 miles across the straits from mid-May through mid-October. They also maintain ferries in St. Ignace and make the 5-mile trip from mid-April to early January.

Near the ferry docks the park maintains a visitors center, but for more information or a list of accommodations on the island in advance, contact Mackinac Island Historic State Parks, P.O. Box 370, Mackinac Island, MI 49757-0370; or call (906) 847-3328.

Straits State Park

Father Jacques Marquette, having already founded Sault Ste. Marie, Michigan's oldest settlement, paddled with a group of Ottawa and Huron Indians from western Lake Superior to what is now downtown St. Ignace in 1671. He established a mission and left with Louis Jolliet in 1673 to search out the "Great Mississippi River." Father Marquette never returned to St. Ignace, as he died on the Lake Michigan shoreline en route back to his mission.

But two years after his death, Native Americans recovered his remains and buried them beneath the Mission Chapel in St. Ignace, and 300 years later the city was selected by a presidential committee as the site for a permanent monument honoring the tricentennial of Marquette's discovery of the Mississippi. The impressive interpretive center is part of Straits State Park, a 181-acre unit in Mackinac County that straddles both sides of the Mackinac Bridge in the Upper Peninsula.

Straits State Park draws 163,000 visitors a year, many of them campers who stay at the park while visiting Mackinac Island. It also has a picnic area, 800 feet of shoreline, and a small amphitheater, but its outstanding features are the fine views found throughout the park of the straits, its islands, and the famous bridge across it.

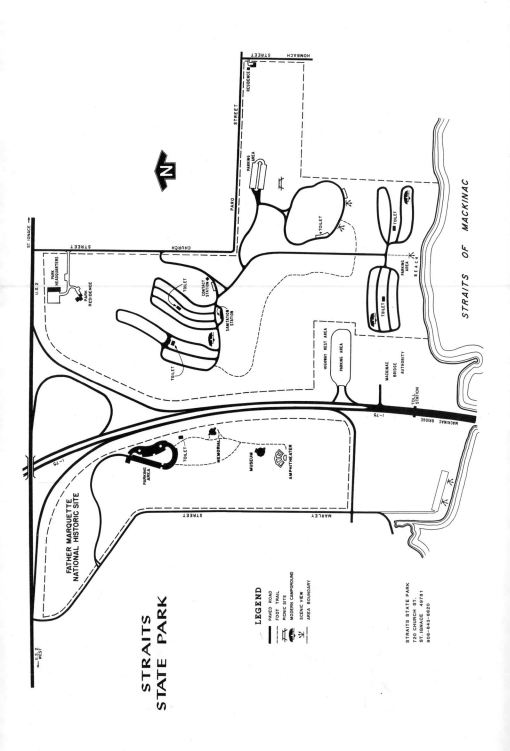

Big Mac from Straits State Park

Camping: The park has 275 modern sites spread out in four campgrounds. North One and North Two are loops up a hill from the shoreline in a partially open section. Some sites are wooded, while many are well-sodded open areas. The popular campgrounds, always the first to fill, are East Loop and West Loop in a well wooded stretch along the Straits of Mackinac. Both loops have a row of sites right on the water with an incredible view of the bridge while the East Loop has a pair of mini-cabins. Although the average stay of campers is less than 2 days, the facility is filled on weekends, usually by Thursday, from July through the Labor Day holiday.

Interpretive Center: Along with the memorial, the Father Marquette National Historic Site features a museum with displays on the explorers and the Native Americans they encountered, an auditorium with a 16-minute film on the life of the Jesuit priest and, perhaps most intriguing, a replica of Marquette's Mississippi journal in both the original French and an English translation. Here you can flip through the pages and read segments of this man's incredible odyssey.

Nearby there is an overlook with public telescopes for a sweeping view of the Mackinac Bridge and amphitheater, where occasionally programs are held. The historic site is open daily June through Labor Day from 10:00 A.M. to 5:00 P.M.

Day-Use Facilities: Straits State Park has a wooded picnic area with playground equipment, tables, grills, and parking for sixty cars. Situated on a bluff above the shoreline, there are also a number of good views of the bridge and waterway. Although the park's shoreline is not suitable for swimming, it does provide another excellent vantage point to view the straits and Mackinac Island.

Access and Information: To reach the park and campground, from I-75 exit east onto Business I-75 toward St. Ignace after crossing the Mackinac Bridge and then immediately turn south (right) onto Church Street to the posted entrance. Head west on US 2 for the Father Marquette historic site and immediately turn south (left) onto Marley Street to the entrance. For more information, contact Straits State Park, 720 Church Street, St. Ignace, MI 49781-1729; or call (906) 643-8620.

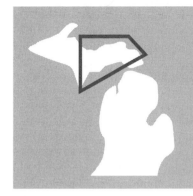

Eastern Upper Peninsula

Brimley State Park

▲ There are seven parks in the Upper Peninsula with shorelines along Lake
⊥ Superior, but Brimley State Park has the distinction of possessing the beach
with the warmest water, maybe the only place where people can swim in this frigid
Great Lake. The 151-acre park in Chippewa County features almost a mile of shoreline along Whitefish Bay, whose shallow bottom and sandbars make for warmer
water in the summer and attract the not-so-timid swimmer.

Brimley is one of the oldest state parks in the Upper Peninsula, having been
established in 1923. The park draws 140,000 visitors a year, mainly for its large
campground and scenic shoreline views of the bay and the Canadian highlands to
the north.

Camping: Brimley has a campground with 270 modern sites in an open area
with a few large shade trees. One row of sites are only a few yards from the
lakeshore. Unseasonably hot weather will fill up the facility, especially with a
heavy influx of Canadians, but during most summers sites are available on both
weekends and weekdays. The park also has a mini-cabin and a rent-a-tent as well as
an organization campground.

Mountain Biking: Just south of the state park and Six Mile Road is the Brimley
Trail, a rail–trail that stretches 32 miles between Sault Ste. Marie and Strongs. Although mostly used by snowmobilers in the winter, the trail is also enjoyed by
mountain bikers in the summer. A one-way trip between the state park and Sault
Ste. Marie to the east is 11 miles.

Fishing: Anglers fish the bay, especially along the western shore around Bay
Mills, for northern pike and walleye. During a few weeks each spring and fall,
perch also congregate in Whitefish Bay. Brimley has a small gravel launch off its
day-use area, but due to sandbars offshore, the park staff recommends it for hand-
carried boats only. There are several private marinas capable of handling larger
boats in Bay Mills.

Lower Falls, Tahquamenon Falls State Park

On the Lake Superior beach at Brimley State Park

Day-Use Facilities: Along with its narrow, sandy beach and shallow swimming area, the park also has a grassy picnic area with a bathhouse and an enclosed shelter that can be rented. The day-use area has a parking lot for 250 cars, with the boat launch located at its north end.

Winter Activities: The park grooms a mile-long ski trail for novice skiers that loops through the campground and the day-use area. Skiers park at a plowed-out campsite, and the fireplace in the enclosed shelter is stocked with wood and used as a warming hut.

Access and Information: From I-75 take exit 386 and head west on M-28 for 7 miles. Turn north (right) on County Road 221 for 3 miles and then east on Six Mile Road in Brimley. The park entrance is a mile east on Six Mile Road. For more information, contact Brimley State Park, P.O. Box 202, Route 1, Brimley, MI 49715-9737; or call (906) 248-3422.

Tahquamenon Falls State Park

Tahquamenon Falls State Park may be second to the Porcupine Mountains in size and eleventh overall in total number of camping sites, but its Upper Falls are the most impressive cascades in Michigan and very possibly the most beloved natural attraction in the state. The falls, nearly 200 feet across with a 50-foot drop, are often cited as the second largest east of the Mississippi River in water volume and third in size, as only Niagara Falls in New York and Cumberland Falls in Kentucky have longer drops. So spectacular are the falls and its wooded setting, especially during fall colors, that it easily makes this unit the most popular park in the Upper Peninsula with more than 500,000 visitors annually.

Everything about Tahquamenon Falls State Park seems to be large. The park contains 38,496 acres and stretches 13 miles from Whitefish Bay in Chippewa County into Luce County. There are 40 miles of hiking trails, almost a dozen lakes and ponds, and three developed areas that contain four campgrounds with 319 sites.

The vast majority of the park is undeveloped, a wilderness setting free from roads, buildings, even powerlines, and the heart of it, the very reason for the spectacular falls, is Tahquamenon River. The river rises from springs north of McMillan and drains an area of more than 820 square miles. It's fed by numerous streams as it winds 94 miles before emptying in Whitefish Bay. The final 16 miles of the river lie in the state park, where it flows over the Upper Falls and then the Lower Falls 4 miles downstream. The amber color of its water is not mud or rust, but tannic acid from the cedar, spruce, and hemlock swamps it flows through.

Native Americans, especially Chippewa tribes, were the first attracted to the Tahquamenon where they farmed, fished, and trapped along its banks. Longfellow immortalized the river as the "marsh of the blueberries," and the poet had Hiawatha build his canoe "by the rushing Tahquamenaw." In the late 1800s the Tahquamenon was the scene of lumbermen who floated thousands of logs to mills. Many became the first permanent settlers of the area.

Today the park is the summer destination for flocks of visitors who travel along M-123 to reach the Upper Falls, Lower Falls, or the Rivermouth Unit on Whitefish Bay. The main attraction is still the marvelous sight and roar of the Upper Falls. But the park lends itself well to a variety of year-round activities including backpacking, hiking, skiing, fishing, and canoeing.

Camping: The park has four separate campgrounds with two in each of its Lower Falls and Rivermouth units and none near the Upper Falls. At the Lower Falls there are 176 modern sites with 81 of them in the Riverbend Campground, including a handful along the river itself. The rest are located in the Overlook Campground, and both areas are well wooded. At the Rivermouth Unit there is a modern campground of 75 sites and a rustic campground of 55 sites. Because the park is a vacation destination, the modern sites are occasionally filled Monday through Wednesday from July through mid-August but available on the weekends. Generally, there are open sites throughout the summer in the rustic facility.

Scenic Viewpoints: The Upper Falls is a day-use area, and from its huge parking lot there is a paved path that winds a quarter mile through a stately beech-maple forest to an impressive overview of the cascades. Here the trail splits, with a fork heading north (right) to a staircase that descends close to the falls' brink. The other spur winds south (left) and ends at the bottom of the gorge via another staircase. The Upper Falls has a maximum flow of more than 50,000 gallons of water per second over the precipice, making the roar of the river impressive. You hear the Upper Falls long before you see them.

In contrast, the Lower Falls lack the overwhelming power of those upstream, but they possess a charm of their own. The Lower Falls are actually a series of seven cascades on both sides of a 25-acre island with a total drop of 30 feet. Access to the falls from the parking area is via a barrier-free, half-mile path. The trail includes an 8-foot-wide ramp that leads from the lot to an observation deck and then continues along the river as the start of the Tahquamenon River Trail to the Upper Falls. Facilities include a picnic area along the banks of the Tahquamenon and a concessionaire that rents rowboats and canoes daily during the summer. The best way to view the Lower Falls is to row or paddle across the river to an island where there is a dock and a mile trail around it.

Hiking: The park has 40 miles of hiking trails, including several interconnecting

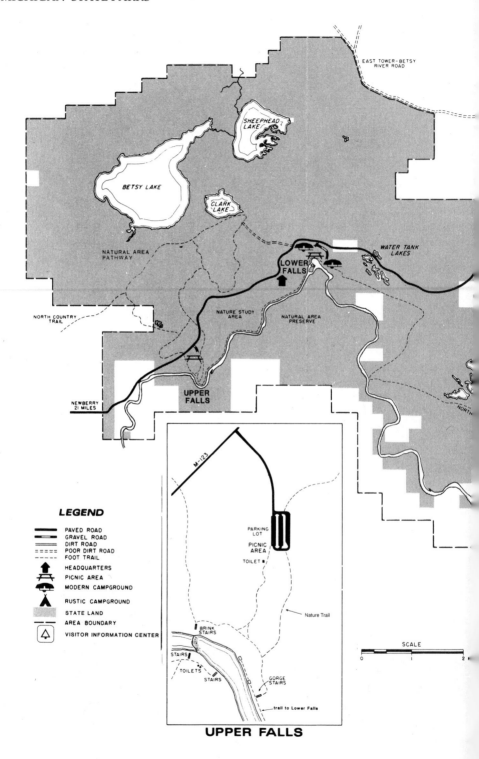

NATURAL AREA PATHWAY

SHEEPHEAD LAKE

BETSY LAKE

CLARK LAKE

EAST TOWER–BETSY RIVER ROAD

WATER TANK LAKES

LOWER FALLS

NORTH COUNTRY TRAIL

NATURE STUDY AREA

NATURAL AREA PRESERVE

NEWBERRY 21 MILES

UPPER FALLS

LEGEND

PAVED ROAD
GRAVEL ROAD
DIRT ROAD
POOR DIRT ROAD
FOOT TRAIL
HEADQUARTERS
PICNIC AREA
MODERN CAMPGROUND
RUSTIC CAMPGROUND
STATE LAND
AREA BOUNDARY
VISITOR INFORMATION CENTER

M-123

PARKING LOT
PICNIC AREA
TOILET

Nature Trail

BRINK STAIRS
STAIRS
TOILETS
STAIRS
GORGE STAIRS

trail to Lower Falls

SCALE
0   1   2

UPPER FALLS

TAHQUAMENON
FALLS
STATE PARK

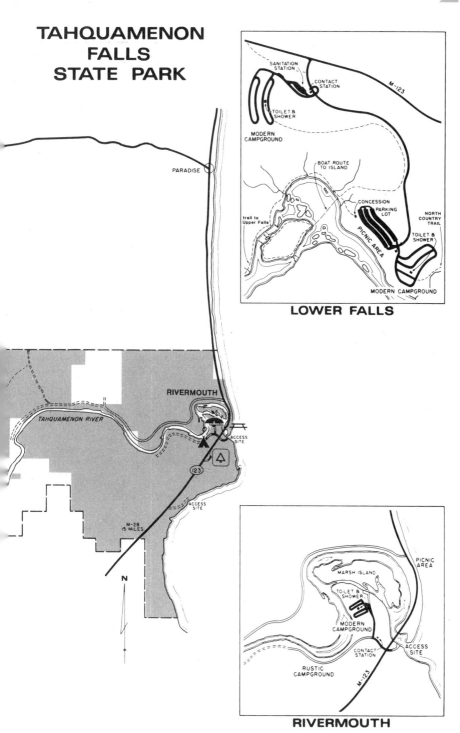

LOWER FALLS

RIVERMOUTH

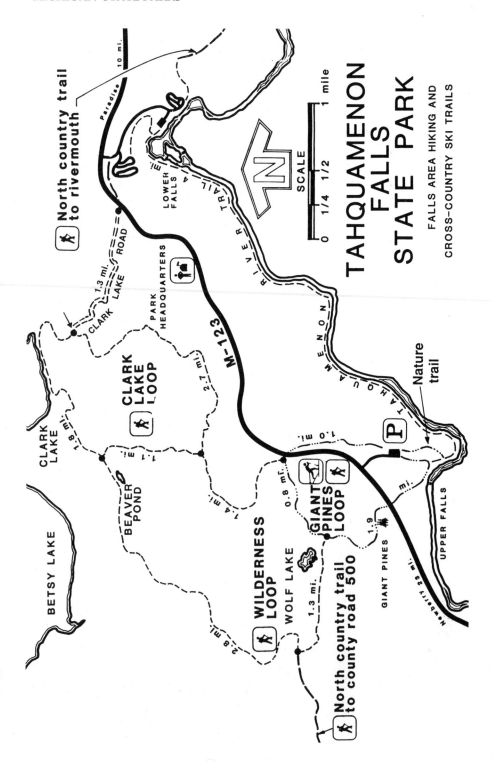

TAHQUAMENON FALLS STATE PARK

FALLS AREA HIKING AND
CROSS-COUNTRY SKI TRAILS

North country trail
to rivermouth

North country trail
to county road 500

CLARK LAKE LOOP

WILDERNESS LOOP

GIANT PINES LOOP

PARK HEADQUARTERS

LOWER FALLS

UPPER FALLS

CLARK LAKE

BETSY LAKE

BEAVER POND

WOLF LAKE

GIANT PINES

Nature trail

M-123

SCALE

0   1/4   1/2   1 mile

loops in the Tahquamenon Natural Area north of M-123 that provide an escape from the crowds around the falls and make for excellent day hikes. The Giant Pines Loop is a 3.7-mile trail that begins and ends at the Upper Falls parking area after passing the falls, a stand of giant pines, and crossing M-123 twice. The Wilderness Loop is a 7.4-mile walk that lies north of M-123 and starts where the Giant Pines Trail crosses the road east of the Upper Falls Unit. The Clark Lake Loop is a 5.6-mile hike that includes a stretch along its namesake lake. A posted trailhead to Clark Lake lies at the end of Clark Lake Road, a rough dirt track that departs from M-123 just west of the Lower Falls Unit. Many hikers prefer walking the 1.3-mile-long road as opposed to driving their car in. The most interesting hike south of M-123, and the most popular one in the park, is the Tahquemenon River Trail, a one-way hike of 4 miles from the Upper Falls to the Lower Falls. This moderately difficult trail skirts the river most of the way, allowing hikers to pass through old-growth forests of beach-maple and hemlock and view stretches of rapids. Beginning at the east loop of the Overlook Campground is the Overlook Nature Trail, a 2-mile walk with interpretive displays that skirts a 90-foot ridge to the Lower Falls and then loops back along a small tributary of the Tahquamenon River.

Backpacking: The North Country Trail, a 3,000-mile link between the Appalachian Trail in New York and the Lewis and Clark Trail in North Dakota, was officially designated in 1980, with the National Park Service coordinating its development. Eventually, the trail will run the length of both the Upper and Lower Peninsulas, but already more than 12 miles of it passes through Tahquamenon Falls. From County Road 500 the trail enters the park to the west and joins the Wilderness Loop before crossing M-123 and following the Tahquamenon River Trail to the Lower Falls Unit. It passes through Riverbend Campground and then cuts through the interior of the park before returning to M-123 at the Rivermouth Unit. From here the North Country Trail follows M-123 across the Tahquamenon River and out of the state park. South of the park the trail continues through the Hiawatha National Forest for another 79 miles until it reaches St. Ignace. To the west the North Country Trail can be followed 40 miles to Muskallonge Lake State Park and then into Pictured Rocks National Lakeshore.

Fishing: The best fishing in the park is found on the Tahquamenon River. Anglers below the Lower Falls, often in canoes or waders, cast for northern pike, muskies, and walleye that measure up to 28 inches in length. Walleyes and brown trout are caught in the river between the two falls, while farther up, above the Upper Falls, there are good populations of perch. There is also a run of steelhead in the Tahquamenon up to the Lower Falls after ice-out in spring and late October. Most anglers fish for the trout either from boats in the lower portions of the river or by surf casting spoons and spawn near the mouth in Whitefish Bay. Betsy, Sheephead, and Clark Lakes can be reached only by short portages and have a no-motor ban on them. Clark is exceptionally shallow but anglers paddle into Betsy and Sheephead for northern pike, perch, and a wilderness fishing experience. The park maintains a boat access site at the Rivermouth Unit, while canoes can be launched in the Lower Falls Unit.

Canoeing: Although the Tahquamenon River is 94 miles long, only about 63 miles of it is paddled by canoeists. A popular put-in is off County Road 415, north of McMillan in Luce County, but there is no camping the first 15 miles as it flows through a willow swamp. There are portages around Dollarville Dam and the falls before the trip ends at the park's Rivermouth Unit. Due to the many swamps it flows through, it's best to avoid the Tahquamenon during black fly season, generally late May through mid-June.

A day trip into the park's wilderness interior begins at the end of the Clark Lake

Kids exploring the Lower Falls, Tahquamenon Falls State Park

access road. From the trailhead it's a quarter-mile portage to the small lake. An unmarked half-mile portage extends from Clark's northern shore to Betsy Lake, and for the adventurous, it's possible to paddle a small river into Sheephead Lake. Camping is not allowed in this area.

Natural Area: The Tahquamenon Natural Area is a dedicated tract of 18,000 acres surrounding Sheephead, Clark, and Betsy Lakes. This nonmotorized area, accessible only by foot trails and canoe portages, contains a portion of the largest peatland landscape in Michigan, as well as a variety of wildlife, including black bear, moose, bald eagles, osprey, and sandhill cranes.

Winter Activities: The Giant Pines Loop is groomed and tracked for cross-country skiers, who park in the Upper Falls Unit. The rest of the trails are not groomed and often deep snow makes wilderness skiing difficult. The path and steps to the Upper Falls are also packed, as the cascade is almost as popular in the winter as it is in the summer. The partially frozen falls, with huge ice formations lining the gorge, is a stunning sight and one of the most popular attractions in the Upper Peninsula for snowmobilers. From a trail that skirts M-123, snowmobilers pull into the Upper Falls parking lot and then walk the half mile to the observation deck above the brink of the cascade.

Access and Information: The Rivermouth Unit is 4 miles south of Paradise on M-123, while the Lower Falls Unit is 12 miles from the small town, where the state highway swings to the west. The Upper Falls Unit is 21 miles from Newberry on M-123 or 2 miles west of the Lower Falls. For more information, contact Tahquamenon Falls State Park, Star Route 48, P.O. Box 225, Paradise, MI 49768; or call (906) 492-3415.

Muskallonge Lake State Park

▲ The narrow, quarter-mile-wide strip of land between Lake Superior and Muskallonge Lake was the original site of the village of Deer Park, a lumber town in the 1800s that included a hotel, store, doctor's office, and, of course, sawmill. The logs were brought in by narrow-gauge railroad and dumped into the inland lake, while ships tied up at a long pier in Lake Superior to be loaded with the finished lumber. Eventually, the white pine ran out, the mill operation moved, and the town was deserted.

Other than a few of the original dock pilings on Lake Superior and a huge sawdust pile near the inland lake, it's hard to imagine Muskallonge Lake State Park as a bustling lumber town. The 217-acre park in Luce County is a wooded area featuring 2 miles of lakeshore, reached by a rough gravel road and seemingly located "a hundred miles from nowhere" as it lies on an isolated stretch between Newberry and Grand Marais.

County Road H-37 (also labeled County Road 497) runs through the middle of the scenic park. To the south you can set up at a lakeshore camp, go fishing, or take a dip in the warm waters of Muskallonge Lake. Cross the gravel road, and you can descend the shoreline bluffs to a sandy and pebbled beach along Lake Superior where rockhounds search for colorful agates. The two lakes combine to give the state park an exceptionally moderate climate year-round, rarely hot in the summer, not as cold as the rest of the Upper Peninsula during the winter. The park's 80,000 annual visitors, however, arrive almost exclusively from spring through fall, as there is little activity during the winter.

Camping: The park has 175 modern sites in a campground along the shores of

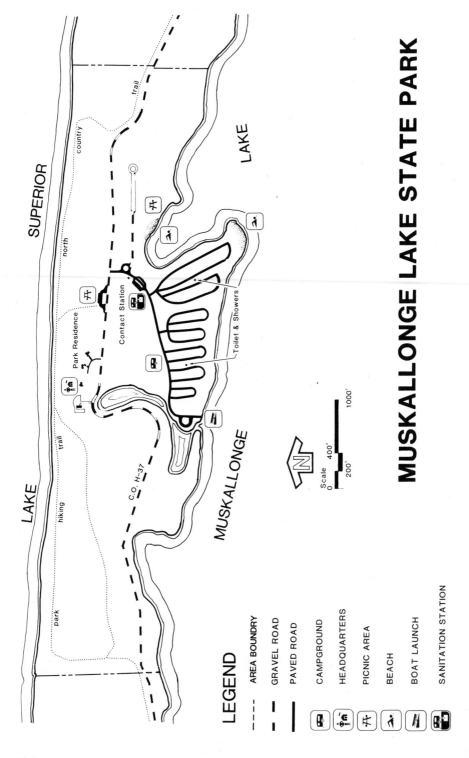

MUSKALLONGE LAKE STATE PARK

LEGEND

- AREA BOUNDRY
- GRAVEL ROAD
- PAVED ROAD
- CAMPGROUND
- HEADQUARTERS
- PICNIC AREA
- BEACH
- BOAT LAUNCH
- SANITATION STATION

Scale
0   200'   400'   1000'

LAKE SUPERIOR

MUSKALLONGE LAKE

park hiking trail

north country trail

Park Residence

Contact Station

Toilet & Showers

C.O. H-37

Muskallonge Lake. The area is well shaded and a number of sites overlook the lake, while others are near a small beach for the campers. Most of the summer a site is easily obtained, but from July 4 to mid-August, the facility is vulnerable to filling up most weekends.

Hiking: Following the Lake Superior shoreline is a portion of the North Country Trail (see Tahquamenon Falls State Park for a description). There are about 1.5 miles of this national trail in the park, and backpackers can follow it west 5 miles from the park to Lake Superior State Forest Campground, or even farther to hook into the Lakeshore Trail in Pictured Rocks National Lakeshore. To the east the Two Hearted River State Forest Campground on the mouth of the famous river is a 10 mile trek. The DNR staff has also added a spur that combines with a portion of the North Country Trail to form a 1.5-mile loop from the Lake Superior parking area to the west end of the park.

Fishing: The 780-acre Muskallonge Lake is known best by anglers for northern pike, perch, and smallmouth bass. In recent years the DNR Fisheries Division has begun stocking the lake with walleye. The park maintains an improved boat launch at the west end of the campground for the inland lake, but there are no launching facilities on Lake Superior. Three resorts, located just outside the park, rent boats and motors and allow campers to tie them up at the park.

Day-Use Facilities: The park has a day-use area on a small bay of Muskallonge Lake east of the campground. The lake is shallow enough so that the water warms up quickly during summer for swimmers. There is parking for twenty vehicles and an adjacent picnic area. Located right off County Road H-37 is parking and a picnic area on Lake Superior. From here visitors can descend a wooden staircase off the bluff to reach the beautiful lakeshore and views of the Great Lake. The lake is generally too cold to swim in but is a popular destination for agate hunters. The best time to search is after a storm or a heavy north wind, which will push a layer of new rocks onto the beach. The most sought-after rock is the Lake Superior agate and examples can be seen in both its rough and polished states at the two stores located near the park.

Access and Information: Muskallonge is 28 miles from Newberry and 18 miles east of Grand Marais. From Newberry head north on M-123 for 4 miles then turn west on H-37 and follow it 14 miles to the park entrance. For more information, contact Muskallonge State Park, P.O. Box 245, Route 1, Newberry, MI 49868; or call (906) 658-3338.

Wagner Falls Scenic Site

▲ Occasionally labeled the "state's smallest state park," Wagner Falls is actually a day-use scenic site of only 22 acres just outside Munising in Alger County. The small unit preserves Wagner Falls, a 20-foot cascade of water less than 200 yards from the parking area via a trail and a boardwalk that ends at an observation deck. A rough trail then winds around the falls to a second set farther up Wagner Creek. The only facility is a small parking area.

Winter Activities: Wagner Falls is a popular attraction in the winter. Between the frozen cascade and the 200-plus inches of snow that the Munising area receives, the short walk to the observation deck can be extremely scenic. Enough visitors view the falls in the winter that the trail is usually well packed, making snowshoes unnecessary.

Wagner Falls

Access and Information: The posted parking area of Wagner Falls is off M-94 at its junction with M-28, 2 miles south of Munising. For more information, contact Indian Lake State Park, P.O. Box 2500, Route 2, Manistique, MI 49854; or call (906) 341-2355.

Laughing Whitefish Falls Scenic Site

Impressive Laughing Whitefish Falls has been preserved as another scenic site in the state park system. The 960-acre unit in Alger County is a day-use park that includes almost a mile of foot trails, a picnic area with a water pump and vault toilets, and three observation decks overlooking the falls.

The cascade was created by an outcrop of resistant sandy dolomite that prevents the Whitefish River from cutting into the softer gray Munising sandstone below. The falls is actually an impressive 30-foot drop to a rock slide that drops away more than 70 additional feet to the bottom of the gorge. It's a half-mile hike from the posted parking area to the first platform overlooking the brink of the falls. From there 158 steps descend past two more platforms to the bottom of the gorge.

Winter Activities: North Sundell Road is not plowed beginning a half mile from the entrance of the state park unit, making Laughing Whitefish Falls a destination for snowmobilers and snowshoers. An occasional snowmobiler finds his way back to the falls, leaving a packed trail up North Sundell Road and then into the park itself to the start of the observation deck and stairway. Snowshoes can either follow the snowmobile trail or cut directly through the woods from North Sundell Road to the day-use area at the end of the park entrance road. In February, when there is no foliage obstructing the view, it is easy to see the towering sandstone walls that box in the Laughing Whitefish River, while the falls themselves are like a frozen fountain. It's roughly a 3-mile trek from the end of North Sundell Road to the cascade, and snowshoes can be rented at Iverson Snowshoes (906-452-6370) in Singleton.

Access and Information: To reach the scenic site, drive to the hamlet of Sundell on M-94 and then head north on North Sundell Road for 2.5 miles. For more information, contact J. W. Wells State Park, N7670 M-35, Cedar River, MI 49813; or call (906) 863-9747.

Indian Lake State Park

Originally, Indian Lake was not a lake at all but a large, shallow bay along Lake Michigan. In time, however, a sandbar formed across the mouth of the bay, and when the level of the Great Lake receded, a lake was born. The lake was originally called "Monistique Lake," according to surveyor's records of 1850, but a Native Amerian tribe lived in log cabins near the outlet, and eventually the earliest European settlers began referring to it as Indian Lake.

The body of water is the Upper Peninsula's fourth largest lake and the main feature, as well as the namesake, of Indian Lake State Park, a 567-acre unit in Schoolcraft County. The park has almost a mile of shoreline along the lake divided between two units, 3 miles apart. The original park was the south unit, acquired in 1932 and developed the following year by CCC crews, then in 1965 the west unit was purchased.

Today both units each contain a campground, a beach on the lake, and a boat launch. Together they draw almost 110,000 visitors annually with the vast majority arriving during the summer.

Camping: Indian Lake has 302 modern and semi-modern sites separated in two campgrounds that are as different as night and day. The original facility, the South Shore Campground, features 158 modern sites in a grassy, lightly shaded area with many of them right on the lakeshore. The West Shore Campground has 144 semi-modern sites with electricity but no restrooms (just vault toilets) or showers. The sites are much more secluded in a hardwoods forest and lie a quarter to a half mile from the lake. The South Shore Campground, which also features a rent-a-tipi and two mini-cabins, is much more popular and tends to fill up almost daily from July through August. The West Shore Campground, on the other hand, usually has open sites available even on the weekends.

Hiking: The south unit has 2 miles of trails, including the Chippewa Trail, a very short path with interpretive stops and an accompanying brochure relating to the wild foods of the Native Americans. The rest of the network forms a loop through the campground and the forested western half of the unit. The most interesting stretch is the mile walk from the park headquarters through an area that is predominantly cedar swamp. The trail then crosses DuFour Creek twice before arriving at the park's day-use area.

Fishing: Indian Lake, the fifteenth largest in the state at 8,659 acres, offers anglers a varied stringer of fish. The lake is 4.5 miles long and 3 miles wide, but its

INDIAN LAKE STATE PARK

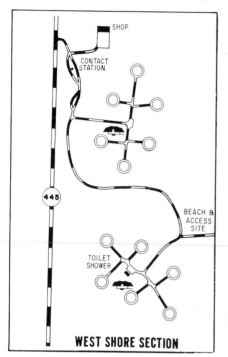

WEST SHORE SECTION

PALMS BOOK STATE PARK

INDIAN LAKE

M-94

M-149

CO. 455

CO. 442

MANISTIQUE

US-2

(WEST UNIT) INDIAN LAKE S. P.

INDIAN LAKE STATE PARK

US-2

THOMPSON

LAKE MICHIGAN

VICINITY MAP

LEGEND

━━━━	PAVED ROAD
▭▭▭	GRAVEL ROAD
≡≡≡	GOOD DIRT ROAD
------	FOOT TRAIL
	HEADQUARTERS
	PICNIC AREA
	CAMPGROUND
	ACCESS SITE
---	AREA BOUNDARY
	STATE LAND

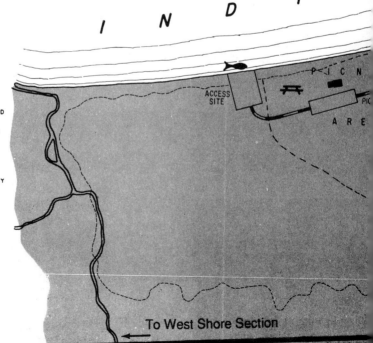

INDI

ACCESS SITE

PICNIC

AREA

To West Shore Section

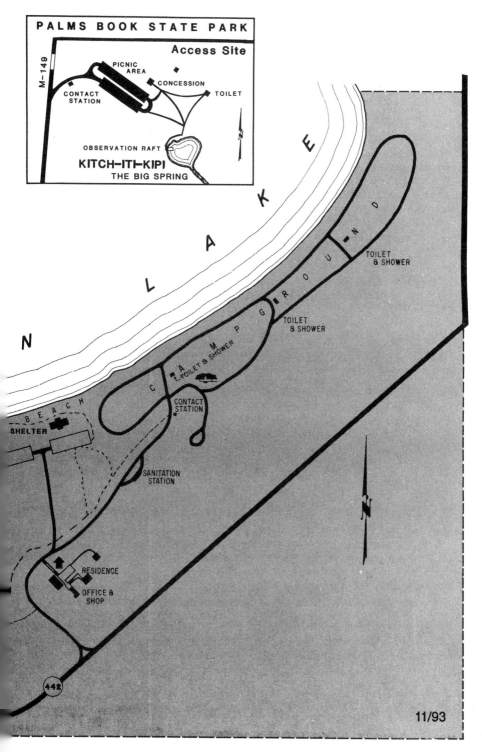

maximum depth is only 18 feet, and more than 90 percent of it is under 15 feet. The lake is best known to fishermen for walleye, and it has been stocked almost annually with the fish. But it also possesses good numbers of yellow perch, especially in its northern basin, northern pike, smallmouth bass, and panfish. Indian Lake has also been stocked in the past with tiger muskellunge. In 1988, the park staff installed a series of log fish crib shelters a third of a mile north of the boat ramp. The cribs are excellent places to drop a line. The state park maintains an improved boat launch at both units, while a concessionaire rents canoes and rowboats within the park daily during the summer.

Day-Use Facilities: The park's day-use area is located in the south unit and features a sandy beach with a swimming area that is only 2 feet deep for more than 300 yards out. Other facilities include tables, grills, parking for 200 cars, and two shelters that can be rented.

Winter Activities: There are no groomed ski trails in the state park itself but nearby is Indian Lake Pathway. The 6-mile state forest network of trails is an easy and popular area to ski in the winter and is groomed on a regular basis by locals. The trailhead is on M-149, a mile west of Palms Brook State Park.

Access and Information: The park is 5 miles west of Manistique on County Road 442 or 3 miles north of Thompson on M-149. To reach the west unit, continue west on County Road 442 and then turn north on County Road 455 to the posted entrance. For more information, contact Indian Lake State Park, Route 2, P.O. Box 2500, Manistique, MI 49854; or call (906) 341-2355.

Palms Book State Park

In the 1920s it was still a black hole hidden in a tangle of fallen trees, obscured to all but John Bellaire. Today that hole is Kitch-Iti-Kipi, or "Big Spring," Michigan's largest spring and the centerpiece of Palms Book State Park, a 308-acre unit in Schoolcraft County. Bellaire operated a five-and-dime store in Manistique when he first visited the spring. He saw through the piles of trash dumped by a local lumber company to the emerald bottom of the pool, where sand bubbled and rolled. Overwhelmed by its beauty, Bellaire convinced state officials to acquire the land, and in 1926 the Palms Book Land Company completed the sale, in which the state purchased 90 acres, including the spring, for ten dollars.

Kitch-Iti-Kipi has since become one of Michigan's most intriguing natural wonders. The natural spring pours out more than 10,000 gallons of water per minute from narrow openings in the underlying limestone that were created by glacial drift. The result is a crystal-clear pond 200 feet long and 40 feet deep. Visitors board a wooden raft with observation holes in the middle and pull themselves across the spring to get a good view of the fantasy world below. Between the swirls of sand and ghostly bubbles rising up, you can view ancient trees with branches encrusted in limestone, huge brown trout slipping silently by, and colors and shapes that challenge the imagination. The spring is especially enchanting in the early morning when a mist lies over the water and the trout rise to the surface.

The spring never freezes, and visitors can operate the raft year-round. Park staff do not plow the access drive, and after the first snow of the winter, they lock the entrance gate. Still, people hike in throughout the winter to visit this alluring attraction. Palms Book, which draws 70,000 visitors annually, does not have a campground.

Riding the raft in winter at Palms Book State Park

Day-Use Facilities: Besides the observation raft, the park features a shaded picnic area, restrooms, and a concession store. Palms Book State Park is bordered by Indian Lake, but its shoreline is undeveloped and forested right to the edge of the water. There is an improved boat launch just north of the park that is reached from a separate entrance at the end of M-149.

Access and Information: The park entrance is 8 miles north on M-149 from US 2. For more information, contact Indian Lake State Park, Route 2, P.O. Box 2500, Manistique, MI 49854; or call (906) 341-2355.

Fayette State Park

In the mid-1800s, iron ore was shipped from the Upper Peninsula to the foundries in the lower Great Lakes at tremendous cost to the companies. Fayette Brown, general manager of the Jackson Iron Company, studied the problem and decided to build a company-owned furnace far from the mine, where the ore could be smelted into pig iron before it was shipped to the steel-making centers. In 1866, Brown chose a spot on the Garden Peninsula overlooking Big Bay De Noc because it possessed a natural harbor for shipping, and the limestone and hardwood forests needed to smelt the ore. He built a company town and gave it his first name—Fayette was born.

It died in 1891 when the company closed down the furnaces, and within a few years Fayette was a ghost town of more than twenty buildings and structures. The land changed hands several times until the state acquired it in 1959 and designated it Fayette State Park, a 711-acre unit in Delta County. The town booms once again

Charcoal kiln, Fayette State Park

during the summer as a scenic historic site overlooking Snail Shell Harbor with its towering white limestone cliffs.

The interpretive area contains a museum and twenty-two other buildings, of which nine are renovated and fully furnished with artifacts from the iron ore days of the late 1800s. Fayette, which attracts 100,000 visitors annually, also features a campground, 3 miles of shoreline on Big Bay De Noc, and an interesting 7-mile network of trails.

Camping: The park has a semi-modern campground that lacks modern restrooms and showers but provides electricity to all eighty sites. The facility is located in a wooded area where trails provide access to the historic town and the park's day-use area. The campground rarely fills up during the summer with the exception of Fourth of July weekend.

Interpretive Center: At its height, some 500 people lived, worked, and enjoyed a good life in Fayette. The town featured not only a furnace complex and numerous charcoal kilns but also baseball fields, a hotel, even an opera house. A walking tour of the area begins in the visitor center, where exhibits and displays review the creation and downfall of the town. The centerpiece of the museum, however, is a scale model of Fayette as it was in the late 1880s. The tour continues in the ghost town, where there are numerous buildings and several other structures, including the kilns and furnaces needed to produce pig iron. Many have been renovated and some, including the Company Office, Opera House, and Machine Shop, feature displays. Although you can visit the town anytime of the year, the museum and buildings are open from mid-May to mid-October daily from 9:00 A.M. to 7:00 P.M. Visitors can cover the ghost town on their own with a walking tour brochure or join a guided tour available from mid-June through Labor Day. In August, the park stages Fayette Heritage Days, an annual festival.

Hiking: Fayette has 7 miles of hiking trails, with the longest loop a 2-mile path

FAYETTE HISTORIC STATE PARK

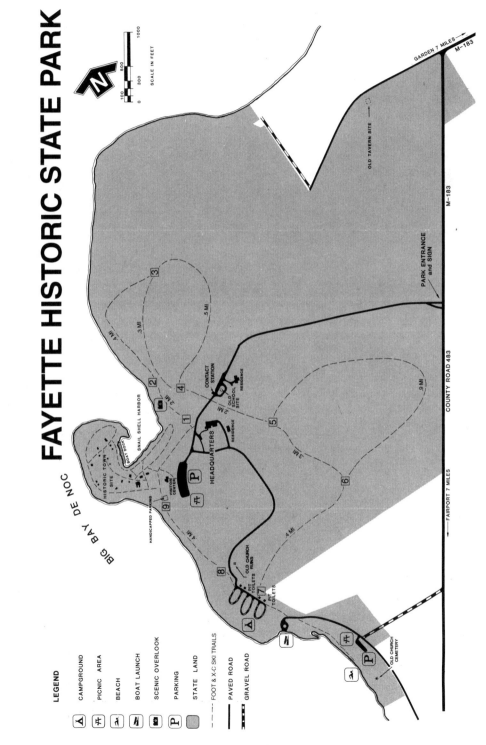

SCALE IN FEET

0   100   300   500   1000

GARDEN 7 MILES — M-183

OLD TAVERN SITE

M-183

PARK ENTRANCE and SIGN

COUNTY ROAD 483

.9 MI

FAIRPORT 7 MILES

OLD CHURCH CEMETERY

.3 MI

.5 MI

.4 MI

CONTACT STATION

RESIDENCE

OLD SCHOOL SITE

.2 MI

2 MI

.1 MI

SNAIL SHELL HARBOR

RESIDENCE

HEADQUARTERS

.3 MI

.4 MI

BOAT DOCK

HISTORIC TOWN SITE

VISITOR CENTER

HANDICAPPED PARKING

.4 MI

OLD CHURCH RUINS

PIT TOILETS

PIT TOILETS

BIG BAY DE NOC

LEGEND

Ⓐ CAMPGROUND

Ⓟ PICNIC AREA

Ⓚ BEACH

Ⓤ BOAT LAUNCH

Ⓢ SCENIC OVERLOOK

Ⓟ PARKING

▨ STATE LAND

- - - FOOT & X-C SKI TRAILS

━━━ PAVED ROAD

▬▬▬ GRAVEL ROAD

Ghost town, Fayette State Park

that begins in the campground and swings through the wooded interior south of the park road before returning. Of the four loops available, however, the most scenic is the 1.5-mile Overlook Trail. The trail begins just up a hill from the parking lot to the townsite and immediately breaks out at the rubbled remains of a massive hay barn that Jackson Iron Company maintained for its horses and oxen. Just around the corner is the first of three overlooks at the edge of the limestone bluffs above Snail Shell Harbor. The second, another quarter mile along the trail, is the best, a panorama of the entire town. It's so close to the edge of the steep-sided bluff that the park has erected a stone fence to prevent any mishaps.

Fishing: Big Bay De Noc is a well-known fishery for perch, smallmouth bass, and northern pike, and in recent years walleye have been planted annually as well as salmon and trout. The park maintains an improved boat launch located in its day-use area. Often during July and August, schools of perch move into Snail Shell Harbor and attract the interest of anglers who fish for them from anchored boats or off a dock located in the small bay.

Day-Use Facilities: Fayette features a beautiful beach on Sand Bay at the south end of the park. The facility includes parking, tables, and a bathhouse, and has a separate entrance just south of the park's main entrance on County Road 483.

Winter Activities: Fayette's trail system is converted during the winter into a 4.5-mile cross-country ski run that is groomed on a regular basis. The terrain for the most part is level, and the runs are rated for novice skiers. This might be the only place in Michigan where you can ski through a ghost town. Snowmobiling is also allowed in certain areas in the park but not on the ski trails.

Access and Information: From US 2 the park is to the south 15 miles on the Garden Peninsula. Follow Country Road 483 to the posted entrance, 8 miles beyond the town of Garden. For more information, contact Fayette State Park, 13700 13.25 Lane, Garden, MI 49835; or call (906) 644 2603.

J. W. Wells State Park

John Walters Wells, a noted lumberman and mayor of Menominee beginning in 1893, took a great deal of Michigan's lumber, but was responsible for a virgin stand of pine that wasn't cut and now remains along Green Bay in Menominee County. The 678-acre area, which also contains a dense forest of beech, cedar, spruce, maple, and even elm, was donated by Wells' children to Michigan in 1924 in memory of their father.

J. W. Wells State Park was established the following year, and today visitors can enjoy the forest and virgin pine from a 7-mile network of trails. But beyond the trees, the park is probably best known for its 3-mile frontage along Green Bay. The shoreline, which includes beautiful stretches of sandy beach, overlooks the clear water of the bay and can be enjoyed from the park's campground, day-use area, or trail system, or by renting one of six frontier cabins. Wisconsin travelers use the park almost as much as Michigan residents and make up a large percentage of Wells' annual attendance of around 100,000.

Camping: Wells has a campground of 178 modern sites in a semi-open grassy area. By far the most popular sites are a row of 33 spots located right on Green Bay. Sites are usually available Sunday through Thursday, but the facility fills up on most weekends throughout the summer due to the increasing number of Wisconsin visitors.

Hiking: Four trails extend to the north and south ends of the park to form a network of 7 miles. The longest is the Cedar River Trail, a 1.6-mile walk that begins at a stone shelter near the campground and follows the lakeshore north to the Cedar River. Looping back off the Cedar River Trail is the Ridgewood and Evergreen Trails. Heading south of the campground past the day-use area is the Timber Trail, a 1.3-mile loop. There are stone shelters on both the Evergreen and Cedar River Trails that were built by CCC crews in the 1930s.

Cabins: Wells has six rustic cabins located near the shoreline in a secluded section of woods, only a short walk from where users must leave their cars. Two of them, Washington and Plum Cabins, are interesting log-and-stone structures built by the CCC that feature barrel stoves for heating and cooking and will accommodate up to twelve persons each. The other four have eight bunks each and all cabin users can use the showers at the campground from May through September. All of the cabins are open year-round and should be reserved in advance.

Fishing: Green Bay is noted by anglers for bass, northern pike, walleye, and trout. The best fishing in the park comes in late March and early April right after ice-out when anglers surf fish for brown trout near the shore. Wells does not have a boat launch, but there are several public ramps in Cedar River 2 miles north of the park.

Day-Use Facilities: The park's day-use area is located in the southern half of the park and includes a beautiful stretch of beach. Along with a bathhouse, the area features a large parking lot and two shelters that can be rented.

Winter Activities: The park grooms and tracks its trails for cross-country skiers in the winter. The runs follow the relatively flat terrain and are rated for novice skiers. The three trailside shelters are also used by skiers as warming huts and are stocked with wood. There is no ski rental concession in the park, but equipment is available in Menominee, 23 miles to the south. Snowmobiling is allowed in Wells except on ski trails.

Access and Information: The park is located right on M-35, 30 miles south of Escanaba. For more information, contact J. W. Wells State Park, N7670 M-35, Cedar River, MI 49813-9616; or call (906) 863-9747.

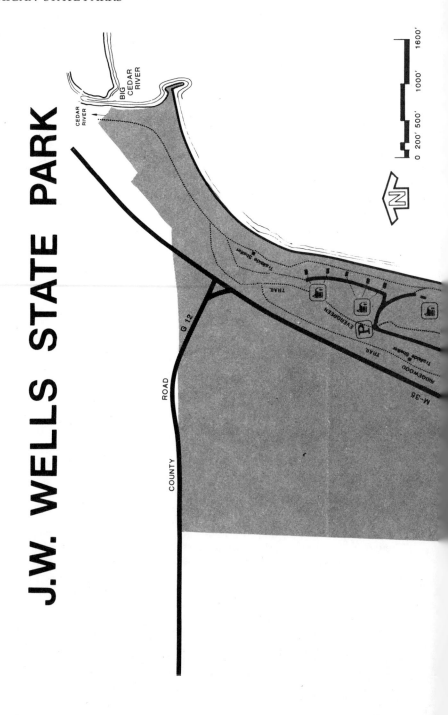

J.W. WELLS STATE PARK

LEGEND

SURFACE ROAD

FOOT TRAIL

CAMPGROUND

RUSTIC CABIN

BEACH

RESTROOMS

HEADQUARTERS

PICNIC SHELTER

PICNIC AREA

SANITATION STATION

STATE LAND

PARKING

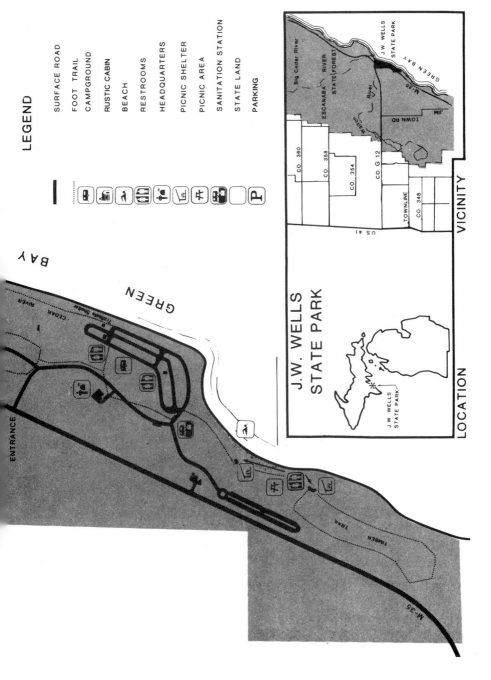

J.W. WELLS STATE PARK

VICINITY

LOCATION

J W WELLS STATE PARK

GREEN BAY

CEDAR RIVER

ENTRANCE

M-35

TIMBER TRAIL

Big Cedar River

ESCANABA RIVER STATE FOREST

TOWN RD

TOWNLINE

CO. 360

CO. 358

CO. 354

CO. G 12

CO. 348

U.S. 41

M-35

GREEN BAY

Porcupine Mountains Wilderness State Park

▲ It's the largest, it's the most remote, its ridges are the steepest, its peaks are the tallest. Without a doubt, Porcupine Mountains Wilderness State Park, a 58,335-acre unit that stretches between Ontonagon and Gogebic Counties, is the crowning jewel of the Michigan state park system. Its dimensions easily swallow up any visitor who departs from the campgrounds and developed areas into its rugged heart. The park is 25 miles long and 10 miles at its widest point. It contains 26 miles of Lake Superior shoreline, four lakes, including the impressive Lake of the Clouds, and numerous rivers, trout streams, and water falls.

But most of all, it's the Porcupine Mountains themselves and the wilderness their ruggedness protects that have become the most cherished quality of the park. Affectionately known as the "Porkies," the range tops off at 1,958 feet at Summit Peak and often is labeled as the "only true mountains in the Midwest." When combined with unbridged stream crossings, a healthy population of black bears and other wildlife, and 90 miles of trails that wind through the backcountry, it's easy to see why backpackers consider the Porcupine Mountains a gem in the state park system.

The rugged terrain protected the Porkies long before man preserved it as a state park. Although Native Americans are said to have gathered "chunks of pure silver" as they traversed the mountains, their mining activity in the area was light, especially compared with that on the Keweenaw Peninsula. The range was the destination of one of the first metal stampedes in the country, when miners arrived in 1845 looking for copper and began the Union Mine on the east side of the park. But the mine never realized a profit, was sold in 1864, and finally was abandoned. For the most part lumbermen also avoided the Porkies, as extracting the trees from the range was an expensive ordeal.

The area emerged in the 1930s as one of the largest remaining wilderness tracts in the Midwest, with most of its virgin pine-hemlock uncut. This unique aspect led

Cross-country skiers at the East Vista, Porcupine Mountains Wilderness State Park

251

Summit Overlook, the highest point in Porcupine Mountains Wilderness State Park

a push for its preservation as a state park in 1945 and is one of the main reasons it draws 400,000 visitors a year.

About a quarter of the visitors are overnight users, a mixture of backpackers and campers who stay in the park's modern campgrounds, rustic campsites, wilderness cabins, trailside shelters, or backcountry camping areas. Anglers, hunters, and downhill and Nordic skiers also come to the park. But most arrivals are day users, people who only want to view the incredible Lake of the Clouds panorama, the picture of Michigan that ends up on more magazine covers than any other scene. Many never stray far from the scenic overlooks, roads, or visitor center. Still, the Porkies have a profound effect on them. Just knowing wilderness exists can bestow a renewed faith in mankind.

Camping: Porcupine Mountains has five campgrounds accessible by road. Its largest is Union Bay Campground with ninety-nine modern sites situated on a grassy shelf overlooking Lake Superior. The campground is located on M-107 on the east side of the park, next to the boat launch on Lake Superior and not far from the visitor center. On the west side, at the end of County Road 519, is Presque Isle Campground, featuring eighty-eight semi-modern sites with restrooms and showers but no electricity. The campground is located in a lightly wooded area, with a handful of sites on a bluff overlooking Lake Superior and all of them an easy stroll from the overlooks at the end of the Presque Isle River, a stunning stretch of waterfalls and rapids. The park also has three rustic facilities called outposts that offer a degree of privacy not found in the larger campgrounds. A mile south of the visitor center on South Boundary Road is Union River Outpost with three sites. Another 6 miles to the west is Lost Creek Outpost with three sites, and 3 miles farther still, White Pine Extension Outpost with seven drive-in sites. Demand on the campgrounds varies from year to year, but the busiest period is Monday and Tuesday with the weekends being considerably slower. The campgrounds often fill up from mid-July to the end of August, and reservations are advisable during this period. There is also an organization camp on the east side of the park on M-107.

Interpretive Center: The first stop for visitors just arriving at the Porcupine Mountains should be the park's impressive visitor center, located a half mile south of M-107 on South Boundary Road. Inside there are exhibits explaining the geological history of the mountains, plus a three-dimensional relief map that every backpacker should study before striking out. There is also a room devoted to the diverse wildlife in the park and a small theater where multislide presentations are repeated throughout the day. The center is the best source of maps and trail information on the backcountry. It is open from May 15 to October 15 from 10:00A.M. until 6:00 P.M., and during the summer months it has a list of vacant cabins available for last-minute rentals.

Backpacking: Porcupine Mountains, with its 90 miles of trails and a network of cabins and shelters in the backcountry, is well suited for multiple-day backpacking adventures. The longest foot route in the park is Lake Superior Trail, a 16-mile hike that parallels the Great Lake shoreline from a trailhead on M-107 to County Road 519 on the west side of the park. Branching off the lakeshore route for the interior of the Porkies are two other lengthy trails. The Little Carp River Trail spans 11 miles from the mouth of the Little Carp River to Mirror Lake, and along the way it passes numerous waterfalls, rapids, and some magnificent stands of timber. The Big Carp River Trail is a 9-mile hike that begins at the mouth of its namesake river and then skirts the river to pass several waterfalls including the stunning Shining Clouds Falls. It ends by climbing the Escarpment for panoramic views of Lake of the Clouds before arriving at the end of M-107. There are a number of trips that backpackers can put together, but a popular 3- or 4-day circuit is formed by combining a portion of the Lake Superior Trail with the Little Carp River Trail and the North Mirror Lake Trail. The 25-mile loop begins and ends near the Lake of the Clouds Overlook, and hikers have the option of renting cabins at a number of locations, including at the mouths of Big and Little Carp Rivers, at Greenstone Falls, and at Mirror Lake. Another scenic 25-mile loop begins with the Lost Lake Trail followed by Government Peak, North Mirror Lake, and the Escarpment Trails before returning to your car on South Boundary Road. Highlights of this 3-day trek include viewing Government Peak, the second highest point in the park, camping near scenic Trap Falls, and the panoramic views from the Escarpment, the rocky ridge above Lake of the Clouds.

Three trailside shelters are available on a first-come, first-use basis. They are located near Lone Rock on the Lake Superior Trail, at the junction of the Big Carp River and Correction Line Trail, and near Trap Falls on Government Peak Trail. There is no cost for the shelters, but they are in heavy demand at the height of the summer, July and August. Trailside camping is permitted throughout the backcountry, but not within a quarter mile of any shelter, cabin, road, or scenic viewpoint. Trailside campgrounds, featuring tent pads and bear poles for hanging food, are located on Lake Superior Trail at both Big and Little Carp Rivers, halfway up the 4-mile-long Union Spring Trail, near Trap Falls, and at Mirror Lake.

Backpackers should keep in mind that the Porkies are a rugged wilderness. Steep grades and numerous unbridged stream crossings are common occurrences on most trails. Hikers must register for a permit and pay a nightly backcountry fee

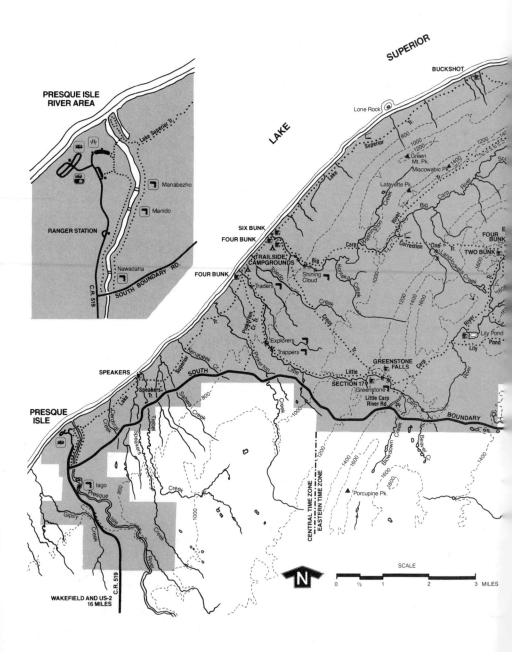

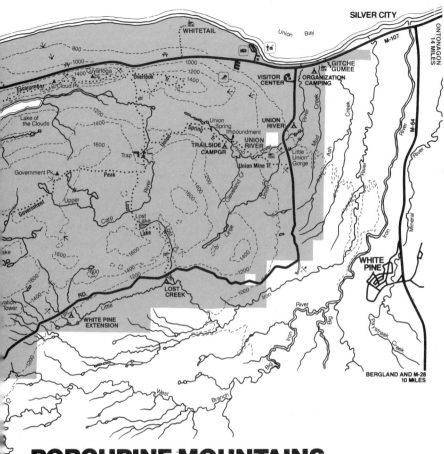

PORCUPINE MOUNTAINS WILDERNESS STATE PARK

LEGEND

——	PAVED ROAD		TRAIL ROAD	··········	FOOT TRAIL
	HEADQUARTERS		CAMPGROUND		SANITATION STA.
	SKI AREA		PARK CABIN		TRAIL SHELTER
	OVERLOOK		OLD MINESITE		WATERFALL

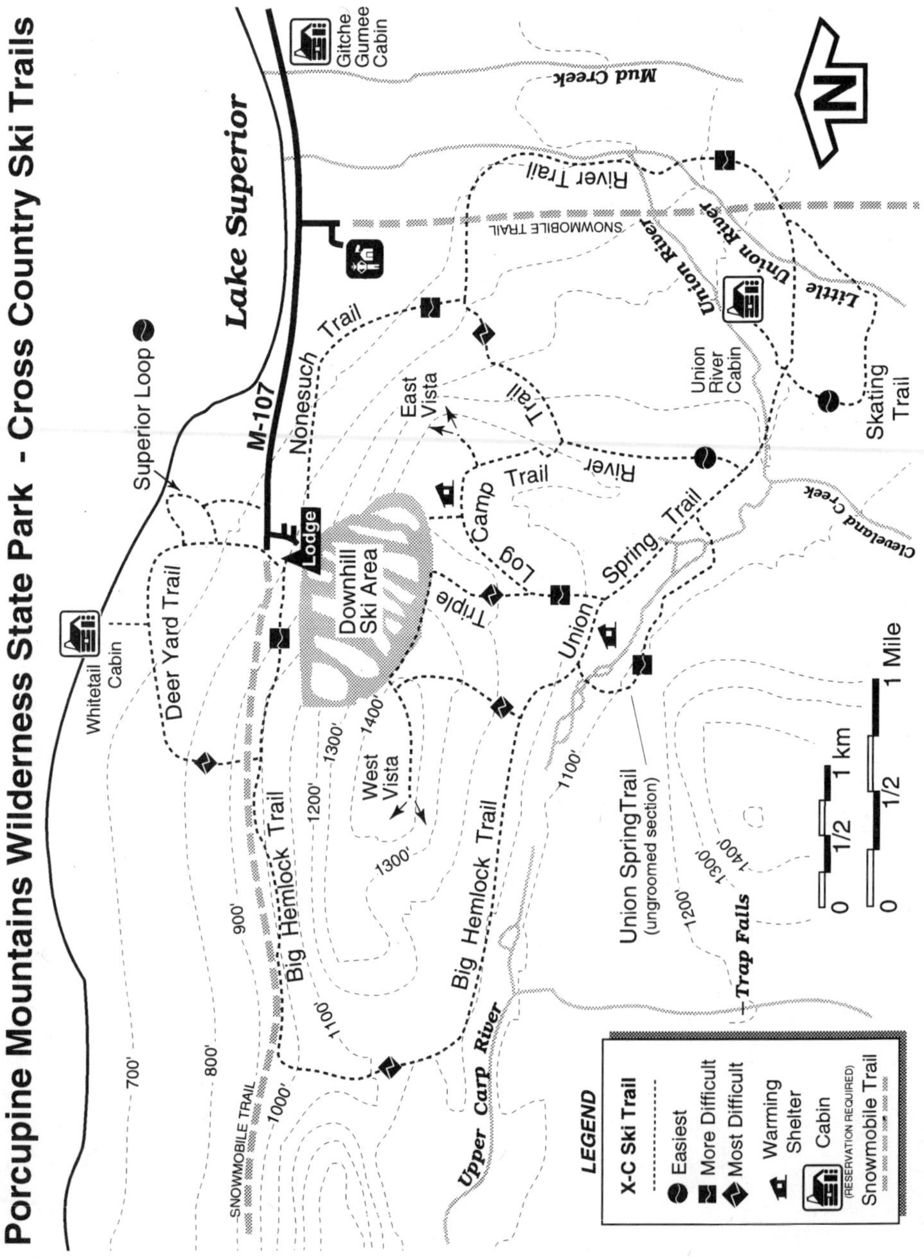

Porcupine Mountains Wilderness State Park - Cross Country Ski Trails

Gitche Gumee Cabin

Mud Creek

Lake Superior

River Trail

SNOWMOBILE TRAIL

Union River

Little Union River

M-107

Superior Loop

Nonesuch Trail

East Vista

Camp Trail

River Trail

Union River Cabin

Skating Trail

Cleveland Creek

Whitetail Cabin

Deer Yard Trail

Lodge

Downhill Ski Area

Triple

Log

Union Spring Trail

Union

1400'
1300'
1200'

1100'

Big Hemlock Trail

West Vista

1300'

Big Hemlock Trail

900'

800'

SNOWMOBILE TRAIL

700'

1000'

1100'

Upper Carp River

Union Spring Trail
(ungroomed section)

1200'

1300'

1400'

1100'

Trap Falls

LEGEND

X-C Ski Trail

Easiest

More Difficult

Most Difficult

Warming Shelter

Cabin
(RESERVATION REQUIRED)

Snowmobile Trail

0   1/2   1 km

0   1/2   1 Mile

N

at the park headquarters or visitor center before beginning any overnight trip. Plan on carrying a lightweight stove to cook on and hang all food at the bear poles that have been installed in backcountry camping areas to avoid attracting black bears. Topographical maps that cover the park and trail advice can be obtained from the visitor center.

Hiking: Not all hiking adventures in the Porkies are overnight backpacking trips. On the perimeter of the state park there are a number of short loops that make for scenic day hikes. Along M-107, west of Union Bay Campground, is the trailhead for the Overlook Trail, which, when combined with a short portion of the Government Peak Trail, forms a 3.5-mile loop to a number of scenic viewpoints above 1,200 feet. The same trailhead is also the east end of the Escarpment Trail, a 4-mile hike along a ridge that includes Cuyahoga and Cloud Peaks and ends at the Lake of the Clouds Overlook on M-107. The views of Lake of the Clouds and the park's interior from this rocky ridge make this trail one of the most scenic in Michigan. Along South Boundary Road, 2 miles south of M-107, is Union Mine Trail. The mile-long loop is marked by signs that point out the history and ruins of the old Union Copper Mine. An interpretive brochure can be picked up at the visitor center. On the west side of the park are the East/West River Trails, which form a 2-mile loop along both sides of the scenic Presque Isle River and pass its three impressive waterfalls. The trails begin in the Presque Isle River Unit.

Mountain Biking: Although most of the Ehlco Mountain Bike Complex lies in the adjoining Ottawa National Forest, a trailhead and a small portion of the 27-mile network is in the Porcupine Mountains. The Ehlco begins at the base of Summit Peak Road and heads northeast along South Boundary Road and then turns east on Forest Road 39 to leave the state park. The rest of the circuit involves riding overgrown logging roads, tiptoeing across beaver dams, and fording a bridgeless West Branch of the Big Iron River before returning to South Boundary Road. Despite very little single track, the route is described as a flat but challenging ride for intermediate to advanced mountain bikers.

Cabins: The Porcupine Mountains have sixteen wilderness cabins for rent throughout the park. The three newest structures, Whitetailed Cabin on Lake Superior, Union River Cabin, and Gitche Gumee Cabin just off M-107, require a walk of only a mile or less from the road and are rented year-round. The rest of the cabins are rented from April 1 through November.

The most popular cabin in the park is Lake of the Clouds Cabin, a half-hour descent from M-107. There are also three cabins on Mirror Lake that are equipped with rowboats and can be reached via South Mirror Lake Trail, a 2.5-mile hike from the end of Summit Peak Road. The largest one, Mirror Lake Eight-Bunk Cabin, is a classic log structure near the edge of the lake. Two other units a short walk from the road are Section 17 Cabin and Greenstone Falls Cabin, located near each other on the Little Carp River and a 1.5-mile hike from the access road off South Boundary Road. All cabins must be reserved in advance through the park headquarters, and reservations are accepted two calendar years in advance beginning January 1.

Fishing: Porcupine Mountains State Park offers a diversity of fishing opportunities but is best known for its steelhead and salmon runs in the spring and fall. Presque Isle River attracts the most attention, with wading anglers either surf fishing or working the mouth of the river, as Manabezho Falls blocks farther runs upstream. The other two rivers offer a unique wilderness aspect for steelheaders who can only reach the area on foot. Little Carp River is a 3-mile walk on the Pinkerton Trail and has naturally produced steelhead that average four to five pounds. Fly fishermen as well as anglers working with spawn and spinners find this river a picturesque setting to catch steelhead. Another mile along the Lake Superior

Trail is the Big Carp River, whose many pools and gravel stretches attract even fewer fishermen.

Rowboats (no motors allowed in the park) are provided with the cabins on Mirror Lake, an 83-acre lake which is best fished spring and fall for splake, brook trout, and rainbow. Trout fishermen can also work Lily Pond either using the cabin rowboat or packing in an inflatable belly boat. Best fishing in midsummer is in Lake of the Clouds, whose cabin also has a rowboat, for smallmouth bass and perch. The Union River Impoundment, a 1.5-mile hike on the Union Spring Trail, was at one time stocked with brook trout, but the program was suspended after the impoundment began to fill in with silt.

The park also has an improved boat launch at Union Pier Campground for anglers who want to troll Lake Superior for lake trout in June and July as well as steelhead, salmon, and brown trout other times of the year.

Canoeing: The Presque Isle River has been described as the most challenging whitewater river in Michigan, an adventure for experienced kayakers or canoeists only. The most common portion paddled is from M-28 to South Boundary Road, a trip of 17.5 miles that ends in the state park. This paddle includes drops and rapids rated Class II to IV, four waterfalls, and a gorge. Because of the difficulty of the trip, most canoeists cover the stretch in 2 days. Below South Boundary Road the three waterfalls make the run unadvisable, while above M-28 the Presque Isle is a much slower river and can be handled by intermediate paddlers.

Scenic Viewpoints: From the end of M-107, it's a short walk to perhaps Michigan's most famous panorama, Lake of the Clouds Overlook. The viewing point is set on the side of a vertical cliff, and from the high point of almost 1,300 feet, it's possible to see the picturesque lake set among forested ridges and much of the Porkies' rugged interior. Another spectacular viewing area is Summit Observation Tower. The deck and observation tower is constructed on Summit Peak, 1,958 feet, and reached by a half-mile walk from the end of Summit Peak Road. The view includes the center of the Porkies and a portion of Mirror Lake.

The other spectacular viewing point in the park is at the end of the Presque Isle River, which enters Lake Superior after a series of waterfalls and surging rapids. At the end of County Road 519 is a day-use parking area where visitors access the gorge via a long stairway. A boardwalk with several observation platforms on the west side can then be followed to view the whitewater, while an impressive swing bridge provides access to a small island at the mouth of the Presque Isle.

Day-Use Facilities: There is a day-use area on each side of the park. Picnic sites along Lake Superior are adjacent to the Union Bay Campground along with an improved boat launch. On the west side there is a picnic area near the mouth of Presque Isle River.

Winter Activities: The Porkies feature a 320-acre downhill ski area whose slopes overlook Lake Superior, providing the park with the finest powder in the Midwest. Located just west of the park headquarters on M-107, the facility includes fourteen slopes with a vertical drop of 600 feet. There are four advanced runs, along with three for beginners and seven for intermediate skiers, that are serviced by a triple chair lift, a double chair, a double T-bar, and tow ropes. The longest run, Sunset, departs from the double chair and winds 1.2 miles through the woods before returning to the chalet at the base.

Fanning out from the downhill ski area is a 26-mile network of cross-country ski trails through a terrain that ranges from rolling to very hilly. The runs are groomed and tracked, and vary from Deer Yard Trail, a 3-mile loop with views of Lake Superior, to Union Spring Trail, an 11.8-mile run. The East and West Vista Trails pass a pair of 1,400-foot highpoints with stunning views of Lake Superior or Lake of the

Backpacker crossing Little Carp River, Porcupine Mountains Wilderness State Park

Clouds and can be reached by purchasing a single ride ticket to the triple chair lift. Cross-country skiers can also reach the Lake of the Clouds Overlook by following M-107, which is unplowed in the winter, but must remember this is also a popular snowmobile route.

Both downhill and Nordic skiers use the park chalet at the base of the slopes. The large warming center features fireplaces, lounge, food service, ski rentals, and a ski shop. The lodge and downhill slopes are open from mid-December through March from 9:30 A.M. to 5:30 P.M. daily. There are fees for both Nordic and downhill skiers that are separate from park entry permits. The lift tickets for the downhill area, however, are the most affordable of any major ski area in Michigan, with children twelve years and younger skiing for free.

Only three of the park's rustic cabins are rented out during the winter. The winter units are Whitetailed Cabin, Union River Cabin, and Gitche Gumee Cabin. Whitetailed and Union River are accessible from the park's groomed-trail system. Gitche Gumee is a 5-minute walk from M-107 and is handicap accessible. All cabins, which feature only woodstoves for heat, must be reserved in advance.

There is no snowmobiling in the interior of the park, but the activity is allowed on M-107 and South Boundary Road, which are not plowed during the winter, and sled rentals are available at the chalet. The Lake of the Clouds Overlook rivals the Tahquamenon Falls as the most popular destination for snowmobilers in the Upper Peninsula.

The park also offers an unusual spring snowshoe season which begins April 1, when the interior cabins become available for rent. For three to four weeks, winter campers ski South Boundary Road or M-107 to the trailheads and then switch to snowshoes to reach the cabins. This is not an adventure to be taken lightly. Although some cabins, like Speakers, are a little more than a mile from where you can leave your car, most are a one-way trip of 6 to 7 miles and the three structures at Mirror Lake can be a journey of up to 12 miles one way. Spring snow is different from year to year, but generally you can count on more than 3 feet of it in the woods in early April.

Access and Information: The park's east entrance is 17 miles west of Ontonagon, via M-64 and M-107. The Presque Isle River Unit is located at the end of County Road 519, 16 miles north of Wakefield. For more information or cabin reservations, contact Porcupine Mountains Wilderness State Park, 412 South Boundary Road, Ontonagon, MI 49953; or call (906) 885-5275.

Twin Lakes State Park

▲ Twin Lakes State Park is often promoted as an excellent "base camp," a place to set up house in order to venture to other Upper Peninsula attractions, most notably Copper Country to the north and the Porcupine Mountains to the west. But this 175-acre park in Houghton County is a natural attraction in itself. Visitors who go beyond the lakeshore campground by crossing M-26 will discover that the vast majority of the park is a heavily wooded and hilly area where, from a pair of lookouts, it's possible to view more than 10 miles north to the blue horizon of Lake Superior.

The park also features a beach and shoreline on Lake Roland, often cited as "the warmest inland lake in the Upper Peninsula." F. J. McLain, a Houghton County commissioner in the 1800s who was instrumental in setting aside the state park that now bears his name, also had a hand in preserving Twin Lakes as a county park. In 1964 the area was designated a state park, and today it draws almost 50,000 visitors annually.

Camping: Twin Lakes has a campground with sixty-two modern sites and a mini-cabin in a wooded area along Lake Roland. Sixteen sites are located right on the lakeshore or have an open view of the lake. They are always the first to be selected by campers. During normal summers it's possible to obtain a site throughout the week with the exception of Fourth of July weekend.

Hiking: Departing from the campground is a 1.5-mile trail that crosses M-26 and makes a loop through the park's undeveloped interior, forested predominantly in maple. Halfway along the loop the trail climbs to a pair of lookout points where hikers can usually view the length of Misery Bay Ravine to Lake Superior.

Fishing: Lake Roland covers 292 acres and reaches depths up to 40 feet. The lake is known by anglers primarily for walleye, crappie, and bass, while an occasional tiger muskie is also landed. The park maintains an improved boat ramp in its day-use area with parking for fifteen vehicles and trailers.

Day-Use Facilities: The day-use area is located on Lake Roland and includes a small, sandy beach, a bathhouse, and two picnic shelters, one enclosed and the other open, that can be reserved and rented.

Winter Activities: During the winter the park expands its trail system to 5.5 miles of cross-country ski runs. The trails form two interconnecting loops in the wooded interior of the park, a 2.2-mile run and a 5.5-mile route, and are occasionally groomed by locals. The terrain ranges from flat to rolling and can be handled by most novice skiers. The ski trailhead is located in the parking area for the DNR headquarters.

Access and Information: The park entrance is 26 miles south of Houghton on M-26 or 3 miles north of the town of Winona. For more information, contact Twin Lakes State Park, Route 1, P.O. Box 234, M-26, Toivola, MI 49965; or call (906) 288-3321 in the summer only.

F. J. McLain State Park

▲ F. J. McLain State Park's outstanding feature is its shoreline, almost 2 miles of frontage that begins at the mouth of Portage Lake Ship Canal and extends northeast along Lake Superior. It's characterized by bluffs overlooking a thin strip of beach and the watery horizon of the world's largest body of fresh water. Arrive at McLain's shoreline at dusk on a clear evening and you witness a spectacular scene—a fiery sunset melting into Lake Superior. So popular is the end-of-day show that lakeside benches were installed on the bluff near the park's campground.

McLain, a 417-acre park located in Houghton County on the edge of Michigan's famed Copper Country, is also a noted area for rock hounds. Agate hunters scour the shoreline for the semiprecious stones, most notably greenstone, and occasionally even find small pieces of native copper. The park draws 200,000 visitors annually with the majority arriving during summer and fall.

Camping: At one time McLain's campground had more than twenty sites on the edge of the shoreline bluff for a spectacular view of Lake Superior, but erosion has reduced the number significantly. Still, the view of the Great Lake is excellent from any of the 103 modern sites located in an area forested lightly in red pine and oak. Scattered through the campground are six mini-cabins that are open year-round.

The facility is popular and from mid-July to late August can be filled any day of the week but particularly the weekends, and always Labor Day weekend. The park also maintains an organization camp.

Hiking: Departing from the campground is Bear Lake Trail, a 3-mile walk that ends near the park headquarters. Along the way the trail skirts Bear Lake and passes a dock, although there is little fishing activity in the shallow body of water.

Breakwater and signal light, F. J. McLain State Park

Cabin: McLain has a rustic eight-bunk cabin situated by itself on the bluff over-looking Lake Superior. To reach it, you drive through the campground to a gated entrance at the end. Bear Lake Trail also passes near it.

Fishing: Although there is no fishing in Bear Lake, shore anglers are attracted to the park's breakwall. Using spawn or spoons, fishermen cast off the wall in spring or fall for steelhead or coho salmon. In the summer there is some fishing activity for whitefish.

Day-Use Facilities: McLain has a small, sandy beach and a bathhouse/shelter located on the Portage Lake Ship Canal. The sand is protected from Lake Superior by a breakwall, which makes for an interesting stroll out toward the Keweenaw Upper Entry Light. Farther east in the day-use area is a picnic area and shelter, along with a 2-mile fitness trail with nine exercise stations.

Winter Activities: The Bear Lake Trail and part of the fitness trail are groomed in the winter, giving the park 4 miles of ski trails. The runs are level and ideal for novice skiers. More advanced skiers tend to favor nearby Swedetown and Maasto Hiihto Ski Trails, which are groomed and tracked by local ski clubs. This far north the ski season often begins in late November and runs through March. Equipment rental is available in Houghton and Calumet.

Access and Information: The park entrance is on M-203, 8 miles north of Hancock. For more information, contact F. J. McLain State Park, Route 1, P.O. Box 82, M-203, Hancock, MI 49930; or call (906) 482-0278.

Fort Wilkins State Park

The Copper Rush of the Keweenaw Peninsula began in 1843, and quickly Copper Harbor became the center of exploration parties, newly formed mining companies, and "a rough population" of enterprising prospectors, miners, and speculators. Due to the seedy nature of the miners and the constant threat of Chippewa tribes wanting to reclaim their lost land, Secretary of War William Wilkins dispatched two companies of infantry to the remote region of Michigan. They arrived in late May of 1844, and by November Fort Wilkins was built.

At the time, Fort Wilkins was the northernmost post in a chain of forts that stretched from the Gulf of Mexico to the tip of the Keweenaw Peninsula and formed a western perimeter of national defense. In reality, however, the fort was of little military importance, as the threat of Native American hostilities never materialized and the troops quickly discovered the Upper Peninsula winters were long and cold. Isolated from the rest of the world with little more than duty and drill to occupy their time, the garrison of 105 men ran into problems of boredom, low morale, and illegal whiskey. In 1845, half the troops were transferred to Texas in preparation for the Mexican War, and in 1846, less than two years after it was built, Fort Wilkins was abandoned.

Although it was briefly reoccupied by soldiers from 1867–70 as an interim home after the Civil War, Fort Wilkins' real value became apparent with the arrival of the automobile in the early 1900s. The abandoned fort, located on a narrow strip of land between rugged Copper Harbor and serene Lake Fanny Hooe, was a beautiful spot to have a picnic or enjoy the outdoors. Almost as soon as the troops left, locals staged concerts, dances, even turkey shoots at the fort, while automobile excursions increased steadily after the turn of the century. In 1921 Fort Wilkins was recognized as an historical landmark by the state and in 1923 designated a state park.

Today the structure is noted for being one of the few surviving wooden forts east of the Mississippi River. But the park also preserves natural beauty as well as human history. The 203-acre unit at the tip of the Keweenaw County includes 2 miles of shoreline along the inland lake and Lake Superior, several islands in Copper Harbor, and even a lighthouse on a point. Fort Wilkins draws more than 150,000 visitors annually. Many stop for the day just to view the fort, while others enjoy the park's campgrounds, trails, or ski runs during the winter.

Camping: Fort Wilkins has a mini-cabin and 165 modern sites divided between the East Campground and the West Campground. Both are in wooded areas, with a row of sites near the shoreline of Lake Fanny Hooe and a trail to the historic fort. Each has its own entrance off US 41 and tend to fill up a few weekends in July and early August. The park also has an organization camp.

Interpretive Centers: The centerpiece of the state park is the restored Fort Wilkins. Although the fort was insignificant militarily, it's an outstanding example of a mid-nineteenth century frontier outpost, as twelve of its nineteen buildings are from the original structure. You can wander through the fort year-round, even ski through it in the winter, but the individual buildings are open mid-May through mid-October from 8:00 A.M. to dusk. Ranging from a kitchen and mess room to a bakery, company barracks, and hospital, many of the buildings contain restored furnishings and artifacts depicting the rough life troops endured here. From mid-June to Labor Day interpreters in period dress give tours daily and add a touch of realism to the fort. Check with park headquarters for a variety of special evening programs held within the fort throughout the summer.

Also part of the state park is the Copper Harbor Lighthouse. The structure was built in 1866 and was occupied until 1919. Today the interior is restored as a lighthouse museum and can be visited through the Spirit of America, a boat tour operator that leaves the Copper City Harbor hourly during the summer from 10:00 A.M. to 5:00 P.M. There is a fee for the boat tour to the lighthouse but none for viewing the fort other than a vehicle entry permit.

Hiking: The park has almost 2 miles of trail, and much of it connects the fort with the campgrounds and day-use area. The Lake Superior Nature Trail begins in the picnic area and forms a circuit that runs along Lake Fanny Hooe, Copper Harbor, and Fanny Hooe Creek before passing the fort.

Fishing: Lake Fanny Hooe is stocked annually with rainbow trout and splake and in the past with walleye. Anglers also catch smallmouth bass. Copper Harbor possesses a fishery consisting of lake trout, salmon, splake, steelhead, and occasionally, even a brown trout is caught. The park maintains a boat launch on Lake Fanny Hooe near the West Campground. There is no ramp on the Lake Superior side of the state park, but the DNR Waterways Division maintains a large public marina in Copper Harbor.

Day-Use Facilities: Just east of the fort there is a pleasant wooded picnic area that includes a shelter that can be rented. Also in the area is a park store and numerous enclosed copper mine shafts that were dug out by the Pittsburgh and Boston Company, but no beach or designated swimming area on Lake Fanny Hooe.

Winter Activities: The park grooms and tracks a 2-mile ski run that is level and begins at a trailhead off US 41 just east of the bridge over Fanny Hooe Creek. The loop includes a section through the fort as well as a very scenic stretch along Lake Fanny Hooe. Nearby is Copper Harbor Pathway, a machine-set trail on the south side of Lake Fanny Hooe that includes the 6.2-mile Kamakazie Run and the 3.1-mile Clark Mine Trail. To reach the pathway trailhead turn right at Fanny Hooe Resort on US 41 and follow the road to where road crews stop plowing. There is no ski rental concession in the park. The other popular winter activity is ice fishing on Lake Fanny Hooe.

FORT WILKINS STATE PARK

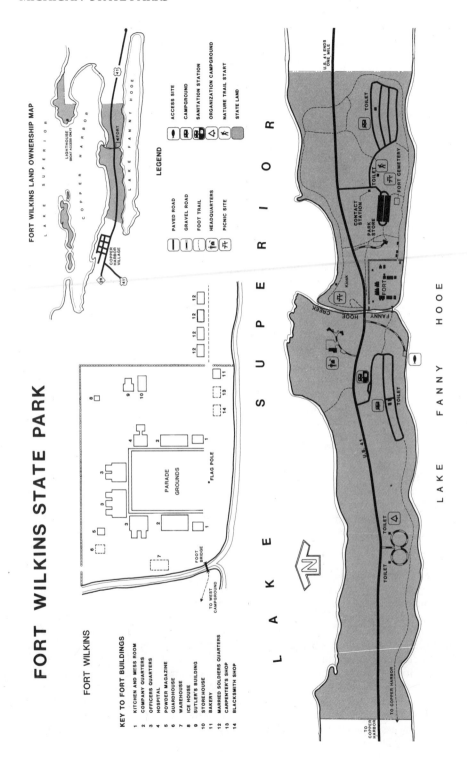

FORT WILKINS LAND OWNERSHIP MAP

LAKE SUPERIOR

COPPER HARBOR

LIGHTHOUSE
(BOAT ACCESS ONLY)

LAKE FANNY HOOE

FORT

COPPER HARBOR VILLAGE

LEGEND

PAVED ROAD	ACCESS SITE
GRAVEL ROAD	CAMPGROUND
FOOT TRAIL	SANITATION STATION
HEADQUARTERS	ORGANIZATION CAMPGROUND
PICNIC SITE	NATURE TRAIL START
	STATE LAND

FORT WILKINS

KEY TO FORT BUILDINGS

1 KITCHEN AND MESS ROOM
2 COMPANY QUARTERS
3 OFFICERS QUARTERS
4 HOSPITAL
5 POWDER MAGAZINE
6 GUARDHOUSE
7 WAREHOUSE
8 ICE HOUSE
9 SUTLER'S BUILDING
10 STOREHOUSE
11 BAKERY
12 MARRIED SOLDIERS QUARTERS
13 CARPENTER'S SHOP
14 BLACKSMITH SHOP

PARADE GROUNDS

FLAG POLE

FOOT BRIDGE

TO WEST CAMPGROUND

LAKE SUPERIOR

LAKE FANNY HOOE

FANNY HOOE CREEK

FORT

U.S. 41

U.S. 41 ENDS ONE MILE

FORT CEMETERY

CONTACT STATION

PARK STORE

Kiosk

TOILET

TO COPPER HARBOR

TO COPPER HARBOR

N

Access and Information: The main entrance to the park, including the fort, East Campground, and the day-use area, is a mile east of Copper Harbor on US-41. For more information, contact Fort Wilkins State Park, P.O. Box 71, Copper Harbor, MI 49918; or call (906) 289-4215.

Baraga State Park

▲ The view of Keweenaw Bay from the Baraga State Park day-use area is excellent. ⊥ To the north of any picnic table is the curving shoreline of the Keweenaw Peninsula, to the east the waterfront of L'Anse, and in between the busy waters of this narrow bay. The view is nice, but the main attraction of this 56-acre park in Baraga County is its location. Of the 50,000 annual visitors to the state park, more than 30 percent are out-of-staters, 10 percent alone from Wisconsin, who set up camp then explore other areas of western Upper Peninsula. Within a 2-hour drive are natural attractions in every direction: the Copper Country of the Keweenaw Peninsula to the north, Porcupine Mountains to the west, and Piers Gorge on the Menominee River to the south.

Camping: US 41 runs through the park and separates the campground from the day-use area on Keweenaw Bay. Baraga has 109 modern sites and 10 semi-modern sites without electricity as well as a mini-cabin and a rent-a-tipi. The campground is in an open area that is well sodded. Obtaining a site is never a problem during the summer, even on the weekends, as the park only fills on Fourth of July weekend.

Hiking: Departing from the campground is the Baraga Nature Trail, a 0.6-mile loop that winds through a morainal landscape of red maple, aspen, and birch. There are sixteen posted stops on the trail, and an accompanying interpretive brochure can be picked up from the park headquarters.

Fishing: Keweenaw Bay is popular among anglers in search of salmon, steelhead, and lake and brown trout. The most activity occurs early spring and late fall when fishermen surface troll the shoreline of the bay, often in less than 10 feet of water. Baraga maintains a boat launch on the bay near the mouth of Hazel Creek in its day-use area. Anglers also fish the small creek for brook trout.

Day-Use Facilities: The park's day-use area is on the east side of US 41 and features 300 feet of sandy shoreline along the Keweenaw Bay. Other facilities include a grassy picnic area and a bathhouse.

Access and Information: The park entrance is located a mile south of the town of Baraga on US 41. For more information, contact Baraga State Park, 1300 US 41 South, Baraga, MI 49908; or call (906) 353-6558.

Lake Gogebic State Park

▲ Lake Gogebic State Park is a crown with two jewels. To the west, the 361-acre ⊥ unit in Gogebic County lies on the edge of the rugged highlands that extend into the heart of the Ottawa National Forest. The ridges and hills, including a high point of 1,545 feet, make up the interior of the park and are forested in hemlock and mixed hardwoods—maple, ash, and elm. To the east, the park ends with 0.75 mile of shoreline on Lake Gogebic, the largest inland lake in the Upper Peninsula and what many consider the most beautiful anywhere in the state.

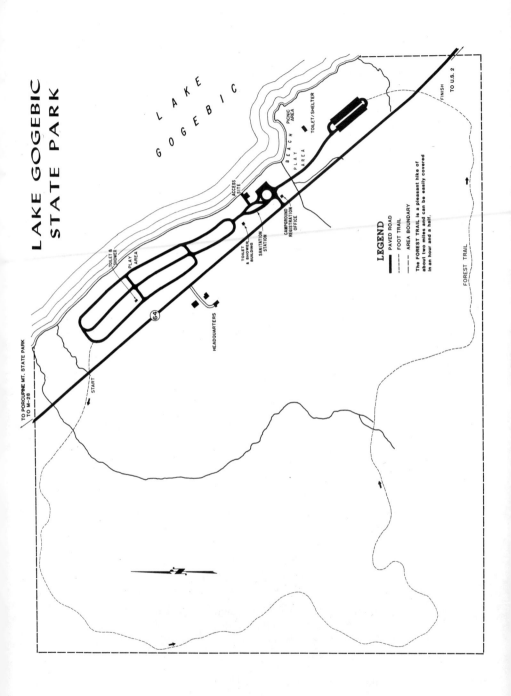

LAKE GOGEBIC
STATE PARK

LAKE
GOGEBIC

TO PORCUPINE MT. STATE PARK
TO M-28

START

TOILET & SHOWER

PLAY AREA

HEADQUARTERS

ACCESS SITE

TOILET & SHOWER BUILDING

SANITATION STATION

CAMPGROUND REGISTRATION OFFICE

BEACH PLAY AREA

PICNIC AREA

TOILET/SHELTER

FINISH

TO U.S. 2

FOREST TRAIL

LEGEND

PAVED ROAD
FOOT TRAIL
AREA BOUNDARY

The FOREST TRAIL is a pleasant hike of about two miles and can be easily covered in an hour and a half.

To the east M-64 follows the lake, and along the shoreline the park is well developed, catering to campers, swimmers, boaters, and anglers. But to the west park users will discover an undeveloped area that is penetrated only by a 2-mile trail. Overall, Lake Gogebic draws 56,000 visitors annually, a far cry from many of the units on the south side of the Mackinac Bridge.

Camping: Lake Gogebic has 104 modern sites in its campground with a large portion of them situated right along the shoreline. The rest have a good view of the water, and all are in a semi-open area that is lightly shaded. There are also 22 semi-modern sites without electricity and a rent-a-tent. Lake Gogebic is a scenic campground, and best of all there are usually sites available, with the exception of Fourth of July weekend and the second week in August.

Hiking: Beginning at a marked trailhead at the back of the campground is the Forest Trail, a 2-mile walk that ends at the parking lot for the day-use area. The trail crosses M-64 twice to wind through the park's wooded and rolling interior, passing a series of interpretive displays. The first mile of the trail can be wet at times as you pass a cedar swamp, but the second half is a dry path through an impressive stand of old-growth maple and hemlock.

Fishing: The largest lake in the Upper Peninsula is also a noted one for walleye fishing. The 14-mile Lake Gogebic covers more than 20 square miles and is stocked annually with walleye. Although there are a variety of ways to fish for walleyes, many anglers prefer drifting or slowly trolling inflated night crawlers or leeches. Working rocky points and dropoffs with lead jigs tipped with minnows is another productive method. Lake Gogebic is also rated quite highly for its population of northern pike and perch. The park maintains an improved boat ramp near the day-use area. Just outside the park along M-65 there are numerous bait shops and resorts that rent boats and motors.

Day-Use Facilities: Lake Gogebic has a small, sandy beach bordered by a large grassy bank in its day-use area. Other facilities include a bathhouse, play area, parking for 100 vehicles, and an exceptionally pleasant picnic area situated on a small point with a nice view of the lakeshore to the north.

Winter Activities: The park's trail system is occasionally groomed for cross-country skiers and makes for a moderately hilly run rated for intermediate skiers. Parking is provided near the park headquarters during the winter, and the entire loop makes for almost a 3-mile ski. There is no warming hut or ski rental concession.

Access and Information: The state park is 25 miles east of Wakefield. Follow US 2 for 16 miles and then turn north (left) on M-64 for 9 miles to the posted entrance. From M-28 turn south at M-64 for 8 miles. For more information, contact Lake Gogebic State Park, P.O. Box 139, H.C. 1, Marenisco, MI 49947; or call (906) 842-3341.

Bewabic State Park

Bewabic State Park is located on the northwest corner of Fortune Lakes—the First Lake, that is. Head south from the park in a canoe or boat and you'll enter the Second Lake, the Third Lake, and finally the Fourth Lake. The chain of small lakes extends south of US 2 and is the most attractive feature of the 315-acre park in Iron County.

Bewabic, which draws only 50,000 visitors a year, also features a campground, a day-use area, and an interesting shoreline along Fortune Lake, plus a small island. But most unusual are the tennis courts. Built in the 1940s when the area was a county park, the courts remained when the state acquired the land in 1966, and now

Log cabin bathhouse on Fortune Lake, Bewabic State Park

Bewabic is the only unit in the state park system where visitors can pack their racket along with their fishing pole.

Camping: The park has a 140 modern sites, 4 semi-modern ones, and a rent-a-tent in a campground located on a hill above the lake. The area is well wooded, and the buffer strips between sites give campers a good deal of privacy. The camp-ground fills up only for Fourth of July weekend during the summer.

Hiking: Bewabic has a pleasant 2-mile foot trail with benches along the way that begins in the campground and drops through the wooded section in the south end of the park before circling back to the day-use area. There is also a very short trail that follows the shoreline of the island just off the day-use area. Visitors use a foot-bridge to reach the trail.

Canoeing: The chain of lakes makes for an ideal day trip, departing from the state park for a round trip that heads out and returns through the four lakes con-nected by small channels. Keep in mind that there are many private cabins on the first two and no public land, other than the state park, on any of the lakes where canoers can camp overnight.

Fishing: A small boat and motor can reach all four Fortune Lakes in a day, and anglers often do in their search for perch, largemouth and smallmouth bass, wall-eye, and bluegill. Most anglers concentrate on First Lake, the largest one at 192 acres with a depth of 72 feet. Bewabic maintains an improved boat launch near the day-use area with parking for twelve vehicles and rigs. Additional parking is allowed along the park drive. Shore fishermen can also wet a line, and perhaps the best spot is off an island connected by a foot bridge to the north end of the park. There is a steep dropoff on the far side of it where it's possible to catch perch and bluegill.

Day-Use Facilities: Bewabic has only a limited stretch of sandy beach on Fortune Lake, but the rest of the day-use facility is a lightly shaded, grassy area that features tables, play equipment, tennis courts, and a shelter that can be rented. There is also a resident flock of Canada geese here that visitors are urged not to feed.

Winter Activities: The campground is not plowed during the winter, and the park sets up a 2-mile ski trail around the facility. Skiers park near the headquarters for the hilly but easy run. There is no snowmobiling in the park, but Fortunes Lakes do draw a number of ice fishermen during the winter.

Access and Information: The park is located 4 miles west of Crystal Falls on US 2. For more information, contact Bewabic State Park, 1933 US 2 West, Crystal Falls, MI 49920; or call (906) 875-3324.

Van Riper State Park

Situated in the heart of the Upper Peninsula, the only unit in Marquette County, is Van Riper State Park. The most popular section of the park, the reason it draws 120,000 visitors annually, is the developed area south of US 41/M-28 along the west end of Lake Michigamme that includes a modern campground, day-use area and beach, and a boat launch along the 0.75-mile of lakeshore.

But the largest part of Van Riper's 1,044 acres lies north of US 41/M-28, and to many, this is the park's most scenic area. Forested predominantly in hardwoods, this is a hilly tract with numerous rock bluffs and is bordered on the west by more than a half mile of the Peshekee River. The lightly used area includes Van Riper's network of hiking trails and a rustic cabin overlooking the river. Like all state parks, Van Riper is open year-round, but without groomed Nordic ski trails, activity during the winter is limited to people renting the rustic and mini-cabins.

Camping: Van Riper has two campgrounds, both at the east end of Lake Michigamme. The modern campground has 149 sites and two mini-cabins, although none of them are directly on the water. There are 40 more sites in the rustic campground, located nearby in a more open area. The modern facility will fill on a handful of weekends during the summer, but there are usually sites available in the rustic campground.

Cabin: Van Riper also has one of the newest rustic cabins in the state park system. The Peshekee River Cabin is an eight-bunk unit featuring a screened porch, which was built in 1993 on a bluff overlooking the river on the north side of US 41/M-28. It's a half-mile drive in from the road and short distance from the park's trail system.

Hiking: The park maintains almost 4 miles of foot trails that wind through the terrain north of US 41/M-28 and are closed to mountain bikers. The trailhead for the River Trail is located just north of the rustic cabin, and from here the path can be combined with a portion of the Old Wagon Trail to form a 2-mile loop. The high point of the hike is at a pair of overlooks that are reached after crossing a gravel road. From either one you can stand at the edge of a rock outcropping and enjoy a grand view of Lake Michigamme.

The 1.5-mile Old Wagon Trail has a trailhead off US 41/M-28 practically across from the entrance of the park and from there extends northwest before merging

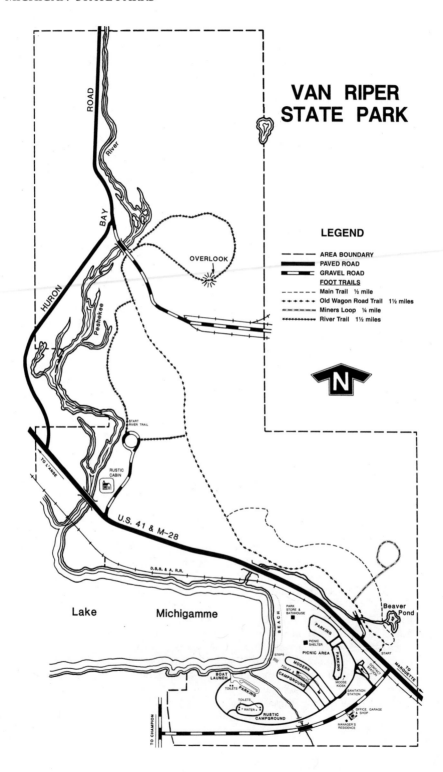

VAN RIPER
STATE PARK

LEGEND

– – –	AREA BOUNDARY
▬▬▬	PAVED ROAD
▬▭▬	GRAVEL ROAD
	FOOT TRAILS
– – –	Main Trail ½ mile
+ + + +	Old Wagon Road Trail 1½ miles
·–··–··	Miners Loop ¼ mile
··········	River Trail 1½ miles

OVERLOOK

START RIVER TRAIL

RUSTIC CABIN

U.S. 41 & M-28

TO L'ANSE

D.S.S. & A. R.R.

Lake Michigamme

Beaver Pond

PARK STORE & BATHHOUSE

BEACH

PARKING

PICNIC SHELTER

PICNIC AREA

PARKING

STEPS

MODERN

TOILET & SHOWER

CONTACT STATION

TO MARQUETTE

START

MODERN CAMPGROUND

MOOSE KIOSK

BOAT LAUNCH

PARKING

TOILETS

SANITATION STATION

OFFICE, GARAGE & SHOP

TOILETS

WATER

RUSTIC CAMPGROUND

MANAGER'S RESIDENCE

TO CHAMPION

A rustic cabin in Van Riper State Park

with the River Trail. Extending from it are the 0.5-mile Main Trail, which features an overlook and an active beaver pond, and the half-mile Miners Loop. Many of the trails now feature interpretive panels.

Interpretive Center: Van Riper is near the spot where fifty-nine moose were reintroduced into the Upper Peninsula in 1985 and 1987. In the parking area of the day-use area is an information kiosk with displays and a self operating video that tells the story of airlifting the moose from the backcountry of Ontario's Algonquin Provincial Park and then trucking them nonstop to a release site 6 miles north of the state park. You can also pick up a "Moose Locator Guide" in the park, and then spend an afternoon driving the forest roads north of US 41/M-28 for the chance of spotting members of the expanding herd.

Fishing: Lake Michigamme spreads over 4,360 acres, reaches depths of up 70 feet, and is known predominantly for its walleye fishery as it is stocked regularly with the species. But anglers also catch smallmouth bass, northern pike, and even an occasional muskie. Peshekee River is subject to very light fishing pressure, mostly upriver from the park, for brook trout. Van Riper maintains an improved boat launch on the southeast corner of Lake Michigamme.

Day-Use Facilities: The park has a large day-use area on Lake Michigamme that features a sandy beach, picnic area, bathhouse, and parking for more than 300 vehicles.

Access and Information: The park entrance to Lake Michigamme is on US 41/M-28, 31 miles west of Marquette or a mile beyond the village of Champion. For more information, contact Van Riper State Park, P.O. Box 66, Champion, MI 49814;

or call (906) 339-4461.

Craig Lake State Park

▲ The most remote unit of the state park system is Craig Lake State Park, a 6,983-acre tract in Baraga County. Craig Lake is a designated state wilderness area and just getting to it is an adventure. The park is reached by following almost 7 miles of poorly marked and very rough logging roads that are often impassable after heavy rains. The drive ends at a small parking area on the southern edge of the park, and to travel any further requires either a paddle or a pair of hiking boots.

Craig Lake is worth all the effort spent reaching it. A rugged area, the park contains six full lakes, parts of several others, and numerous small ponds, along with a variety of wildlife including deer, black bear, beaver, loons, and even a portion of the newly transplanted Upper Peninsula moose herd. Its centerpiece is Craig Lake, a 374-acre body of water featuring six islands and high granite bluffs along its

One of many islands in Craig Lake

northern shoreline. The park is managed as a primitive unit with bans on motorized vehicles and boat motors and is totally undeveloped except for its trail network and two cabins left by the previous owners.

Most of the park was acquired in the early 1950s by Frederick Miller of Milwaukee, a wealthy sportsman who was president of the Miller Brewing Company. After naming three of the lakes after his children (Craig, Clair, and Teddy), Miller built a good-sized lodge on Craig Lake along with a much smaller cabin for his caretaker. He introduced muskellunge in Craig Lake as well as bass and walleye. Miller died a few years after acquiring the land, and eventually the state purchased the area from a logging company. The wilderness tract was dedicated a state park in 1967. Although the park is open year-round, only skiers and snowshoers who are quite familiar with the area should enter it during the winter.

Camping: The only designated camping facilities in the park are tent pads located on Craig and Crooked Lakes. The Sandy Beach Camping Area is located on the east shore of Craig Lake, south of the portage trail to Crooked Lake, and consists of three tent pads. The Eagle Nest Camping Area is on Crooked Lake, just off the east end of the portage trail, and features two pads above the lake. Dispersed camping is allowed anywhere with the exception of the immediate cabin area. Canoers and hikers must self-register at the first portage trail to Craig Lake where there is a drop pipe for the nightly backcountry camping fee.

Cabins: The two cabins are located on the west shore of Craig Lake and are reached by either a portage and paddle across the lake or a 1.5-mile hike. Situated near each other, the largest cabin sleeps 14 and has a huge recreation/dining room with a stone fireplace. The smaller cabin sleeps six and has a woodstove in its main room. The cabins are available from May 15 to October 15 and due to their popularity, especially among anglers, they should be reserved several months in advance.

Hiking: There are more than 10 miles of trails in the park, including a portion of the North Country Trail. The NCT basically merges into an 8-mile loop that circumnavigates Craig Lake. The hike around the lake is extremely scenic and includes a number of high rocky bluffs with the most impressive one less than a mile north of the cabins. You also cross the short portages to Clair and Crooked Lakes and a footbridge over the West Branch of the Peshekee River. The loop is accessible from the portage between the parking area and Craig Lake.

Canoeing: The park provides enough lakes for an enjoyable weekend of paddling. From the parking lot, the portage to Craig Lake is 0.2 mile along a wide path. At the north end of the lake, near the outlet of the West Branch of the Peshekee River, is the posted portage to Clair Lake, a 0.3-mile walk. Most paddlers head toward Crooked Lake, reached from a marked portage on the east side of Craig Lake. The trip is a half-mile hike, while Crooked Lake is an interesting body of water of many bays, narrows, and inlets.

Fishing: Craig Lake is renowned for its muskellunge that require patience and time of anglers who often troll for the large fish with surface lures. Most anglers are content to catch walleyes, northern pike, and smallmouth bass. Clair Lake has an excellent fishery for smallmouth bass, while anglers also work Teddy, Crooked, and Keewaydin Lakes. Parking areas lie quite near Teddy and Keewaydin, while Crooked and Clair can only be reached by a portage from Craig Lake. Due to the park's unique populations of large predator fish and its wilderness state, there are a number of special rules for fishermen to follow. Boat motors, even electric ones, are banned throughout the park. Anglers can use only artificial lures, and all northern pike and muskies must be released. The minimum size to keep bass is 18 inches,

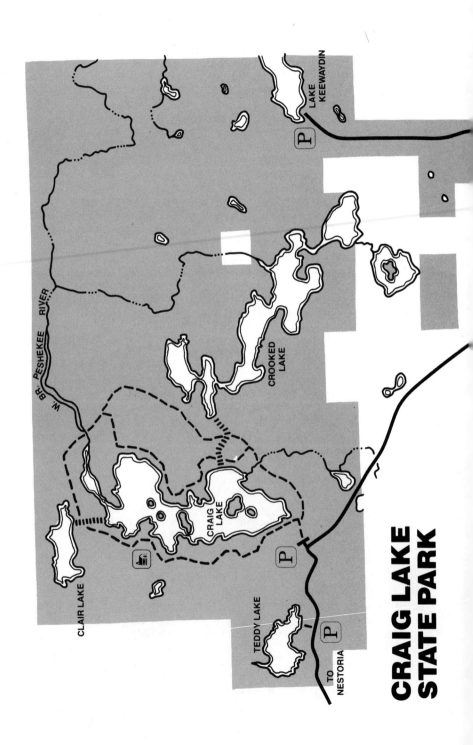

LAKE KEEWAYDIN

W. BR. PESHEKEE RIVER

CROOKED LAKE

CLAIR LAKE

CRAIG LAKE

TEDDY LAKE

TO NESTORIA

CRAIG LAKE
STATE PARK

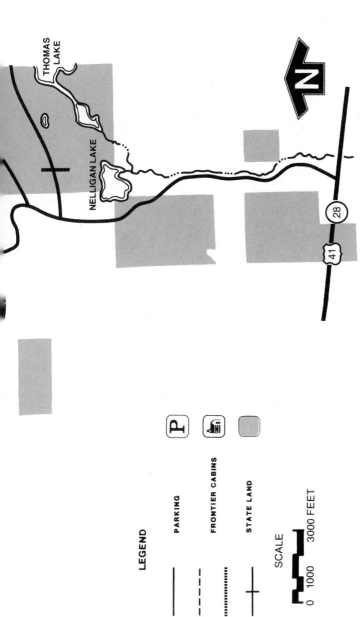

CRAIG LAKE STATE PARK RULES and SERVICES

1. Special Fishing & Motor Boat Regulations apply to all lakes in Craig Lake State Park. See your copy of the "Michigan Fishing Guide", under Special Provisions — Baraga County.

2. Carry out what you carry in. Please do not leave paper, cans, bottles, or other trash in the park.

3. Roads — Some may be impassable .... or passible by 4-wheel drive vehicles only. Contact the manager at Van Riper State Park for current road conditions at Craig Lake.

4. Camping — A fee for rustic camping applies in Craig Lake State Park. Camps must be set up a minimum of 150 feet from the waters edge.

5. Frontier Cabins are available for rent. Contact the manager at Van Riper State Park.

6. PLEASE NOTE — The Island on Clair Lake is PRIVATE PROPERTY (not state-owned). Please respect their property and their privacy.

LEGEND

ROADS

TRAILS

PORTAGES

GATE ON ROAD

PARKING 🅿

FRONTIER CABINS

STATE LAND

SCALE
0 1000 3000 FEET

THOMAS LAKE

NELLIGAN LAKE

N

28

41

Paddling Craig Lake

and walleye, 13 inches. The daily limit is two, singly or combined. Anglers will find trolling for muskies good to the end of June, while lead jigs with twister tails is a common lure used for walleye.

Access and Information: Keewaydin Lake Road, the main road into the park, is 7.9 miles west of the Van Riper State Park entrance on US 41/M-28, and is posted. But following the lightly marked network of logging roads to the parking areas of Keewaydin, Craig, and Teddy Lakes is challenging. All visitors should first obtain a map of the park from the Van Riper State Park headquarters. For more information or cabin reservations, contact Van Riper State Park, P.O. Box 66, Champion, MI 49814; or call (906) 339-4461.

Quick Reference to Facilities and Recreation

The following table is a quick reference to what each park offers (by reading across) as well as which parks offer a particular facility or recreation activity (by reading up and down).

Reference Key

Campground
M—modern campground (includes electricity, flush toilets, showers and sanitation station)
R—rustic campground (usually includes vault toilets and hand-pump water)
B—both types of sites available

Rent-a-Tent
•—park participates in Rent-a-Tent or Rent-a-Tipi program

Cabins
•—rustic cabins available for rent by either families or groups

Day-Use Facilities
•—picnic area with tables, water, grills, and often play equipment
B—picnic area and a boat rental concession on a lake or river
C—picnic area and bicycle paths

Picnic Shelter
•—picnic shelter with tables (in most cases can be rented and reserved in advance)

Interpretive Center
•—nature center, museum, or outdoor interpretive area

Boat Launch
I—improved boat launch (includes a concrete ramp capable of handling boats over 16 feet in length and a parking area for trailers)
U—unimproved boat launch (gravel or dirt ramp)
H—access for hand-carried boats only

Fishing (only the major species caught in each park are listed)
W—walleye, northern pike, or perch
B—smallmouth or largemouth bass
P—panfish such as bluegill, crappie, and sunfish
S—salmon, steelhead, or lake trout
T—inland rainbow trout, brown trout, or brook trout
M—muskellunge

Fishing Pier
•—fishing pier, breakwall, or a dock from which it is possible to fish without the use of a boat

Hiking
•—network of hiking trails or a nature trail
B—overnight backpacking opportunities/trailhead for an extended trail

Mountain Biking
•—designated mountain bike area or trail

Canoeing
•—canoeing opportunities in a river or a chain of lakes
R—canoe rental concession

Swimming
•—beach and swimming facilities

Equestrian Facilities
•—network of bridle paths
C—bridle paths and equestrian campground
S—stable concession

Skiing
•—trails for cross-country skiing
R—ski rental concession
D—downhill skiing facilities

Snowmobiling
•— open to snowmobiling in designated areas

Rifle Range
•—rifle or archery range

Handicapped Facilities
•—handicapped facilities available

Southeast Michigan

	Campground	Rent-a-Tent	Cabins	Day-Use Fac.	Picnic Shelter	Interp. Center	Boat Launch	Fishing	Fishing Pier	Hiking	Mtn. Biking	Canoeing	Swimming	Equest. Fac.	Skiing	Snowmobiling	Rifle Range	Handicapped Fac.
Sterling SP	M			B			I	WP	•	•	•	R	•					•
Maybury SP				C	•	•		P	•	•	•			S	R			•
Island Lake RA	R		•	B	•		H	TB		•	•	R	•			•		•
Brighton RA	B		•	B	•		I	TB		•	•	R	•	SC	•		•	
Proud Lake RA	M			•	•		I	T		•		R	•	•	R	•		•
Highland RA	R		•	•	•		I	W		•	•		•	S	•	•		
Dodge No. 4 SP				B	•		I	BW					•					•
Pontiac Lake RA	M	•		•	•		I	BW	•	•	•		•	SC		•	•	•
Seven Lakes SP	M			B	•		I	BWM	•	•	•	R	•			•		•
Holly RA	M	•	•	B	•		I	PB		•	•	R	•			•	•	•
Ortonville RA	R		•	•	•		I	BPW		•	•		•			•	•	•
Metamora–Hadley RA	M			B	•		I	B	•	•		R	•			•	•	•
Bald Mountain RA			•	•	•		I	BPT	•	•	•		•			•	•	•
Wetzel SP																•	•	
Algonac SP	B			•	•		I	W	•							•	•	
Lakeport SP	M			•	•								•					•

Heartland

	Campground	Rent-a-Tent	Cabins	Day-Use Fac.	Picnic Shelter	Interp. Center	Boat Launch	Fishing	Fishing Pier	Hiking	Mtn. Biking	Canoeing	Swimming	Equest. Fac.	Skiing	Snowmobiling	Rifle Range	Handicapped Fac.
Lake Hudson RA	R			•	•		I	M										
Cambridge SHP				•		•												
W. J. Hayes SP	M			B			I	BPW				R	•			•		•
Waterloo RA	B		•	•	•	•	I	BPT		B	•	R	•	C	•	•		•
Pinckney RA	B			B	•		I	BPW	•	B	•	R	•	S	•	•		•
Lakelands Trail SP				C						•	•			S	•	•		
Yankee Springs RA	B		•	•	•		I	WP		•	•	R	•	C	•	•		•
Sleepy Hollow SP	M			B	•		I	BPW	•	•	•	R	•			•	•	
Fort Custer RA	M		•	•	•		I	BW		•	•	R	•	•	•	•		•

	Campground	Rent-a-Tent	Cabins	Day-Use Fac.	Picnic Shelter	Interp. Center	Boat Launch	Fishing	Fishing Pier	Hiking	Mtn. Biking	Canoeing	Swimming	Equest. Fac.	Skiing	Snowmobiling	Rifle Range	Handicapped Fac.
Ionia RA	B			•	•		I	BWT	•	•	•	R	•	C	•	•	•	•
Wilson SP	M	•		•	•			MB					•					
White Pine Trail SP				C						•	•				•	•	•	
Mitchell SP	M			•	•	•	U	WPB	•				•		•			•
Newaygo SP	R						I	WB					•					

Lake Michigan

	Campground	Rent-a-Tent	Cabins	Day-Use Fac.	Picnic Shelter	Interp. Center	Boat Launch	Fishing	Fishing Pier	Hiking	Mtn. Biking	Canoeing	Swimming	Equest. Fac.	Skiing	Snowmobiling	Rifle Range	Handicapped Fac.
Warren Dunes SP	M			•	•					•			•		•			•
Warren Woods NA				•						•								
Grand Mere SP							H	BP		•			•		•			•
Van Buren SP	M			•	•								•					
Kal–Haven Trail SP				C						•	•				•	•	•	
Saugatuck Dunes SP				•	•					•					•	•		
Holland SP	M			C	•		I	WBS	•				•					•
Grand Haven SP	M			C	•			WS	•				•					•
P. J. Hoffmaster SP	M			•	•	•				•			•	•	•			•
Muskegon SP	B			•	•		I	WBS	•	•			•		•			•
Duck Lake SP				•	•		I	WP					•					•
Silver Lake SP	M			•	•		I	BS	•				•					
Hart–Montague Trail SP				C						•	•				•	•	•	
Charles Mears SP	M			•	•			WS	•	•			•					•
Ludington SP	M			C		•	I	MWS	•	•	•		•		•	•		•
Orchard Beach SP	M			•	•			S	•				•		•			•

Lake Huron

	Campground	Rent-a-Tent	Cabins	Day-Use Fac.	Picnic Shelter	Interp. Center	Boat Launch	Fishing	Fishing Pier	Hiking	Mtn. Biking	Canoeing	Swimming	Equest. Fac.	Skiing	Snowmobiling	Rifle Range	Handicapped Fac.
Port Crescent SP	M			•	•		H	WSB	•	•		•	•		•	•		•
Sanilac HS						•				•								
Albert E. Sleeper SP	M			•	•					•	•		•		•	•		•

	Campground	Rent-a-Tent	Cabins	Day-Use Fac.	Picnic Shelter	Interp. Center	Boat Launch	Fishing	Fishing Pier	Hiking	Mtn. Biking	Canoeing	Swimming	Equest. Fac.	Skiing	Snowmobiling	Rifle Range	Handicapped Fac.
Bay City State RA	M	•		•	•	•		P	•	•	•		•					•
Tawas Point SP	M			•	•			WS		•			•					
Rifle River RA	B		•	•	•		I	TBW	•	•	•	•	•		•	•		•
Harrisville SP	M	•		•	•		H	S		•			•					
Negwegon SP	under development									•			•					
Thompson's Harbor SP										•	•							
P. H. Hoeft SP	M			•	•			S		•			•		•			•
Cheboygan SP	M		•	•	•		H	BTW		•			•		•			•
Onaway SP	M			•	•		I	WM		•								
Clear Lake SP	M		•	•	•		I	BT		•			•		•			•

Northwest Michigan

	Campground	Rent-a-Tent	Cabins	Day-Use Fac.	Picnic Shelter	Interp. Center	Boat Launch	Fishing	Fishing Pier	Hiking	Mtn. Biking	Canoeing	Swimming	Equest. Fac.	Skiing	Snowmobiling	Rifle Range	Handicapped Fac.
South Higgins Lake SP	M			B			I	WSB		•	•	R	•		•			•
North Higgins Lake SP	M			•	•	•	I	WSB		•	•		•		•			•
Interlochen SP	B	•		B	•		I	BWP		•		R	•					•
Traverse City SP	M			•				S					•					
Leelanau SP	R			•	•					•					•			
Young SP	M			•			U	SBP		•			•		•			•
Fisherman's Island SP	R			•			H	S		•			•		•			•
Petoskey SP	M			•						•			•					•
Hartwick Pines SP	M	•		•	•	•	H	TPB		•	•				•	•		•
Otsego Lake SP	M			•			I	BMW				R						•
Burt Lake SP	M	•		B	•		I	SWB		•			•					•
Aloha SP	M	•		•	•		I	WB	•				•					•

Straits of Mackinac

	Campground	Rent-a-Tent	Cabins	Day-Use Fac.	Picnic Shelter	Interp. Center	Boat Launch	Fishing	Fishing Pier	Hiking	Mtn. Biking	Canoeing	Swimming	Equest. Fac.	Skiing	Snowmobiling	Rifle Range	Handicapped Fac.
Wilderness SP	M	•	•				I	B		•	•		•		•	•		
Colonial Michilimackinac SP				•		•												•
Mill Creek SP				•		•				•								•

	Campground	Rent-a-Tent	Cabins	Day-Use Fac.	Picnic Shelter	Interp. Center	Boat Launch	Fishing	Fishing Pier	Hiking	Mtn. Biking	Canoeing	Swimming	Equest. Fac.	Skiing	Snowmobiling	Rifle Range	Handicapped Fac.
Mackinac Island SP				C		•				•	•		•	•	•			•
Straits SP	M			•		•												•

Eastern Upper Peninsula

	Campground	Rent-a-Tent	Cabins	Day-Use Fac.	Picnic Shelter	Interp. Center	Boat Launch	Fishing	Fishing Pier	Hiking	Mtn. Biking	Canoeing	Swimming	Equest. Fac.	Skiing	Snowmobiling	Rifle Range	Handicapped Fac.
Brimley SP	M	•		•	•		H	W		•	•		•		•	•		•
Tahquamenon Falls SP	B			B	•		I	WSM				B		R	•	•		•
Muskallonge Lake SP	M			•			I	WB				B	•					•
Wagner Falls SS										•								
Laughing Whitefish Falls SS				•						•					•			
Indian Lake SP	M	•		•	•		I	WBP		•		R	•		•			•
Palms Book SP				•			I											•
Fayette SP	R			•		•	I	WSB		•			•		•	•		•
J. W. Wells SP	M		•	•	•			WSB		•			•		•	•		•

Western Upper Peninsula

	Campground	Rent-a-Tent	Cabins	Day-Use Fac.	Picnic Shelter	Interp. Center	Boat Launch	Fishing	Fishing Pier	Hiking	Mtn. Biking	Canoeing	Swimming	Equest. Fac.	Skiing	Snowmobiling	Rifle Range	Handicapped Fac.
Porcupine Mountains Wilderness SP	B	•	•	•	•	•	I	SBTW				B	•	•	DR	•		
Twin Lakes SP	M			•	•		I	WB		•			•		•			
F. J. McLain SP	M			•	•	•		S		•	•		•		•			•
Fort Wilkins SP	M			•	•	•	I	S		•					•			
Baraga SP	M	•		•			I	ST		•			•					•
Lake Gogebic SP	M	•		•	•		I	W		•			•		•			•
Bewabic SP	M	•		•	•		I	WBP		•	•	•			•			
Van Riper SP	B			•	•	•	I	W		•		•	•					•
Craig Lake SP			•					WBM				B	•					

index

ABOUT THE AUTHOR

A resident of Clarkston, Michigan, Jim DuFresne is torn between two loves—exploring the outdoors by foot, canoe, and kayak, and writing about the areas he explores to lure others out to enjoy them as well. He has hiked extensively in the upper Midwest, the Rockies, New Zealand, Australia, and Nepal, as well as in Alaska, where he was, for several years, sports/outdoor editor for the *Juneau Alaska Empire*.

DuFresne has written fourteen books, including *Michigan Off the Beaten Path; Michigan's Best Outdoor Adventures with Children; Isle Royale National Park; Glacier Bay National Park; Tramping in New Zealand* and *Alaska: Travel Survival Kit*. He is a member of the Outdoor Writers of America Association and the Michigan Outdoor Writers Association and covers outdoor recreation for Booth Newspapers, a chain of eight dailies in southern Michigan.

THE MOUNTAINEERS, founded in 1906, is a nonprofit outdoor activity and conservation club, whose mission is "to explore, study, preserve, and enjoy the natural beauty of the outdoors. . . . " Based in Seattle, Washington, the club is now the third-largest such organization in the United States, with 15,000 members and five branches throughout Washington State.

The Mountaineers sponsors both classes and year-round outdoor activities in the Pacific Northwest, which include hiking, mountain climbing, ski-touring, snowshoeing, bicycling, camping, kayaking and canoeing, nature study, sailing, and adventure travel. The club's conservation division supports environmental causes through educational activities, sponsoring legislation, and presenting informational programs. All club activities are led by skilled, experienced volunteers, who are dedicated to promoting safe and responsible enjoyment and preservation of the outdoors.

If you would like to participate in these organized outdoor activities or the club's programs, consider a membership in The Mountaineers. For information and an application, write or call The Mountaineers, Club Headquarters, 300 Third Avenue West, Seattle, Washington 98119; (206) 284-6310.

The Mountaineers Books, an active, nonprofit publishing program of the club, produces guidebooks, instructional texts, historical works, natural history guides, and works on environmental conservation. All books produced by The Mountaineers are aimed at fulfilling the club's mission.

Send or call for our catalog of more than 300 outdoor titles:

The Mountaineers Books
1001 SW Klickitat Way, Suite 201
Seattle, WA 98134
1-800-553-4453
e-mail: mbooks@mountaineers.org
website: www.mountaineers.org

Other titles you may enjoy from The Mountaineers:

MICHIGAN'S BEST OUTDOOR ADVENTURES WITH CHILDREN,
Jim DuFresne
Seventy-five hiking, biking, canoeing, camping, skiing, beachcombing, birding.
and fishing adventures.

ADVENTURE CYCLING IN MICHIGAN: Selected On- and Off-Road Rides,
The Adventure Cycling Association
A guide to thirty-nine classic on- and off-road bike routes, with information about
the area and expert advice on safety, equipment, and road and trail rules.

ISLE ROYALE NATIONAL PARK, 2nd Ed.: Foot Trails & Water Routes,
Jim DuFresne
A guide for hikers and canoeists to Lake Superior's most isolated wilderness.

MAKING CAMP: the Complete All-Season, All-Activity Guide,
Steve Howe, Alan Kesselheim, Dennis Coello, and John Harlin
A comprehensive camping how-to compiled by *Backpacker Magazine* field experts
for anyone traveling by foot, boat, bicycle, or skis, through all kinds of terrain,
year-round.

EVERYDAY WISDOM: 1001 Expert Tips for Hikers, *Karen Berger*
Expert tips and tricks for hikers and backpackers, covering everything from
packing and planning to field repairs and emergency improvisations.

MOUNTAIN BIKE EMERGENCY REPAIR, *Tim Toyoshima*
A handbook that shows how to make temporary trailside repairs with few or no
tools, and then permanent repairs with proper tools.